THE DAILY STUDY BIBLE

INDEX VOLUME

Edited by C. L. Rawlins

THE SAINT ANDREW PRESS
EDINBURGH

First published in 1978 by
THE SAINT ANDREW PRESS
121 George Street, Edinburgh

© The Saint Andrew Press

ISBN 0 7152 0378 9 (Limp)
ISBN 0 7152 0379 7 (Cased)

Printed in Great Britain by
Robert MacLehose & Company Ltd

CONTENTS

INTRODUCTION

The Daily Study Bible hardly needs an introduction. Since its inception twenty five years ago, 'the little red commentaries'[1] have circulated in their thousands around the world and are to be found from archbishops' palaces to the more humble homes of ordinary people on five continents.

It was in the year of the Coronation that the then relatively unknown lecturer in New Testament studies at the University of Glasgow provided, at short notice, his first commentary; there was no indication then that it would be the precursor of a full series or that it would be selling on a world-wide scale a quarter of a century later. But so it was, and within six years it was complete—an extraordinary event which even pre-planned series with multiple authors and the full backing of fully staffed publishing houses has not equalled. And so the name of William Barclay became an household name with more than sixty books to his credit, countless articles in periodicals both popular and technical, and radio and television appearances which attracted record listening and viewing.[2]

And what is the DSB (as it is familiarly called)? Precisely what its title asserts: a *daily* study of the Bible. It is not just a commentary, if by that term one implies full critical and exegetical treatment of the text, nor if one understands it to mean a fully-worked exposition. To be sure, these matters are not excluded from these studies, and behind them there lies a masterful comprehension of biblical learning, as his other works show.[3] But in this series we have Barclay the pastor rather than Barclay the Professor of Divinity and Biblical Criticism, an important aspect which several critics have overlooked when they have spoken of the unevenness of treatment in this or that part. As the author himself declares, in setting out his aims in the General Introduction, it is 'to make the results of modern scholarship available to the non-technical reader in a form that does not require a theological education

to understand; and then to make the teaching of the New Testament books relevant to life and work today . . . they are meant to enable men and women to know Jesus Christ more clearly, to love him more dearly, and to follow him more nearly'.[4]

In other words, the books (seventeen in all, extending over more than four thousand pages) provide us with exposition which is informative, devotional and relevant, as any *daily* encounter with the scriptures should be. And how informative! For those with the inclination and discipline to take them seriously they are a veritable gold-mine. In these practiced hands the world of the New Testament comes vibrantly alive, alive with the authentic ring of first-hand experience and the touch of the craftsman-writer. Through these pages we are introduced to the air breathed by the early Christians, made to sit where they sat, and helped to see things as they saw them. The message to them thus becomes the message to us, for Dr Barclay is a most practical writer, a pastor *par excellence*. Ever ready to enlighten and enliven the most casual reference or mundane comment, his main task is to home-in on the real meaning and present-day reality of the passage under consideration. As he says himself, 'Christianity is truth, but it is truth in action'.[5] Relevance might be his second name. But how devotional, too! In some commentators' hands the Bible is handled with clinical precision: introduced, analysed, explained —and the net result is a descriptive piece which would grace any museum. . . . Barclay is not such a writer. His work radiates an infectious love for Christ and mankind, and thus through his books there develops a powerful encounter between both. But it is an encounter, and his ethic is one, therefore, of 'reciprocal obligation',[6] towards God and man.

In all this he is clear and frank. Where there are problems he says so; where there are difficulties he admits them; where there are discrepancies, weaknesses, contradictions even, he states them, fully and carefully. If a statement conflicts with present-day modes of thought or practice he does not baulk the issue or weaken his stance; the reader is left always in a position to be

responsive to God and his Word. The whole thrust of his exposition is to bring the would-be Christian under the inexorable demands of Christ, demands which are humbling and demanding in a total sense, as Barclay is at pains to declare.

He does not dilute the reality of sin, the danger of compromise or the existence of God's wrath; nor does he obscure the glorious reality of his love and kindness, his willingness to forgive and heal, his power to deliver from enslaving habits, and the hope he inspires. All these, and much more, are found finely stated and illustrated in these commentaries. His exposition is carefully balanced, more so than many—whether 'liberal' or 'conservative'—are prepared to admit. These, with his simplicity and directness of style,[7] are some of the reasons for his great success and usefulness.[8]

This *Index* is simply an aid to the greater and more effective use of the preceding seventeen books. Its format demonstrates the method and strengths of Barclay the commentator. He is primarily a *biblical* theologian. Not only in the sense that his life and energies have been spent in the service of the Bible, by studies linguistic and archaeological, exegetical and practical, classical and modern, but also in the sense that he allows the Bible to create its own theological ethos, dictate its own theological style, provide its own theological language, direct, in a word, its own theological ends. The interpretive rules (or hermeneutic) he uses are themselves biblically oriented. He is not a manipulator of scripture, but one manipulated by it; his authority is of one 'under authority'.[9] In all his writings the axiom of scripture interpreting scripture predominates. In this way he preserves the integrity of scripture and the interrelatedness of its several parts.

Any commentator of whole books of the Bible is placed under the severe discipline of facing unavoidably a wide range of subjects and problems. The second section of this *Index* manifests Barclay's ability to grapple with major and contentious issues fairly and competently. He is not evasive, but brings all matters under the searchlight of the full biblical revelation and record, whether they be matters of the moment

or ones of more lasting consequence, personal or public.

Nor does he work in isolation from contemporary scholars or those of past ages. In the third section his indebtedness to their knowledge and experience (never divorced!) is shown. Thanks to great industry, wide reading and a phenomenal memory,[10] his works are replete with quotations and anecdotes of all sorts: practical, philosophical, religious, secular, antiquarian, modern, prose, poetry, and in several languages. From the Hebrides to the Antipodes he draws from a rich fund which never fails to interest or inform. In the final two sections of the *Index* we see much of the sources of Dr Barclay's exposition. Here etymology and ancient practice join hands in a creative act of enlightenment of scripture which could otherwise remain meaningless to the modern reader.

Users of this *Index* should be aware of the 'chain-reference' method whereby they can trace a great deal of information about the subject of their enquiry from small beginnings. In a writer of Barclay's stature this is particularly important, for his use of language is rich and fluent; he moves swiftly through adjectives and synonyms.[11] I have not sought to centralize subjects under single heads, so readers should be alive to a fairly diverse form of reference. For example, those wishing to understand his emphasis on right doctrine should refer to 'Doctrine', 'Belief', 'The Faith', 'Creeds', and 'Orthodoxy'. Further aspects may be explored in other sections, such as under Personal Names (e.g. Jesus or Paul), key scripture references (e.g. Rom. 3:21-25 for 'justification'), or foreign words; by this method the user will be enabled to reach a comprehensive viewpoint of Dr Barclay's thought.

This volume is sent out with the prayer that it may be found to be a worthy servant of the series and the One to whom the whole series looks as both Lord and Master.

A number of people have helped in various ways, to whom I record my deep appreciation and gratitude: Mr Tim Honeyman (Secretary of the Church of Scotland Publications Committee) and Mr Maurice Berrill (its former Publisher) have both supplied much help and encouragement notwithstanding some

delays; Mrs Beryl Barnes produced an admirable typescript from a difficult manuscript; my wife Veronica willingly shouldered many extra jobs in addition to her professional and domestic tasks; but above all to Dr Barclay himself whose tireless efforts bring to us the ripe fruits of learning year after year.

C. L. RAWLINS

Postscript

Some months after the above was written, news reached me of the death of Dr Barclay. He had seen it, and it had met with his approval, but the Foreword he had promised remains unwritten.

From around the world there has come a flow of appreciations for this great man, undoubtedly one of the foremost communicators of the Christian faith of the century. They will continue, as his work will continue, for it is based on the unchanging expression of God's will and purposes in Christ Jesus. Let this small volume stand as part of the living memorial in William Barclay's honour, who counted not the praise of men but only of God himself.

C. L. R.

NOTES

1. They were revised and reset in 1974–76.
2. See 'Barclay the Broadcaster' by the late Ronald Falconer, in *Biblical Studies: Essays in Honour of William Barclay*, edited by J. R. McKay and J. F. Miller (William Collins & Sons, 1976, pp. 15–27).
3. See the 'Table of Events and Selected Works' in *Men and Affairs* (A. R. Mowbray & Co., pp. 147–149).
4. Richard of Chichester's prayer is quoted in the General Introduction to both the original and the revised editions of the series.
5. 12.100, a passage which particularly emphasizes the need for Christian action.

6. See, for example, **11**.160f. Dr Barclay twice uses this phrase in the DSB, but the concept pervades the whole of his thought both ethically and theologically.

7. See the Editor's Preface in *Men and Affairs*, pp. viiif.

8. David Edwards, formerly one of Dr Barclay's editors but now Dean of Westminster Abbey, refers to this in the Preface to *Testament of Faith* (A. R. Mowbray & Co., 1975, pp. vii–xii).

9. Matt. 8:9; significantly, Barclay finds the centurion who originally voiced these words 'one of the most attractive characters in the gospels' (**1**.300). Johnston McKay and James Miller, in the Editors' Preface to *Biblical Studies*, refer (somewhat clumsily) to Barclay's 'biblicality' (p.9).

10. See Dr Barclay's modest admission of this in *Testament of Faith* (p. 22f.); David Edwards highlights it in his Preface (p. viii).

11. Note Edwards' reference to this as 'his extraordinary appetite for words' (op. cit., p. ix).

EXPLANATION OF USE

For reasons of space the seventeen volumes of the *Daily Study Bible* have each been given a numerical reference (1–17); these references are printed in *bold type* throughout the book; the key to these will be found at the foot of every page. The main exposition of a passage is printed in italics, thus references to Philippians 3:1 will appear as: **11**.7, 15, *50–53*; **14**.336. It will be found that volume **11** is *Philippians, Colossians and Thessalonians* and volume **14** is *James and Peter*; the primary passage will be found at pages 50–53 of the former volume.

INDEX OF OLD TESTAMENT REFERENCES

Genesis

1–2	13.36
1:1	5.37
1:2	1.22; 5.83; 14.339
1:3	5.7, 28, 45; 17.181
1:6–7	17.47
1:6	5.28; 14.339; 17.181
1:7	16.155
1:9	17.181
1:11	5.28
1:14–18	11.44
1:14	17.181, 209
1:26–27	2.278; 3.287; 11.117f
1:26	1.178; 13.17; 15.75, 97; 17.181
1:27	1.13–14; 3.240; 12.94
1:28	13.23; 14.88
1:31	3.182; 12.94
2:7	6.274; 9.157
2:8–16	17.220
2:8	16.70
2:9	16.69
2:16–17	16.69
2:18	3.343
2:22–23	9.98
2:23–24	2.200, 203
2:24	3.240; 9.56
3	17.82
3:1–19	9.150
3:1	16.70
3:6	17.221
3:8–10	6.17
3:8	3.102; 17.17
3:12–13	14.52
3:17	8.110
3:21	6.90
3:22–24	16.69
3:24	16.158
4:1–15	13.131; 15.189
4:1	6.209; 11.63; 15.54, 185
4:7	6.38
4:10	13.187
5:1	1.12
5:24	13.133; 14.239; 16.122; 17.70
6–8	13.140
6:1–8	1.321; 3.34; 14.240
6:1–5	14.322
6:1–4	15.183; 17.48
6:1–2	3.71; 9.99
6:2	14.239; 15.158
6:5	14.325
6:9	13.142
6:12–13	14.240
8:21	11.86
9:2	14.88
9:3	12.94
9:4	5.224; 17.31
9:18–27	12.79
10:1	1.12
11:10	1.12
11:27	1.12
12:1–3	8.12; 9.252
12:1	9.221; 13.142; 17.151
12:2–3	8.67
12:3	4.34; 10.24
12:7	13.62
14:14	9.15
14:17–20	13.67

14:18–20	13.72	21:7	13.147
15:5	17.26	21:12	8.128
15:6	8.66	22:1–18	13.151
15:8–21	6.34	22:1	1.62, 224; 14.42
15:13	16.9; 17.188	22:12	8.116
15:18	17.53	22:16–18	13.62
16–17	10.41	24:1	6.35
16:13	4.102	24:50	12.76
17:5–6	13.62	25:11	6.90
17:5	5.90; 11.38f; 16.98	25:23	8.128
17:7–8	10.28	25:25–26	4.17
17:7	17.206	25:28–34	13.183
17:9–10	11.55	25:34	16.133
17:9	15.78	26:17–25	11.157
17:10–11	8.66; 11.138	26:17–22	9.216
17:12	11.57	26:24	16.25
17:15–22	13.146	27	5.28; 17.181
17:17	6.34; 8.70; 13.146	27:1–39	13.183
17:25	11.57	27:2	13.153
18–19	14.327	27:28–29	13.153
18:1–8	6.26; 13.192	27:36	16.133
18:1	6.90	27:39–40	13.153
18:9–15	13.146	28:12	5.94
18:10–14	8.128	28:16	17.36
18:12	13.146	29:35	8.47
18:18	13.62	32:12	17.26
18:23	9.15	32:28	5.90; 11.39, 58; 16.98
18:25	16.121	32:29	17.180
19:1–11	1.371; 14.327; 15.185	32:30	13.3
19:4–11	17.71	32:32	9.80
19:12–28	15.185	33:18–19	5.147
19:12–26	14.327	35:1–5	6.79
19:12–14	9.221; 17.152	35:17–18	11.58
19:16	14.328	35:20	1.24
19:28	17.112	37:34	1.93
19:29	14.327	37:35	15.36
19:30–38	12.79	38	1.17
21	10.41	40:8	1.16
21:1–8	13.146	41:42	16.143; 17.23

43:11	17.7
45:22	14.115
47:29	13.153
48:7	1.24
48:9–22	13.153
48:15–16	13.153
48:22	5.147
49	14.31
49:1	15.59
49:3	14.31
49:4	16.133
49:5–7	14.31
49:8	8.47; 16.133
49:9	16.169
49:14–15	14.31
49:17	17.25
49:18	14.31
49:19	14.31
49:20	14.31
49:22–26	14.31
49:27	14.31
50:5	1.314
50:20	14.272
50:22–26	13.153

Exodus

1:15–22	13.155
2:1–10	13.155
2:11–14	13.156
2:14–22	13.157
3:1–5	4.251
3:1	17.143
3:2–5	3.37
3:6	3.290
3:10	8.12
3:14	16.29
4:1–17	6.45
4:10	13.156
4:12	1.375
4:22	3.71; 6.27; 8.124; 11.119
6:6–7	2.340; 3.333; 10.109
6:12	11.55, 139
6:20	13.155
7:11	12.194
7:14–18	17.71
7:17–21	17.127
7:20–25	17.125
7:20–21	17.44
8:5–14	17.125
8:5–11	17.130
8:7	12.194
8:16–18	17.125
8:20–24	17.125
9–16	8.130
9:3–6	17.125
9:8–11	17.125f
9:11	12.194
9:22–26	17.125
9:24	17.44, 117, 134
10:12–19	17.125
10:21–23	17.44, 127
10:29–30	17.125
12	3.323, 332; 4.262
12:5	14.185
12:11–13	5.81
12:11	3.334
12:12–48	13.158
12:15ff	9.45
12:21–23	2.340
12:22	6.259
12:34	2.339
12:38	12.194
13:1–10	2.286; 4.140; 17.99
13:2	4.24
13:7	9.45

13:9	2.286; 14.271		20	10.29
13:11–16	2.286; 4.140; 17.99		20:5	6.38; 14.104
13:16	2.286		20:7	1.158
13:19	13.153		20:8–11	4.60
13:21–22	2.161; 9.88		20:9	4.213
14	13.158		20:10	2.208
14:19–31	9.88		20:11	6.77
14:21	17.128		20:13	1.138
15:1–9	17.119		20:14	1.146
15:11	17.94		21:1–6	6.77
15:20	16.105		21:23–25	1.163
15:24	11.43; 15.197		21:33	4.188
16:1–21	1.218		22:1	4.235
16:2	11.43		22:4, 7	4.235; 17.153
16:7	14.259		22:9	6.77; 17.153
16:10	3.210; 5.69; 8.125		22:13	6.61
16:11–21	4.144		22:26–27	1.167
16:11–15	9.88; 16.94		22:28	6.77; 7.164
16:15	5.215; 16.95		23:1	5.254
16:18	9.230		23:7	8.57
16:19	17.42		23:16	5.248
16:29	5.122		24:1–8	4.266; 9.189; 10.109; 13.81, 91, 108; 14.170; 15.204
16:33–34	16.94			
17:1–7	13.33			
17:3	15.197		24:3–8	3.339; 8.24; 13.4
17:6	5.251		24:3	10.109; 11.142
19–20	16.24		24:7	10.109; 13.81
19:4	17.85		24:10	17.213
19:5–6	14.198		24:15	1.234
19:5	5.59		24:16–18	17.35
19:6	11.10; 16.35		24:16–17	5.69; 8.125
19:9	3.210		24:16	14.259
19:10	17.30		24:18	3.22
19:12–13	13.185		25–31	13.95
19:14	17.30		25:1–7	13.95
19:16	16.43, 155; 17.42		25:8	13.95
19:17	5.30		25:9	17.10
19:18	13.188		25:18–21	16.158
19:22	14.106		25:22	13.97

25:23–30	3.63
25:31–37	16.44
25:40	13.88; 17.10
26:31	16.158
26:33	11.10
27:1	17.211
28:4	16.45
28:16	17.212
28:17	17.214
28:30	13.99
28:41	6.217
29:4	14.234
29:5	16.45
29:7	15.69
29:20–21	14.170
29:38–42	5.81
29:43	8.125; 14.259
30:2	17.211
30:13	2.168
30:19–21	14.107
30:34–38	17.161
31:13	5.30
31:18	2.159
32:6	9.88
32:28	12.194
32:30–32	3.132
32:32–33	16.123
32:32	8.123; 17.196
33:9–11	13.159
33:9	3.210
33:12–32	6.159
33:17	6.5
33:18–22	8.125
33:19	8.130
33:20	5.73; 13.3; 17.222
33:23	17.222
34:5	2.161
34:7	6.38
34:14	14.104

34:15–16	14.102; 16.108
34:15	5.143; 17.106
34:22	5.248
34:29	2.159
34:30	9.190
34:33	9.192
35–40	13.95
36:5–7	13.95
40:13	15.69
40:34–38	17.35
40:34–35	17.122
40:34	2.161; 5.69; 14.259

Leviticus

1:4	1.52
1:9, 13, 17	11.86
2:13	3.234
4:2	13.45
4:7	17.11
4:13	13.45
5:7	14.233
6:5	4.235
6:30	14.233
8	13.78
8:30	14.170
11–15	3.165; 10.32
11	2.111; 3.166, 172; 7.81; 8.182; 10.20; 13.196
11:10	17.30
11:12	1.271
11:13–21	2.112
11:22–23	3.116
11:44	14.188
12	4.24
12:3	5.242; 11.57

12:8	**2**.245; **3**.273; **4**.24;
	6.10
13–14	**4**.58
13	**3**.44
13:45–46	**1**.296, 365; **4**.58, 218
13:47–52	**15**.205
13:47	**3**.44
14	**1**.299; **3**.45
14:1–7	**14**.170
14:22	**2**.245; **3**.273
14:33	**3**.44
15:14	**2**.245; **3**.273
15:19–33	**4**.113
15:25–27	**1**.346; **3**.129
15:29	**2**.245
16	**13**.97, 101
16:4	**14**.107; **16**.45
16:12	**17**.40
16:15	**13**.103
16:19	**6**.77
16:21–22	**13**.103
16:27	**13**.197
16:29	**13**.98
16:31	**1**.233
16:32	**15**.69
16:33	**13**.98
17:11–14	**17**.10
17:11	**13**.107
18:5	**8**.138
18:8	**9**.44
18:16	**3**.150
19:2	**14**.188; **15**.29
19:9	**2**.16
19:13	**14**.118
19:15	**14**.63
19:18	**1**.165; **2**.278; **3**.295;
	4.140; **14**.111; **15**.44
19:23–25	**3**.282
20:5	**1**.330
20:7	**14**.188; **15**.29
20:10	**1**.146; **6**.2
20:14	**17**.149
20:21	**3**.150
20:26	**11**.11; **14**.188; **15**.29
21:6	**11**.10
21:9	**17**.149
21:16–23	**13**.78
23:10–11	**3**.323; **9**.150
23:21	**7**.21
23:27–32	**13**.101
23:39	**5**.248
23:40	**5**.249
24:5–9	**2**.23; **4**.70
24:9	**3**.63
24:16	**3**.49; **6**.76, 234
24:19–20	**1**.163
25:23	**5**.59
25:39–42	**6**.23
26:5	**5**.168
26:11–12	**9**.223; **17**.203
26:21–26	**17**.9
26:26	**17**.7
26:41	**11**.55, 139
27:30	**2**.293; **11**.10
27:32	**6**.56; **11**.10

Numbers

4:3	**6**.36
5:2	**4**.218
5:6–7	**1**.57
5:7	**4**.235
6:1–21	**7**.138; **12**.119
6:22–27	**16**.135
8:4	**17**.10
9:12	**6**.261
9:15	**17**.121

11:12	5.74	19	3.165; **13**.103
11:16–30	**14**.262	19:2	2.239; 3.266
11:16–17	4.133; **12**.70	19:11	4.139; 7.80
11:24–25	4.133	19:16	2.296; 4.156
12:3	1.98	20:1–13	**13**.33
12:6–7	**13**.29	20:1–11	9.88
12:7–8	**13**.159	20:4	**16**.80
12:8	**15**.145	21:4–9	5.134
13–14	**13**.36; **15**.182	21:4–6	9.89
13:23	2.251	21:11	4.295
13:26–	**15**.158	22–24	**14**.333; **15**.190
14:29		22:22	3.22; **12**.194; **17**.81
13:33	**14**.322	23:19	**12**.170
14:18	6.38	24:14	**15**.59
14:24	**14**.35; **16**.25	24:17	**17**.228
14:30–32	9.88	24:29	**15**.197
14:32–33	**15**.182	25	**14**.333; **15**.190
15:22–31	**13**.45	25:1–9	9.88
15:30–31	2.41	25:1–5	**16**.66
15:37–41	1.192, 347; 2.286;	25:3	8.24
	3.295; 4.113	25:11–13	**11**.60
15:38–40	3.130	27:17	6.59
15:38	3.299	27:18–21	6.105
16	9.89	28:3–8	**13**.116
16:1–35	**15**.191	28:9	2.24
16:3	**16**.80	28:26	7.21
16:5	**12**.177	29:7–11	**13**.101
16:23–26	**17**.152	29:7	**13**.99
16:26	**12**.177	30:2	1.158; 2.116
16:41	**11**.43	31:8	**14**.333; **15**.190
16:46	8.24; **17**.40	31:16	**15**.190; **16**.67, 80
17:7	**17**.121	32:10–13	**15**.182
18:2	**17**.121	35:30	6.14
18:14	2.17		
18:16	4.24		
18:19	3.234	*Deuteronomy*	
18:20–21	**13**.76		
18:21	4.224	1:16	5.254
18:28	2.276	1:17	5.187

2:24	**8.124**	12:9	**13.33**
3:6	**8.124**	13:1–5	**6.48; 14.315, 319;**
3:9	**1.260**		**14.89; 17.131**
3:24	**14.271**	13:6	**5.74; 7.61**
4:2	**17.231**	13:8–11	**8.124**
4:11	**13.185**	13:13	**9.104; 11.212**
4:12	**5.73, 197**	14:1	**8.124**
4:23	**13.91**	14:2	**5.59; 14.166**
4:24	**13.189**	14:21	**2.112**
4:34	**14.42**	14:22	**2.293; 4.224**
5:23–27	**13.185**	15:4	**14.173**
5:32–33	**6.157**	15:7–11	**1.169; 9.235**
6:4–9	**1.192; 2.286; 3.295;**	15:9	**1.246**
	4.140; 17.99	15:11	**3.326; 6.113**
6:4	**3.295; 4.140; 8.60;**	15:23	**5.224**
	9.252	16:13–16	**5.248**
6:5	**2.278**	17:2–7	**13.124**
6:8	**2.286; 3.295**	17:6	**5.195; 6.14; 15.112**
6:13	**1.70; 4.44**	17:7	**6.234; 9.48**
6:16	**1.69; 4.44**	17:12	**13.46**
7:6	**5.59; 14.166**	18:3–4	**2.17**
7:13	**17.6**	18:15	**2.9; 4.115; 5.78, 206,**
7:19	**14.42**		**252; 6.72**
8:3	**1.68; 4.43**	18:18	**5.206, 252; 6.72;**
8:8	**2.251**		**17.71**
9:3	**5.30**	18:20	**14.315**
9:19	**13.186**	19:10	**14.173**
9:26	**14.271**	19:15	**2.188; 5.195; 6.13;**
9:27	**14.35**		**15.112; 17.70**
9:29	**14.267**	19:18	**1.164**
10:12	**9.207**	19:19	**9.221**
10:16	**11.55**	19:21	**1.163**
10:20	**4.44**	21:1–9	**2.362**
11:4–9	**3.295**	21:3	**2.239; 3.266**
11:13–21	**1.192; 2.286; 3.295;**	21:17	**4.204**
	4.140; 17.99	21:19	**2.143**
11:13	**4.140**	21:22–23	**2.372; 6.260**
11:14	**14.121; 17.6**	21:23	**7.27; 9.17; 10.26**
11:18	**2.286**	22:10	**9.221**

1 Matt, v.1	**3** Mark	**5** John, v.1	**7** Acts	**9** Cor
2 Matt, v.2	**4** Luke	**6** John, v.2	**8** Rom	**10** Gal, Eph

22:12	1.347; 2.286; 4.113
22:13–24	6.2
23:3	1.17
23:18	11.54; 17.227
23:21–22	1.159
23:24–25	2.253
23:25	2.21; 3.63; 4.69
24:1	1.151; 2.197, 200; 3.238–40; 4.211
24:5	4.194
24:7	9.48
24:14–15	14.118
24:19	2.16
25:1–3	9.253
25:4	9.79; 12.116
25:5–10	2.277; 3.289
25:5–6	4.41, 249
25:7	2.143; 14.263
26:18	5.59
27:4	5.157
27:14–26	11.142
27:26	10.26, 30
28:6	6.59
28:35	17.126
28:51	17.6
29:4	8.145
29:17–18	17.44
29:18	13.182
29:23	15.185
29:28	14.37
30:6	11.55, 139
30:12–13	8.138
30:14	14.57
30:15–20	1.278; 5.146
30:19	16.109
31:16	2.276; 5.143; 14.102; 16.108; 17.106
31:29	6.157
32:4	2.140
32:6	6.27; 8.124
32:8	15.183
32:9	5.59
32:11–12	17.85
32:15	12.18
32:16	14.104
32:21	8.122, 142; 14.104
32:31	2.140
32:32	15.185
32:35f	13.125
32:39	2.276; 5.186; 14.112
32:43	8.198; 13.19; 17.165
33:1	12.134
33:17	16.171
33:27	5.30
34:1–4	14.181
34:5–6	2.159; 6.90, 177
34:5	14.293

Joshua

1:2	8.12; 11.10; 12.227
1:5	13.194
2:1–21	13.161; 14.78
2:1–7	1.17
2:9–11	13.161
3:10	16.48; 17.22
3:17	17.128
5:14–15	13.17
6:1–20	13.160
6:17	8.124
6:25	13.161
7	8.79
7:1–26	8.124
7:19	6.48
7:21	1.239
9	1.73
9:6	13.90

10:11	**17.**134
14:7	**3.**281
19:28–29	**3.**178
24:15	**1.**278; **5.**146; **16.**109
24:29	**6.**178; **8.**12; **12.**227; **14.**35, 293; **16.**25
24:32	**5.**147; **13.**153

Judges

2:2	**13.**90
2:8	**11.**10; **16.**25
2:17	**17.**106
2:22	**14.**42
3:1, 4	**14.**42
4–5	**13.**163
4:4	**16.**105
5:14	**11.**58
5:19–21	**17.**132
5:31	**16.**51
6–7	**13.**163
6:49	**16.**25
7:21	**14.**115
8:23	**6.**236; **10.**108
8:27, 33	**17.**106
9:8–15	**3.**89
9:13	**12.**79
10:4	**6.**118
11–12	**13.**163
13–16	**13.**163
13:18	**17.**180
13:20	**13.**18
13:22	**10.**129
14:12	**14.**116
18:30	**17.**25
20:16	**6.**55
20:26	**1.**234

Ruth

1:4	**1.**17
1:22	**1.**24
2:14	**6.**146

1 Samuel

1	**13.**163
1:16	**17.**59
2:1–10	**4.**15
2:2	**2.**140; **17.**120
2:6	**5.**187; **14.**112
2:12	**17.**59
2:27	**12.**134
3:1–14	**6.**126
3:14	**2.**42
6:7	**2.**239
7:6	**1.**234
9:1–2	**11.**58
9:6	**12.**134
9:16	**15.**69
10:1	**15.**69
10:2	**1.**38
12:12	**6.**236
15:22	**3.**296; **13.**114
16:1–13	**13.**163
16:1	**1.**24; **16.**133
16:3, 12	**15.**69
16:13	**16.**133
17:12	**1.**24
17:34–36	**6.**61
18:4	**16.**46
20:6	**1.**24
21:1–6	**2.**23; **3.**63; **4.**70
22:2	**2.**140
23:14–15	**1.**24
23:18	**13.**90

24:5–11	**16**.46
24:14	**11**.54
25:17, 25	**17**, 59
26:21	**16**.65
28:14	**2**.276
29:4	**1**.225; **3**.22; **17**.81

2 Samuel

3:18	**3**.281; **14**.293
7:14	**3**.71; **9**.223; **13**.19; **17**.206
9:7, 13	**6**.142
10:4	**16**.143
11–12	**1**.17
12:1–14	**16**.145
12:1–13	**3**.50
12:1–7	**3**.85, 89
13:28–29	**12**.79
14:4	**3**.268
16:7	**17**.59
17:23	**6**.118
18:15	**13**.164
19:22	**1**.225; **3**.22
19:26	**6**.118
22:5	**11**.212
22:32	**2**.140

1 Kings

2:22	**16**.133
3:7	**6**.59
4:25	**2**.251; **5**.93
5:4	**1**.225; **3**.22; **17**.81
6:20	**17**.212
6:23–30	**16**.158
7:49	**16**.45
8:2	**5**.248
8:10–11	**2**.161; **3**.210; **14**.259; **17**.122, 203
8:11	**5**.69
8:17–18	**15**.87
8:18	**1**.101
8:53	**14**.35
8:66	**16**.25
11:14, 23	**17**.81
11:29–32	**2**.240; **3**.339; **4**.239; **7**.154; **13**.13
11:30–32	**3**.264
11:36	**16**.25
12:21	**11**.58
12:22	**12**.134
12:29	**17**.25
13:22	**17**.72
14:13	**16**.121
16:31	**16**.105
17–18	**14**.132
17:1–7	**17**.79
17:1	**14**.132; **17**.42, 71
17:17ff	**13**.166
18	**6**.45
18:1	**14**.132
18:13	**16**.106
18:15	**17**.42
18:17–40	**1**.64
18:19	**6**.143; **16**.106
18:26	**1**.196
18:37	**6**.100
18:42	**14**.132
19:1–8	**4**.126; **6**.126; **13**.164; **17**.79
19:3	**1**.64
19:4	**17**.143
19:8	**3**.22

19:9–12	2.159
19:10–18	8.144
19:11	17.20
19:12	16.50
19:13	1.281
19:15–16	15.69
19:19	1.281
20:8	14.263
20:35–43	12.102
21	16.106
21:10	11.212; 17.59
21:11	14.263
21:13	11.212; 17.59
22	14.314f
22:11	16.171
22:19	13.17; 16.151, 153

2 Kings

1:8	1.44, 282; 3.16
1:9–10	17.71
2:11	2.159; 17.70, 72
2:12	2.287
3:14	17.42
4:8ff	13.166
4:18–37	4.86
4:29	4.134
5	3.127
5:5	14.116
5:6	5.186; 17.42
5:7	14.112
5:22	1.239; 14.116
6:17	3.24
6:26	3.268
6:31ff	13.164
6:32	14.263
7:3–3	1.365

8:13	11.54
9:13	2.239; 3.266
9:22	16.106
9:27	17.132
9:36	16.25
10:10	16.25
15:5	1.365
17:6	5.149
17:23	14.37
17:24	5.149
17:28	5.159
17:29	5.157, 159
18:4	5.134
18:17–37	17.22
19:15	16.158
19:34	16.25
19:35–36	12.150; 13.18
20:1–7	13.164
20:6	16.25
20:20	6.43
21:1–9	9.221
21:10	16.25
22:14	16.105
23:3ff	9.221
23:10	1.141; 3.231
23:29–30	17.132
24:14–16	14.37
25:26	14.39

1 Chronicles

5:26	14.37
9:33	17.34
17:4	16.25
21:1	17.59
24:5, 7–18	16.153
29:10–12	16.179

2 Chronicles

3:7	**16.**158
5:13–14	**2.**161
7:1–13	**17.**35
7:2	**2.**161
11:6	**1.**24
13:5	**3.**234
13:7	**17.**59
13:19	**6.**106
24:6	**16.**25
24:20–2	**2.**298; **4.**159; **13.**166
25:6–31	**16.**153
26:18	**6.**77
28:3	**1.**141; **3.**231
32:3–8, 30	**6.**43
33:6	**3.**231
33:13	**1.**58
34:17	**12.**70

Ezra

2:61–63	**4.**40; **13.**68
2:62	**1.**12
4:1	**11.**58
10:8	**6.**47

Nehemiah

1:7	**16.**25
6:1	**1.**231
6:11	**15.**50
7:63–65	**4.**40; **13.**68
8:1–8	**2.**282
9:1	**1.**234
10:29	**16.**25
13:15–19	**5.**182
13:28	**5.**150

Esther

3:10	**17.**23
6:6–11	**16.**144
8:2	**17.**23

Job

1:6–9	**17.**81
1:6–7	**1.**226; **3.**22, 71
1:6	**14.**322; **16.**153
1:8	**14.**35; **16.**25
1:11–12	**17.**81
2:1–6	**17.**81
2:1	**14.**322; **16.**153
2:2	**3.**22
2:6–7	**12.**54
2:7	**17.**126
3:21	**17.**51
4:4	**9.**143; **10.**158; **13.**122
4:7	**1.**181; **3.**47, 173
4:16	**6.**126
4:18	**11.**124; **14.**322
5:13	**9.**34
5:17	**14.**246; **16.**145
8:6	**1.**181
9:3	**17.**192
9:33	**13.**89
11:4	**1.**181
11:7	**11.**16; **14.**295
13:15	**14.**125
13:26	**6.**3
14:1	**4.**13
14:7–12	**6.**93
15:14	**4.**13
15:15	**11.**124
16:19	**14.**125
19:25–27	**9.**139

19:25	**14.**125	8:2	**2.**249
21:20	**17.**111	8:4–6	**13.**23
22:29	**14.**109	8:4	**2.**26
23:3	**3.**25	8:5	**13.**24
25:4	**4.**13	8:6–8	**14.**89
26:6	**17.**51	9:10	**1.**205; **4.**143; **5.**62;
26:13	**15.**62		**6.**210; **15.**53
27:9	**6.**48	9:13	**16.**52
28:17	**16.**156	9:18	**1.**91
28:19	**17.**214	10:7	**8.**55
28:22	**17.**51	14:1–3	**8.**55
28:28	**9.**207	14:1	**1.**140; **3.**314f
29:3	**6.**13	15	**3.**293
31:12	**17.**51	15:3	**1.**274
33:4	**1.**22	16:5	**14.**174
37:4	**16.**155	16:8–11	**14.**181
37:9–10	**17.**20	16:9–11	**6.**92; **9.**139
38–41	**8.**27	16:10	**5.**117
38:7	**14.**322	16:11	**6.**158
38:31	**16.**48	18	**16.**25
40:15–24	**17.**77	18:2	**2.**140
42:7	**16.**25	18:10	**16.**158
42:12	**14.**125	18:15	**17.**20
		18:31	**2.**140
		18:49	**14.**127
Psalms		18:50	**8.**198
		19:1–2	**16.**159
1:1	**1.**88	19:4	**8.**141
2	**14.**181	19:9	**9.**208
2:2	**17.**73, 132	19:10	**17.**57
2:5	**10.**18	20:7	**1.**206; **5.**60f; **6.**210;
2:7	**1.**60; **4.**38; **13.**19, 47		**15.**54
2:8–9	**16.**110	21:3	**14.**49
2:8	**1.**70	22	**2.**368; **12.**220; **14.**181
2:9	**17.**75, 78, 182	22:7–8	**2.**368
5:9	**8.**55	22:16	**11.**54
6:5	**6.**91; **9.**138; **14.**237;	22:18	**2.**368; **6.**255
	16.181	22:20	**11.**54
8	**13.**23	22:22	**6.**210; **13.**27

22:25–31	2.368	40:3	16.176	
23	12.201	40:6–9	13.113f	
23:1–2	1.211; 6.53	40:11	12.25	
23:1	14.215; 17.38	41:9	3.335; 6.142	
23:2	17.39	42:1	5.154; 14.192	
23:5	3.255; 6.110	42:2	16.48; 17.22	
24:1	1.250	42:3	14.338	
24:4	14.107f	42:6	1.260	
24:5	12.18	42:7	3.255; 17.86	
25:11	15.54	42:11	11.83	
26:3	6.158	43:5	11.83; 12.19	
26:6	14.107	45:7–8	13.19	
27:1	6.13	46:1	1.211	
27:2	17.148	46:4	17.220	
27:3	6.152	46:7	1.211	
27:10	9.199	46:9	17.4	
27:11	6.157	46:10	2.163	
29	17.55	47:8	16.151	
29:10	10.142	50:3	14.341	
30:9	6.92; 9.138; 14.237; 16.181	50:10	1.250; 17.191	
30:11	10.50	50:12	1.250	
31:3	15.54	50:14	13.115	
31:5	4.288	50:20	14.111	
32:2	5.93; 17.108	51:1–7	17.30	
32:5	1.57	51:16	5.113; 8.58; 13.115	
32:6	17.86	51:17	1.95	
33:2	16.174	53:1	15.200	
33:3	16.176	55:12–14	6.143	
33:6	1.22; 5.29	55:22	14.272	
34:6	1.91	57:3	12.25	
34:8	14.192	66:18	6.48	
34:15	6.48	68:5	14.61	
35:10	1.91	68:6	15.103	
35:19	6.187	68:8	13.188	
36	16.25	68:10	1.91	
36:1	8.55	68:17	17.53	
36:9	5.154; 17.39, 216	68:18	10.143	
37:25	1.181; 3.246	68:20	14.112	
		69:4	6.187	

69:9	5.114; 8.197; 11.60	89:3	11.10; 15.25
69:21	6.259	89:4	6.128
69:22–23	8.145	89:6	14.322
69:28	16.123; 17.196	89:10	15.62; 17.58
72:4	1.91	89:12	3.210
73:9	14.85	89:17	16.171
73:13	14.108	89:20ff	3.298; 6.178
73:23–26	14.174	89:20	11.10
73:23–24	3.292; 6.92; 9.139	89:27	11.119; 16.33; 17.206
73:27	5.143	90	12.134
74:12–14	17.77	90:4	3.108; 14.250, 342;
74:13	17.47		17.188
75:4	16.171	90:15	16.9; 17.188
75:8	3.255; 17.111	91:6	12.214
77:18	13.188; 16.155	91:7–10	1.181
77:20	6.53	91:11–12	1.69
78:1–3	2.69	92:5	17.119
78:24–25	16.95	94:11	9.34
78:24	5.215	94:12	14.246; 16.145
78:45	17.130	95:7–11	13.33, 37
78:70	11.10; 14.293	95:7	6.53
79:3	17.72	96:1	16.176
79:5–10	17.12	97:1	17.172
79:10	14.338	97:7	13.19
79:13	6.53	98:1	16.176; 17.119
80:1	6.53; 16.158; 17.38	98:2	17.120
80:8	6.172	98:5	16.174
82:6	6.77	99:1	16.158
83:13–14	14.85	99:3	17.120
83:13	17.20	100:3	6.53; 14.216
85:2	1.56	101:5	14.111
86:9	17.120	101:7	17.228
86:11	6.158	102:25–27	17.195
86:14–16	12.25	102:25–26	17.15
87:4	17.58	102:26–27	13.19
88:5	6.92	103:2	4.219; 17.28
88:10–12	6.92; 9.138; 14.237;	103:15	14.48
	16.181	103:22	16.159
88:11	17.51	104:2	16.122, 151; 17.75

104:3	16.155; 17.54		118:6	13.194
104:4	13.19		118:22–23	3.283; 4.247; 8.135
104:30	1.22		118:22	2.264; 14.194
105:6	6.25; 14.166		118:25	2.239; 5.249
105:26	14.293; 16.25		118:26	2.2, 239; 3.266
105:30	17.130		118:29	5.249
105:33	2.151		119:30	6.158
105:41	5.251		119:103	17.57
105:43	14.166		119:174	14.192
106:1	17.169		120–134	3.324
106:2	1.196		121:3	15.207
107:18	16.52		121:6	3.119
107:20	5.29		121:8	6.59
107:30	5.210		122	3.324
107:41	1.91		124:4	3.255; 17.86
109:6	17.81		124:8	15.87
109:14	6.38		130:8	1.19
110	14.181		132:10	16.25
110:1	2.279; 3.298; 4.252; 13.19		132:15	1.91
			133:1	11.14; 14.209
110:4	13.67, 71, 72, 80		135:1	17.169, 171
111:1	17.169		135:4	5.59
111:2	17.119		135:20	17.171
111:9	17.120		136	1.390; 2.342; 3.338
112:1	17.169		136:5–6	5.168
112:3	9.235		137	14.37
112:9	9.235; 16.171		137:8	17.153
113–118	2.342; 3.338; 5.249; 6.116; 17.169		139:1–4	5.163
			139:12	17.219
113–114	3.338		139:14	17.119
113:1	17.169		140:3	8.55
114:7	13.188		141:2	16.174
115–118	3.338		141:8	6.152
115:17	6.92; 9.138; 14.237		144:9	16.176
116:8	9.173		144:10	16.25
117:1	8.198; 17.169		145:1	10.108
118	3.267		145:15	1.176
118:1	5.249		145:17	17.120
118:5–6	6.116		145:19	6.48f

11 Phil, Col, Thes   **13** Heb   **15** John, Jude   **16** Rev, v.1
12 Tim, Tit, Phlm   **14** Jas, Pet   **17** Rev, v.2

146:1	**17.**169	11:28	**14.**117
147:1	**17.**169	11:30	**16.**69
147:7	**16.**174	11:31	**14.**261
147:15	**5.**29	13:3	**14.**55
148	**16.**159, 182	13:12	**16.**69
148:1	**17.**169	13:14	**17.**220
148:4	**16.**155	13:24	**16.**145
148:14	**16.**171	14:27	**17.**220
149:1	**16.**176; **17.**169	15:1–4	**14.**82
150:1	**17.**169	15:4	**16.**69
		15:11	**17.**51
		15:17	**9.**220
		15:29	**6.**49
Proverbs		16:6	**9.**207
		16:22	**17.**221
1:7	**9.**207; **14.**209	16:27	**14.**85
1:9	**14.**49	16:32	**1.**98; **12.**252
2	**11.**117	17:15	**8.**57
3:6	**6.**208	17:28	**14.**55
3:11–12	**13.**177	19:14	**12.**76
3:12	**16.**144	20:1	**12.**79
3:13–26	**5.**31	20:27	**5.**251
3:18–20	**5.**31	22:2	**14.**63
3:18	**6.**208; **16.**69	23:6	**1.**246
3:24	**12.**186	23:13–14	**16.**145
3:27–28	**14.**118	23:29–35	**12.**79
3:34	**8.**37; **14.**105, 270	24:29	**1.**165
4:5–13	**5.**31	25:21	**1.**165
4:9	**14.**49	26:11	**14.**335
6:23	**6.**158	27:1	**14.**113
8	**11.**117	27:6	**16.**145
8:1–9:2	**5.**31f	27:20	**17.**51
8:22–30	**5.**31f	28:13	**1.**57
9:10	**9.**207	28:22	**1.**246
10:11	**17.**220	29:15, 17	**16.**145
10:12	**14.**253	29:20	**14.**55
10:17	**6.**158	29:33	**14.**110
10:19	**14.**55	30:5–6	**17.**231
10:25	**1.**290	31:6	**12.**79
11:9	**6.**208		

1 Matt, v.1	**3** Mark	**5** John, v.1	**7** Acts	**9** Cor
2 Matt, v.2	**4** Luke	**6** John, v.2	**8** Rom	**10** Gal, Eph

35:12	14.63
36:9	17.221

Ecclesiastes

2:5	16.70
2:15–16	16.84
2:24	9.154
3:12	9.154
5:2	1.196
5:18	9.154
7:20	14.82
8:15	9.154
9:2	16.84
9:4–5	9.138; 16.84
9:7	3.38; 9.154
9:8	16.122
9:10	6.92; 9.138; 14.237

Song of Solomon

3:11	14.49
5:2–6	16.147
6:3	17.203
6:10	17.75
8:7	9.125

Isaiah

1:9–10	17.71
1:9	15.185
1:11–20	13.115
1:11–17	5.112
1:15	6.48; 12.65
1:16–17	12.256
1:16	1.54; 14.107
1:18	16.49; 17.30
1:21	17.142
1:30	16.70
2:2–4	17.216
2:2	15.59
2:4	16.10
2:12	7.25
3:9	15.185
3:16–17	17.154
3:18–24	14.221
4:3	17.196
5:1–7	3.281; 4.245; 6.172
5:7	2.261
5:8	14.117
6	13.17
6:1	16.151
6:3	5.69; 16.127, 162
6:4	17.122
6:5–6	14.107
6:5	10.102; 17.36
6:6	17.41
6:8	1.360; 8.12
6:9–13	8.145
6:9–10	2.68; 3.92; 4.99; 6.132; 8.145
7:3	8.145
8:12	8.145
8:7–8	17.137
8:13–15	2.265
8:13–14	14.195
8:13	14.229
8:14	8.135
8:17	13.27
8:18	8.145
9:1–2	1.75
9:2–7	3.298
9:7	3.193; 6.128
9:12	8.145
9:18	14.85

9:19	**8.25**	22:15–25	**16.**133
10:22–23	**8.**120, 133	22:22	**2.**145; **16.**128
11:1–9	**3.**298	23	**2.**12
11:1	**1.**40; **3.**193; **16.**2, 170;	23:1, 14	**14.**115
	17.228	23:16–17	**17.**142
11:2	**16.**31, 116	24:21–22	**14.**237
11:4	**16.**51; **17.**178, 182	24:21	**17.**47
11:6–9	**3.**24; **16.**10	24:23	**16.**153; **17.**47
11:10	**8.**198; **16.**2, 170	25:6	**17.**174
11:12	**17.**19, 216	25:8	**16.**11; **17.**203
11:13	**16.**10	26:1	**17.**210
11:16	**17.**128	26:3	**1.**261
12:3	**5.**154, 249	26:19	**2.**276
13:6–16	**3.**304; **7.**25	27:1	**15.**62; **17.**58, 77
13:6	**14.**115; **17.**16	27:12	**16.**8
13:8	**17.**16	27:13	**3.**319; **17.**42
13:9	**4.**257; **6.**197; **8.**25;	28:1–2	**14.**49
	11.204; **14.**344	28:2	**17.**134
13:10–13	**4.**257; **14.**344	28:7	**14.**315
13:10	**2.**303; **3.**319; **16.**7;	28:9–12	**9.**131
	17.14	28:16	**2.**265; **8.**121, 135, 139;
13:13	**2.**303; **17.**15		**14.**194
13:19–22	**16.**8, 149	29:6	**14.**341
13:19	**15.**185	29:10	**8.**145
14:12	**15.**183; **16.**111; **17.**59,	29:13	**3.**167
	80	29:14	**9.**17
14:13	**17.**133	30:21	**6.**157
14:31	**14.**115	30:30	**14.**341
15:2–3	**14.**115	31:4	**6.**61
16:7	**14.**115	32:15	**16.**10
19:2	**17.**5	33:15	**3.**294
20:3–4	**7.**154; **14.**36	33:18	**9.**17
20:3	**16.**25	33:24	**16.**11
20:4	**16.**143	34:4	**3.**319; **17.**14, 15
20:7	**14.**293	34:8–10	**17.**112
21:9	**17.**111	34:9–10	**17.**170
22:5	**11.**204	34:11–15	**17.**150
22:9–11	**6.**43	35:1	**16.**10
22:14	**2.**42	35:5–6	**6.**72

35:6	**5.**186	45:22	**17.**217
35:7	**5.**154	45:23	**1.**369; **8.**187
35:8–10	**3.**319	48:12	**16.**48, 52, 81
35:8	**6.**157	48:13	**5.**30
35:10	**17.**203	48:20	**17.**152
37:16	**16.**158	49:2	**16.**51
37:32	**8.**133	49:6	**5.**55; **6.**63; **16.**8;
38:10	**16.**52		**17.**217
38:18	**6.**92; **9.**138; **14.**237;	49:10	**1.**67; **5.**154; **17.**37
	16.181	49:23	**16.**130
39:13	**9.**138	49:24–26	**2.**36
40:3–5	**4.**6, 32	50:3	**17.**14
40:3	**1.**44; **5.**78f	50:9	**14.**229
40:6–8	**14.**189	51:2	**14.**222
40:6–7	**14.**48	51:3	**16.**10
40:7	**17.**20	51:5	**16.**8; **17.**217
40:11	**6.**54; **14.**215; **17.**38	51:6	**17.**195
40:24	**17.**20	51:9	**15.**62; **17.**47, 58, 77
40:25	**16.**127	51:17	**3.**255; **17.**111
40:31	**7.**11; **17.**85	52:6	**6.**210
41:5	**17.**14	52:7	**8.**141
41:8	**6.**25, 178	52:11	**9.**223
42:1–4	**2.**33	52:13–	**14.**181
42:1	**1.**60; **4.**38	53:12	
42:6	**5.**55; **6.**63	52:15	**5.**79; **8.**203
42:9–10	**16.**176	53	**1.**60; **5.**81; 7.69, 129;
43:2	**17.**86		**9.**18; **14.**185, 214
43:15	**16.**127	53:1–2	**6.**131; **8.**141
43:18–19	**17.**204	53:4	**1.**310f
43:21	**14.**198	53:7	**5.**81; **14.**120; **16.**171
44:1–2	**16.**25	53:9	**5.**93; **17.**108
44:3	**1.**48; **5.**154	54:5	**5.**143; **9.**246; **14.**101;
44:6	**16.**48, 52, 81; **17.**204		**16.**108; **17.**76, 172
44:9–17	**17.**21	54:11–12	**17.**200
45:1	**2.**33	54:12–13	**16.**9
45:3	**6.**5; **13.**60	55:1	**5.**154; **17.**230
45:4	**14.**166; **16.**25	55:2	**5.**212
45:14	**10.**122; **16.**8, 130	55:5	**17.**217
45:20–22	**16.**8	55:6	**5.**246

55:11	1.369; **5**.29	66:15	**17**.20
56:1	3.294	66:19	**17**.217
56:6–8	**17**.217	66:22	**17**.197
56:7	**2**.247; **3**.274f	66:24	3.232
56:8	6.63		
56:11	3.178		
56:12	**9**.154		
57:15	**14**.110		
57:19	**10**.111		
58:11	**5**.250		
59:7–8	**8**.55	*Jeremiah*	
59:20–21	**8**.152	1:4–5	**8**.12
59:21	**5**.83	1:5	**6**.77, 216
60:10–20	**17**.201	2:2	16.63
60:12	1.304; **10**.122	2:7	**5**.59; **14**.173
60:14	**16**.130	2:13	**5**.154; **17**.220
60:19–20	**17**.216	2:21	6.172
60:19	6.13	2:23	**14**.173
61	4.48	2:35	1.57
61:1	**5**.84; **15**.69	3:2	**14**.173
61:2	**15**.36	3:6–11	**2**.49
61:6	**16**.35	3:6–10	**17**.76
62:2	**16**.99	3:14	**17**.172
62:5	**9**.246	3:17	**17**.217
63:1–3	**17**.181	3:18	**16**.10
63:3	**17**.116	3:20	**14**.101; **16**.108
63:6	**16**.8	4:13	**17**.20
63:16	**6**.27	4:24	**17**.15
64:4	3.292	5:24	**14**.121
64:6	**17**.30	6:10	**11**.55, 139
64:8	**6**.27	6:14	1.281; **14**.314
65:1	**8**.142	7:11	**2**.247; **3**.274
65:6–7	6.38	7:22	**5**.112
65:14	**14**.115	7:25	3.281; **8**.12; **11**.10;
65:17	**8**.109; **17**.197		**12**.227; **14**.36
65:19	**17**.203	7:34	**17**.167
65:20–22	**16**.10	8:3	**17**.51
65:25	**16**.10	8:11	1.281
66:15–16	**14**.341; **16**.7	8:13	**2**.251

8:16	17.25	27:22	7.154
9:14–15	17.44	28	14.315
9:23–24	9.22	28:10–11	2.240; 3.339
11:17	8.149	29:5	16.70
11:19	5.81; 16.171	30:7	11.204
11:20	16.109	30:9	3.193; 16.2
13:1–11	4.239; 7.154; 13.13	30:23	17.20
13:8	14.49	30:24	15.59
15:2	17.97	31:3	5.220
15:19	14.134	31:8–9	5.186
16:9	17.167	31:12	16.10
16:18	5.59	31:18	1.53
16:19–21	17.217	31:31–34	13.92
17:13	5.154	31:33	17.203
17:15	14.338	31:34	13.118
17:19–27	5.182	33:14–18	3.298
17:21–24	4.60; 5.122	35:5–7	12.119
17:24	3.39	37:17	15.22
18:1–6	8.132	47:2	17.137
21:8	1.278	47:4	2.12
22:4	3.193	48:47	15.59
22:13	14.119	49:18	15.185
23:1–4	6.54	49:36	17.20
23:3	8.145	50:8	17.152
23:5ff	3.298	50:13	8.24
23:5	3.193; 16.2	50:29	17.153
23:14	14.315; 15.185	50:39	17.150
23:15	17.44	50:40	15.185
23:16	14.312	51:6	17.152
23:19	17.20	51:7–8	17.111
23:20	15.59	51:7	17.137
23:29	5.29; 17.181	51:13	17.134
23:32	14.315	51:34	17.77
25:10	17.167	51:36	17.128
25:15	17.111	51:37	17.150
25:22	2.12	51:45	17.152
27	3.339	51:48	17.165
27:1–11	4.239; 13.13	51:56	17.4
27:1–6	2.240	51:63–64	17.166

11 Phil, Col, Thes	**13** Heb	**15** John, Jude	**16** Rev, v.1
12 Tim, Tit, Phlm	**14** Jas, Pet		**17** Rev, v.2

B

Lamentations

1:12	6.254
1:15	17.116
1:30	1.30
3:24	14.174
3:30	1.165
4:6	15.185
5:16	14.49
5:21	12.44

Ezekiel

1:6	16.157
1:7	16.50
1:10	16.157
1:13	16.155
1:18	16.157
1:22, 26	16.157
1:28	5.69; 16.51; 17.54
2:1	8.220
2:9–10	16.165
3:1, 3	17.57
3:12	16.43
3:14	17.143
3:15	16.39
3:18	6.17
3:23	16.51
3:27	17.225
4	7.154
4:1–8	3.339
4:1–3	4.239; 13.13
4:16	17.7
5:1–4	3.339; 4.239; 7.154; 13.13
7:2	17.19
7:19	8.25
8:3–18	9.221

8:3	17.143
8:18	6.48
9:1–7	17.23
9:6	2.242; 14.261
10:2	17.41
10:8	14.263
10:20, 22	16.158
11:24	17.143
13:3	14.312
13:16	14.314
14:14, 20	8.145
14:21	17.9
14:22	8.145
15	6.172
16	17.172
16:15	17.142
16:37–39	16.143
16:46, 49, 53, 55	15.185
17:22ff	3.110
17:23	4.179
18:4	8.26; 10.82
18:18	6.17
18:23	14.343
18:31	5.131
19:10	6.172
20:34	9.223
20:37	6.56
20:43	14.173
21:2	13.23
22:27	1.281
23:26–29	16.143
24:6	17.167
26–27	17.158
26:3–7	2.12
26:13	17.166
26:16	16.46
27:3	17.154
27:28–30	17.164

28:12–22   2.12
28:17   16.151
30:2   13.23
31:1ff   3.110
31:6   2.76; 4.179
32:7–8   3.319
32:7   17.14
33:12   1.56
34   6.54
34:9–10   15.194
34:23ff   3.298
34:23   14.215; 16.2; 17.38
34:24   16.25
36:25   5.79
36:26–27   1.48; 5.84, 131
37:9   6.274
37:14   1.48
37:24   3.298; 14.215; 16.2;
           17.38
37:25   6.128; 16.25
37:27   9.223; 17.203
38–39   17.194
38   17.60
38:8   17.133
38:14–39   16.8
38:19   17.13
38:21   17.133
38:22   17.134
39:2, 4   17.133
39:15   1.314
39:17–19   17.184
39:17   17.133
39:29   1.48
40:2   17.209
40:3   17.67, 211
40:6   17.67
41:21   17.212
43:1–2   17.151
43:2   16.48, 50

43:3   16.51
43:16   17.212
44:7, 9   11.139
44:13   14.106
45:2   17.212
47:1–12   5.154, 251
47:1–7   17.220
47:12   17.221
48:20   17.212
48:30–35   17.210
48:31–35   17.201
48:35   16.135

Daniel

2:34f, 44f 2.265; 8.135
2:44   17.187
3   9.119; 13.129
3:19–28   13.164
3:19–25   1.117
3:24–25   8.166
4:10, 21   3.110
5:29   16.144
6:17   17.23
6:18, 23   13.164
7:1–14   5.185f; 16.36
7:1–8   6.121
7:3–7   17.88
7:8   17.94
7:9   16.48f
7:10   17.196
7:13–14   17.115
7:13   2.355; 5.185; 6.121;
           16.45
7:14   6.128; 17.187, 217
7:20   17.94
7:27   16.9; 17.187
8:9–12   17.60, 62

8:10	**17**.77	6:6	**1**.335; **2**.24; **3**.296;
8:26	**17**.225		13.115
9:11	**14**.35; **16**.25	8:13	**5**.112
9:27	3.309	9:1	**14**.102; **16**.108; **17**.106
10:5	**16**.46	9:3	**5**.59
10:6	**16**.49f; 103	10:1	**6**.172
10:13, 20f	**16**.54	10:8	**17**.16
11	**17**.194	11:1	**1**.35f; **3**.71; **8**.124
11:31	3.309; **15**.62	11:8	**15**.185
12:1	**16**.54, 123	11:10	**17**.54
12:2–3	**16**.9	12:5	**16**.39
12:3	**14**.134; **16**.111	13:5	**8**.114
12:7	**17**.69	13:15	**17**.20
12:10	**17**.225	14:6	**8**.149
12:11	**2**.306; **3**.309; **15**.62		

Joel

Hosea

		1:7–18	**17**.49
1:5	**17**.4	2–3	3.304
1:6, 9	**14**.197	2:1–11	**17**.49
1:10	**8**.121, 133; **14**.197;	2:1–2	**4**.257; **6**.197; **7**.25;
	16.48; **17**.22		14.344; **16**.7
1:11	**16**.10	2:1	**17**.16, 42
2:1	**14**.197	2:10	3.319; **17**.13, 44
2:3	**16**.143	2:11	**17**.16
2:4	**6**.28	2:23	**14**.121
2:8	**17**.6	2:28	**1**.48
2:9	**16**.143	2:30–31	**2**.303; **4**.257; **11**.204;
2:12	**2**.251		14.344; **16**.7
2:18	**3**.24; **16**.10	2:30	**14**.341
2:19–20	**16**.76; **17**.172	2:31	**17**.14
2:22	**17**.6	2:32	**8**.121, 140
2:23	**8**.133; **14**.197	3:2, 12	**17**.116
4:6	**6**.208	3:13	**17**.115
4:17	**8**.29; **16**.145	3:15	3.319; **16**.7
5:6	**5**.112	3:16	**17**.54
5:8	**11**.58	3:18	**5**.251; **17**.220

Amos

1:14	**17.20**
3:2	**8.114; 11.11**
3:7	**2.5; 3.281; 6.51;**
	8.12; 11.10; 12.49,
	227; 13.12; 14.36;
	14.293; 15.170;
	16.25, 168
3:8	**17.54**
3:10	**14.116**
3:12	**6.60**
4:11	**15.185**
5:4	**6.208**
5:11	**14.117**
5:16–20	**3.304**
5:18–20	**4.257; 7.25**
5:18	**11.204**
5:27	**7.60**
7:7–9	**17.67**
7:14–15	**3.28**
8:3	**14.115**
8:4–7	**14.117**
8:8	**17.13**
8:9	**3.319; 17.14**
9:3	**17.47**
9:5	**16.39**
9:8–10	**8.145**
9:11	**16.2**
9:13	**5.168**
9:14	**12.79**

Micah

1:1–4	**17.16**
1:8–11	**16.143**
2:12	**8.145**
3:3	**17.148**
3:8	**5.83**
3:11	**14.315**
4:1	**15.59**
4:4	**2.251; 5.93**
4:6	**13.182**
5:2–4	**16.2**
5:2	**1.24, 30**
5:3	**8.145**
6:6–8	**8.58; 13.115; 14.61**
6:8	**3.294**
7:6	**3.313**
7:8	**6.13**
7:12	**3.319**
7:18	**1.56**

Nahum

1:3	**17.19**
1:4	**17.20**
1:5–6	**14.341**
1:5	**17.15**
3:4	**17.142**
3:5	**16.143**
3:14	**17.167**

Habakkuk

2:3	**13.127**
2:4	**3.294; 10.26**
2:14	**6.208**
2:20	**17.36**

Jonah

3:10	**1.54**

Zephaniah

1:3	**17**.44
1:7	**7**.25
1:12	**9**.45
1:14–18	**2**.303; **4**.257; **14**.344
1:14–16	**11**.204
1:14	**16**.7; **17**.16
1:16	**17**.42
2:9	**15**.185
2:11	**5**.158
2:13–15	**17**.150
3:3	**1**.281
3:8	**8**.25
3:9	**17**.217
3:12–13	**8**.145
3:13	**17**.108

Haggai

2:6	**13**.188; **17**.13
2:7–9	**16**.9
2:9	**17**.201

Zechariah

1:5	**6**.33
1:6	**3**.281; **14**.36
1:18	**16**.171
2:1	**17**.67
2:5	**17**.210
2:12	**5**.59
2:13	**17**.217
3:1–5	**17**.30
3:1–2	**17**.81
3:2	**3**.22
3:10	**2**.251

4:2	**16**.45
4:10	**16**.172
5:3	**1**.370
6:1–8	**16**.2
6:1–5	**17**.19
7:6–10	**14**.61
8:2	**14**.104
8:20–23	**17**.217
8:22–23	**16**.130
9:9	**2**.240; **3**.264; **4**.240; **6**.117f
9:14	**17**.20, 42
10:6–11	**3**.319
10:11	**17**.128
11:10	**2**.337
11:16	**6**.62
12:6	**14**.85
12:10	**6**.261; **16**.36f
12:11	**17**.132
13:1	**5**.79, 154
13:4	**1**.282
13:7	**2**.343
14	**17**.60
14:1–11	**16**.8; **17**.194
14:1–4	**17**.116
14:8	**5**.154; **17**.220
14:9	**17**.217
14:13	**16**.7; **17**.5
14:16–18	**5**.248

Malachi

1:2–3	**8**.128
1:8–9	**14**.63
1:11	**5**.158
2:7	**16**.54
2:9	**14**.63

---

1 Matt, v.1	**3** Mark	**5** John, v.1	**7** Acts	**9** Cor
2 Matt, v.2	**4** Luke	**6** John, v.2	**8** Rom	**10** Gal, Eph

2:10	6.27	3:5	14.119
2:16	1.151; 11.196	4:1	11.204; 14.341
2:17	14.338	4:4	14.35, 293
3:1–4	5.108	4:5–6	1.44; 2.6, 136, 164;
3:1–3	16.7; 17.16		3.213; 4.19, 90;
3:1	1.69; 2.242; 3.12;		5.78; 16.6
	17.70	4:5	17.70

INDEX OF NEW TESTAMENT REFERENCES

(Page numbers in italics indicate the main treatment of the N.T. passages)

Matthew

1:1–17	**1**.9, *11–18*; **3**.298; **4**.12, 40f
1:2	**4**.3
1:5	**13**.161
1:16	**4**.41
1:18–25	**1**.*18–23*; **4**.12
1:21–23	**1**.6
1:21	**8**.20; **14**.176
1:24–25	**14**.20
2:1–2	**1**.*23–27*
2:2	**1**.9; **17**.21
2:3–9	**1**.*28–30*
2:9–12	**1**.*31–33*
2:13–15	**1**.*33–36*
2:13	**17**.79
2:14–15	**1**.6
2:15	**4**.137
2:16–18	**1**.6, *36–38*; **3**.149
2:17	**4**.137
2:19–23	**1**.*38–40*
2:22	**7**.93
2:23	**1**.6; **4**.137
3:1–6	**1**.*43–46*
3:2	**1**.51
3:3	**4**.6; **5**.79
3:7–12	**1**.7, *46–58*; **2**.3; **3**.20; **7**.141
3:8	**14**.72
3:9	**6**.26
3:11	**5**.84; **7**.141; **15**.108
3:12	**17**.117
3:13–17	**1**.*58–60*
3:16–17	**15**.108
3:17	**3**.20
4:1–11	**1**.*61–70*
4:1	**3**.6; **17**.82, 143
4:2	**1**.234
4:3–4	**5**.204
4:3	**17**.82
4:5	**17**.82
4:8–9	**16**.33
4:8	**17**.82
4:10	**2**.150; **17**.82
4:11	**17**.82
4:12–17	**1**.*70–76*, 364
4:12	**5**.2
4:18–22	**1**.*76–79*
4:21	**14**.9
4:23–25	**1**.*80–83*
5–7	**1**.8; **4**.76
5:1	**1**.86–87, 198
5:3	**1**.*88–92*; **4**.5; **14**.66
5:4	**1**.*93–95*; **14**.108; **15**.36; **17**.204
5:5	**1**.*96–98*; **10**.51
5:6	**1**.*99–102*; **17**.36
5:7	**1**.*102–105*; **2**.194; **14**.70
5:8	**1**.*105–108*; **2**.119; **14**.108; **15**.75; **16**.122; **17**.34, 222
5:9	**1**.*108–110*
5:10–12	**1**.*110–118*
5:10	**12**.198

5:12	1.179; **17**.172	6:5–8	1.*191–198*
5:13–16	**2**.54	6:5	1.186
5:13	1.85, *118–122*	6:9–15	1.*198–200*
5:14–15	1.*122–125*	6:9	1.*200–210*
5:14	**16**.53	6:10–11	1.364
5:15	1.85; **3**.98	6:10	1.*210–214*, 258, 267;
5:16	1.*125f*; **14**.72, 204		**2**.86, 289; **3**.42;
5:17–20	1.6, *126–133*; **2**.282,		4.54f; **14**.347
	285	6:11	1.*215–219*
5:18	1.85	6:12	1.103, *219–224*; **3**.276;
5:21–48	1.*133–137*		**14**.228
5:21–22	1.*137–141*; **15**.83	6:13	1.*224–232*; **9**.196;
5:21	1.9, 134		**17**.82
5:22	1.140; **3**.231	6:14–15	1.103, *219–224*; **2**.195;
5:23–24	1.*142f*; **12**.65		**3**.276; **14**.22, 71, 228
5:25–26	1.*144–146*	6:14	**14**.134
5:26	**4**.171	6:15	**12**.65
5:27–28	1.*146*	6:16–18	1.*232–238*, 335
5:27	1.9, 134	6:16	1.186
5:28	**14**.331	6:19–21	1.*238–243*
5:29–30	1.*147–150*; **11**.150	6:19	**14**.116
5:29	1.140; **3**.231	6:21	**2**.218
5:30	1.140; **2**.183; **3**.231	6:22–23	1.*243–247*
5:31–32	1.85, *150–157*; **4**.212	6:24	1.*248–254*; **14**.103;
5:31	**3**.237		**15**.57; **16**.109
5:33–37	1.*158–162*; **2**.292;	6:25–34	1.*254–261*; **14**.272
	14.126	6:26–30	**2**.54
5:33	1.134	7:1–5	1.85, *261–265*
5:34–37	**14**.22	7:1–2	**2**.89; **6**.6; **14**.66, 71,
5:34	1.9		121
5:38–42	1.*162–172*	7:2	**3**.98; **17**.153
5:38	1.9, 134	7:3–5	**6**.6
5:43–48	1.*172–178*	7:6	1.*265–269*; **3**.178;
5:43	1.9, 134		**11**.54
5:47	**9**.163	7:7–12	1.85
6:1–18	1.*179–185*	7:7–11	1.85, *270–272*
6:1	1.*185f*	7:7	**4**.8; **5**.246
6:2–4	1.*187–191*	7:11	**3**.27
6:2	1.186	7:12	1.*272–277*

1 Matt, v.1	**3** Mark	**5** John, v.1	**7** Acts	**9** Cor
2 Matt, v.2	**4** Luke	**6** John, v.2	**8** Rom	**10** Gal, Eph

7:13–14	**1**.*277–280*		9:20–22	**1**.*345–348*
7:15–21	**14**.72		9:21	**8**.20; **14**.176
7:15–20	**1**.*281–288*; **16**.63		9:23–26	**1**.*342–345*
7:15	**16**.63		9:24	**6**.86
7:16–20	**14**.22		9:27–31	**1**.*349–351*
7:16	**3**.271		9:27	**3**.298
7:21–23	**1**.*288–290*		9:30	**1**.298; **6**.97
7:21	**3**.271		9:31–34	**1**.325
7:22	**12**.177		9:32–34	**1**.*351–352*
7:24–27	**1**.*290–294*; **2**.54; **4**.82		9:35	**1**.*352–354*
7:28–29	**1**.133		9:36	**1**.*354–356*; **3**.7; **6**.54; **14**.269
8	**1**.358			
8:1–4	**1**.*295–300*		9:37	**1**.*356–357*
8:5–13	**1**.*300–307*; **5**.174		10	**1**.8
8:9	**8**.54f		10:1–4	**1**.*357–362*
8:10	**6**.64		10:1	**2**.166
8:11	**1**.6, 210; **6**.64; **17**.174		10:2	**14**.8
8:14–15	**1**.*307–309*		10:3	**5**.94; **14**.8
8:14	**2**.175		10:4	**4**.3
8:16–17	**1**.*309–310*		10:5–8a	**1**.*362–366*
8:16	**1**.2		10:5–6	**1**.6; **4**.6; **6**.63
8:17	**1**.311		10:6	**14**.269
8:18–22	**1**.*311–315*		10:8b–10	**1**.*366–368*
8:23–27	**1**.*316–319*		10:11–15	**1**.*368–371*
8:25	**8**.20; **14**.176		10:15	**15**.185
8:28–34	**1**.*319–323*		10:16–22	**1**.*372–378*; **6**.155
8:28	**1**.319; **12**.182		10:16	**1**.281; **6**.61
9	**1**.358		10:17–22	**6**.182
9:1–8	**1**.324, *325–328*; **3**.2		10:18–19	**7**.174
9:9–13	**4**.64		10:22	**14**.176
9:9	**1**.5, *328–332*; **14**.8		10:23–29	**6**.182
9:10–13	**1**.324, *332–335*; **2**.183		10:23	**1**.*378–382*
9:11	**1**.7		10:24–25	**1**.*382–384*
9:13	**1**.18		10:26–31	**1**.*384–390*
9:14–17	**1**.325		10:26	**3**.98
9:14–15	**1**.*335–337*		10:28	**1**.140, 312; **3**.231; **14**.112
9:16–17	**1**.*337–340*; **2**.54			
9:18–31	**1**.*340–342*; **6**.100		10:29	**4**.161, 171
9:18–19	**1**.*342–345*		10:32–33	**1**.*390–392*; **2**.42;

	12.170; **15**.68; **16**.123	12:30	*2.39–41*
10:33	**15**.119	12:31–33	*2.41–45*
10:34–39	1.*393–397*	12:31–32	**4**.161
10:34	**6**.185	12:34–37	*2.45–47*
10:36	**1**.228; **3**.75; **4**.103	12:36–37	**14**.82
10:37–39	**2**.151	12:38–42	*2.48–50*
10:39	**6**.124; **17**.84	12:38–40	**2**.129
10:40–42	1.*397–400*	12:39	**16**.108
10:42	**1**.179	12:43–45	**2**.20, *50–52*
11	**11**.1	12:45	**14**.335
11:1–6	*2.1–4*; **5**.245; **6**.163	12:46–50	**2**.20, *52f*; **14**.9
11:4	**5**.196	13	**1**.8; *2.53–56*
11:5	**14**.66	13:1–9	*2.56–63*; **14**.57, 189
11:7–11	*2.4–7*	13:8	**6**.154
11:12–15	*2.7–9*	13:10–17	*2.63–71*
11:16–19	*2.9–10*	13:12	**3**.98
11:16–17	**2**.54	13:13	**4**.99
11:20–24	*2.11–13*	13:14–15	**6**.132
11:23–24	**1**.371	13:18–23	*2.56–63*
11:24	**15**.185	13:19	**15**.24
11:25–27	*2.13–15*	13:24–30	*2.71–75*; **12**.179;
11:27	**15**.67		**17**.115
11:28–30	*2.15–18*	13:31–32	*2.75–78*; **4**.179
11:29	**10**.51	13:33	*2.78–83*
11:30	**10**.51; **11**.157; **15**.104	13:34–35	**1**.6; **2**.63–71
12	*2.18–20*	13:36–43	*2.71–75*; **12**.179
12:1–8	**2**.19, *21–27*, 42	13:37–43	**17**.115
12:7	**1**.335	13:39	**17**.82
12:9–14	**2**.19, *27–32*	13:43	**16**.122
12:10–13	**4**.72	13:44	*2.83–86*
12:14	**1**.7; **2**.19	13:45–46	*2.86–88*
12:15–21	*2.32–34*	13:46	**17**.215
12:15	**1**.2	13:47–50	*2.88–90*; **12**.179
12:16	**1**.298	13:51–52	*2.90f*
12:22–29	**2**.19, *34–39*	13:53–58	*2.91f*
12:23	**1**.15; **3**.298	13:55	**3**.6; **4**.13; **14**.9, 14,
12:24	**1**.7		19; **15**.170
12:25–29	**15**.78	13:57	**5**.172
12:28	**12**.90	13:58	**1**.3

14:1–12	2.*92–98*		16:13	5.230; **15.32**
14:3–12	**1.71**		16:16	**15.68**
14:3	7.93		16:17–19	2.*139–146*
14:5–12	4.36		16:18	**14.195**
14:12–21	**1.1; 3.2**		16:20–23	2.*147–150*
14:13–21	2.*98–103*		16:21	**2.227; 14.263**
14:13	4.117		16:23	**1.65; 2.150**
14:14	1.354		16:24–26	2.*151–155*
14:15–21	2.125		16:24–25	2.107
14:15	4.87		16:24	6.155
14:19	2.125		16:25	**6.124; 17.84, 118**
14:22–27	2.*104–106*		16:27–28	2.*155f*
14:27	**16.52**		16:28	1.381
14:28–33	2.*106f*		17:1–8	2.*156–163*; **14.310**
14:30	8.20		17:1	**14.9**
14:33	16.146		17:2	**16.51; 17.54**
14:34–36	2.*108*		17:7	**16.52**
14:36	1.347		17:9–13	2.*164f*
15:1–9	2.*109–117*		17:9	1.298
15:1–6	2.215		17:14–20	2.*165–168*
15:10–20	2.*118–120*; **11.145**		17:20	**2.75; 3.275**
15:13	1.7		17:22–23	2.*164f*, 227
15:17	**11.145**		17:24–27	2.*168–172*
15:21–28	2.*120–124*; **5.175**		17:27	4.172
15:21	2.125		18	**1.8; 2.*172–174***
15:22	**1.9, 15, 349; 3.298**		18:1–4	2.*174–176*
15:24	**1.6; 6.64**		18:2	3.7
15:28	1.363		18:3	**5.127; 12.44**
15:29–39	2.*124–128*		18:5–7	2.*176–181*
15:32	**1.354f; 4.87**		18:8–9	2.*181–184*
16:1–4	2.*128–130*		18:8	3.43
16:1	14.102		18:9	**1.140; 3.231**
16:3	1.7		18:10	**1.321; 2.*176–181*;**
16:4	16.108			**3.35; 13.18; 16.54**
16:5–12	2.*130–132*		18:12–14	2.*184–186*; **14.269**
16:6	2.79		18:12	**6.54, 283**
16:12	1.7		18:15–18	2.*186–190*
16:13–23	1.7		18:16	5.195
16:13–16	2.*133–138*		18:17	**1.7**

18:19–20	*2.190–192*
18:19	6.180
18:21–35	*2.192–195*; **14**.71
18:24	4.172
18:35	1.102; **12**.65
19:1–9	*2.195–205*
19:3–9	1.157; **3**.240
19:4–6	17.106
19:10–12	*2.205–210*
19:13–15	*2.211–212*; **3**.7
19:16–22	*2.213–216*
19:19	2.201
19:20	2.213
19:21	1.313
19:23–26	*2.216–219*
19:24	17.2
19:27–30	*2.220f*
19:27–29	16.154
19:28	14.269; **17**.193
20:1–16	*2.221–226*
20:2	4.171
20:17–19	*2.227f*
20:17	3.7
20:20–28	*2.228–235*
20:20–23	3.253
20:20	1.3; **5**.16; **6**.256
20:21	17.148
20:29–34	*2.235–237*
20:30–31	1.15, 349
20:30	2.280
20:34	1.354; **4**.87
21:1–11	2.9, *237–243*
21:35	1.6
21:5	10.51
21:9	1.9, 15; **2**.280; **3**.298; **4**.252
21:12–14	*2.243–248*
21:12–13	5.4, 107
21:13	5.111
21:15–17	*2.248–250*
21:15	1.9, 15; **3**.298
21:18–22	*2.250–257*
21:23–27	*2.257–259*
21:23	14.263
21:28–32	*2.259f*, 271
21:31–32	2.187
21:33–46	*2.260–265*, 271
21:33	1.250
21:41	1.7; **14**.166
21:42	8.135; **14**.194
22:1–14	2.271
22:1–10	1.333; *2.265–268*
22:2, 10–11	17.172
22:11–14	*2.268–271*
22:15–22	*2.271–274*
22:16	14.62
22:21	14.205
22:23–33	*2.274–277*
22:30	14.324
22:34–40	*2.277–279*
22:41–46	*2.279f*
23	1.7, 8
23:1–4	*2.284f*
23:2	1.7
23:4–7	14.81
23:4	15.104
23:5–12	*2.285–287*
23:5	1.347; **3**.295, 299
23:12	11.38; **14**.110
23:13–26	2.288
23:13	*2.288f*
23:15	1.140; *2.289–291*; **3**.231
23:16–22	*2.291–293*
23:23–24	*2.293f*
23:25–26	*2.295f*
23:27–28	*2.296f*

23:29–36	2.*297–299*	24·37, 39	2.312; **14.**122, 123
23:33	1.140; 3.231	24:42–51	2.*316–318*
23:37–39	**2.***299f*	24:42–43	16.119
23:37	3.263; **5.**3, 106	24:44	17.61
24–25	1.8	24:48–51	16.132
24	1.7; 2.*300–302*	25:1–13	1.7; 2.*318–321*
24:1–31	2.*301–304*	25:1	17.172
24:1–2	2.302, *304f*	25:14–30	1.7, 179, 184; 2.*321–*
24:3	2.*312f*; **14.**122		*324*; 4.172
24:4–5	2.304, *311*	25:15	1.250
24:5	5.199; **15.**64	25:21, 23	4.39
24:6–8	2.304, *308f*	25:25	2.84
24:8	16.7	25;29	3.98
24:9–10	2.*309f*	25:31–46	1.7–8, 180; 2.*324–326*;
24:9	17.10		17.195
24:11–13	2.304, *311*	25:35	**14.**255
24:11	12.92; **15.**4	25:40	3.225; **13.**199
24:12	**15.**3	25:41	3.23
24:13	**14.**125, 176; **16.**40	25:43	**14.**255
24:14	1.6; 2.*312f*; **14.**347;	26:1–5	2.*327f*
	17.109	26:3	**14.**263
24:15–22	2.302, *305–308*	26:6–13	2.*328–331*
24:15	**15.**62	26:14–16	2.*331f*
24:21	17.17, 29	26:15	3.328
24:23–26	2.304, *311*	26:17–19	2.*338–340*
24:23	17.61	26:18	5.102
24:24	5.199	26:20–25	2.*333f*
24:27–28	2.*312f*	26:26–30	2.*341–343*
24:27	2.312; **14.**122, 123	26:29	17.174
24:29–31	2.*308*	26:31–35	2.*343f*
24:29	17.14	26:31	6.54
24:30	16.36	26:33–35	2.106
24:31	16.43; **17.**42	26:33	6.285
24:32–41	2.*313–316*	26:35	8.100; **14.**90
24:32–35	2.*314f*	26:36–46	2.*347–350*
24:33	**14.**121	26:38–46	**14.**272
24:36–51	**14.**123	26:39	**15.**115
24:36–41	2.*315f*	26:40	11.166
24:36	11.205; **14.**123	26:41	16.119

11 Phil, Col, Thes   **13** Heb   **15** John, Jude   **16** Rev, v.1
12 Tim, Tit, Phlm   **14** Jas, Pet   **17** Rev, v.2

26:42	**15.**115	27:62–66	*2.374*
26:45	**5.**102	27:66	**6.**266; **16.**166; **17.**23,
26:47–50	*2.334–336*		191
26:50–56	*2.350–352*	28:1–10	*2.375f*
26:52	**17.**97	28:2	**4.**291
26:53	**6.**67; **17.**182	28:3	**17.**121
26:56	**14.**154, 268	28:9	**6.**270
26:57–58	*2.344–347*	28:10	**6.**271
26:57	*2.352–356*; **14.**263	28:11–15	*2.377*
26:59–68	*2.352–356*	28:16–20	*2.377f*
26:61	**5.**115	28:18	**1.**9
26:63	**1.**161; **6.**245	28:19–20	**1.**6, 363; **6.**64
26:64	**16.**36	28:20	**6.**192; **7.**10; **17.**232
26:65–66	*2.357*; **6.**235		
26:69–75	*2.344–347*; **14.**90		
27:1–2	*2.353, 356–362*		
27:1	**14.**263		
27:3–10	*2.336–338*	*Mark*	
27:3–5	**3.**330; **7.**16	1:1–4	*3.11–15*
27:3	**14.**263	1:3	**4.**6; **5.**78f
27:9	**1.**6	1:5–8	*3.15–18*
27:11–26	*2.353, 356–362*	1:8	**15.**108
27:11	**1.**9	1:9–11	*3.18–21*; **15.**108
27:14	**6.**245	1:11	**6.**127
27:15–26	**6.**248	1:12–13	*3.21–24*
27:17, 22	**2.**361	1:12	**1.**64; **3.**6
27:27–31	*2.362–364*	1:13	**17.**82
27:32–44	*2.365–367*	1:14–15	*3.24–26*
27:34	**4.**284	1:14	**1.**210; **5.**2, 141; **7.**11
27:35	**1.**6; **14.**267	1:15	**1.**51; **4.**54
27:37	**1.**9	1:16–20	*3.26–29*
27:45–50	*2.367–370*	1:19–20	**5.**16; **10.**149; **14.**9
27:50	**2.**369; **3.**364; **4.**288;	1:19	**14.**273
	6.258	1:20	**3.**254; **4.**16; **6.**229
27:51–56	*2.370f*	1:21–28	**1.**308
27:54	**1.**301; **6.**193, 205	1:21–22	*3.29–32*
27:56	**5.**16; **6.**256; **14.**8, 16	1:21	**4.**187
27:57–61	*2.371–374*	1:22	**1.**133; **3.**6
27:57	**2.**219	1:23–28	*3.33–36*

1:25	3.115	3:21	1.3, 228; 2.52; 4.102;
1:27	3.6		7.15, 96; 9.144, 208;
1:29–31	3.*36–38*		11.188; 14.9, 19
1:29	14.9	3:22–27	3.*77–79*
1:32–34	3.*39f*	3:27	17.190
1:34	1.2, 298	3:28–30	3.*79–81*; 4.161
1:35–39	3.*40–42*	3:31–35	3.*81–83*; 14.9, 19
1:38	1.210	3:34	16.49
1:40–45	3.*42–46*	3:35	15.102
1:41	1.354f; 4.87; 5.9;	4:1–2	3.*84–87*
	6.39	4:1	1.317
1:43	6.97	4:3–9	3.*88–90*
2:1–12	1.1; 3.2	4:10–12	3.*90–94*
2:1–6	3.*46–48*	4:11–12	2.68
2:1	1.326	4:12	6.132
2:5	14.131	4:13–20	3.*94–97*
2:7–12	3.*49–52*	4:15	17.82
2:14	14.8; 17.107	4:21–25	3.98
2:13–14	3.*52–55*	4:21	3.*97–100*
2:14–17	1.332	4:22–23	3.*101f*
2:15–17	3.*55–58*	4:24	3.*103f*
2:17	3.8	4:25	3.*104–106*
2:18–20	3.*58–60*	4:26–29	3.*106–109*
2:19	17.172	4:29	17.115
2:21–22	3.*60–62*	4:30–32	3.*109–112*
2:23–28	3.*62–66*	4:33–34	3.*112–114*
2:23	5.4	4:35–41	3.*114–117*
2:27	2.26	4:35	1.317
3:1–6	3.*66–70*; 4.72	4:38	3.7
3:5	1.3; 3.7; 10.156;	4:41	3.6
	16.49	5:1–20	3.184
3:7–12	3.*70–72*	5:1–19	1.322
3:10	1.2	5:1–13	3.*117–120*
3:13–19	3.*73–75*, 360	5:1	1.319
3:14–15	3.219	5:7	1.322
3:14	1.360f; 4.74	5:14–17	3.*121–124*
3:17	5.16; 14.8	5:18–20	3.*124–126*
3:18	5.94; 14.8	5:21–43	6.100
3:20–21	3.*75–77*	5:21–24	1.342; 3.*126–128*

11 Phil, Col, Thes	**13** Heb	**15** John, Jude	**16** Rev, v.1
12 Tim, Tit, Phlm	**14** Jas, Pet		**17** Rev, v.2

5:22	**5.**9		7:9–13	**2.**215; **3.***169–171*
5:25–29	**3.***128–131*		7:11	**3.**8
5:26	**1.**346; **4.**113		7:14–23	**3.***171–175*; **11.**145
5:30–34	**3.***131–133*		7:15	**12.**244
5:35–39	**3.***133–136*		7:19	**11.**145
5:37	**5.**16; **14.**9		7:22	**10.**47
5:40–43	**3.***136f*		7:24–30	**3.***176–179*
5:41	**3.**8		7:24	**2.**125
5:43	**1.**298		7:31–37	**3.***179–182*
6:1–6	**3.***137–141*		7:31	**2.**125f
6:3	**3.**6; **14.**9, 14, 15, 19; **15.**170		7:33	**6.**41
			7:34	**3.**6, 8
6:4	**5.**172		7:36	**1.**298
6:5–6	**1.**3		8:1–10	**3.***182–185*
6:6	**3.**7		8:2	**4.**87
6:7–11	**3.***141–144*		8:11–13	**3.***185f*
6:12–13	**3.***144–146*		8:12	**3.**6
6:14–15	**3.***146–148*		8:14–21	**3.***187–189*
6:16–29	**3.***148–154*		8:22–26	**3.***189–191*
6:17–29	**4.**36		8:26	**1.**298
6:17	**7.**93		8:27–33	**1.**7
6:30–44	**1.**1; **3.**1f, 27		8:27–30	**3.**180, *191–193*
6:30–34	**3.***154–156*		8:27	**5.**230
6:30	**4.**117		8:29	**2.**137
6:31–44	**2.**125		8:31–33	**3.***199–201*
6:31	**3.**7		8:31	**3.**220, 252
6:34	**3.**6f; **6.**39, 54; **14.**215, 270		8:33	**3.**7
			8:34–37	**2.**151
6:35–44	**3.***157–159*		8:34–35	**3.***201–203*
6:39	**2.**125; **5.**4		8:35	**6.**124; **17.**84
6:40	**3.**7		8:36	**3.***203–205*
6:44	**3.**184		8:37	**3.***206f*
6:45–52	**3.***159–161*		8:38–9:1	**3.***207–209*
6:45	**5.**208		8:38	**14.**102; **15.**119; **16.**108
6:51	**3.**6			
6:53–56	**3.***161–163*		9:1	**1.**381f; **2.**155, 314; **14.**310
7:1–4	**3.***163–167*			
7:3	**14.**107		9:2–8	**3.***209–211*; **14.**310
7:5–8	**3.***167–169*		9:2	**5.**16; **14.**19

9:4	17.71		10:32	3.7
9:5	5.4		10:35–45	2.228
9:7	6.127		10:35–40	3.*253–256*
9:9–13	3.*212–214*		10:35	1.3; 5.16; **14.**9
9:14–18	3.*214–216*		10:37	17.148
9:14	5.9		10:41–45	3.*256–259*
9:19–24	3.*216–218*		10:41	14.9, 190
9:22	1.354		10:42–44	14.267
9:25–29	3.*218–220*		10:45	14.317; **16.**177
9:30–31	3.*220f*		10:46–52	3.*259–262*
9:31	3.252		10:47ff	1.349; 3.298
9:32–35	3.*221–224*		11:1–6	3.*262–265*
9:36–37	3.*224f*		11:1–2	3.8
9:38–40	3.*225–228*		11:1	2.238
9:38	5.16		11:7–10	3.*266–268*
9:40	2.40		11:9	**11.**2
9:41–42	3.*228–230*		11:11	3.*268f*; **16.**49
9:43–48	3.*230–233*		11:12–14	2.251; 3.*269–272*
9:43	1.141		11:12	3.7
9:44–48	1.141		11:13	2.252
9:45	1.141		11:15–19	3.*272–275*
9:47	1.141		11:15–17	5.4, 107
9:49–50	3.*233–236*		11:17	5.111, 113
10:1–12	3.*236–240*		11:20–21	2.251; 3.*269–272*
10:9	9.62		11:22–26	3.*275–278*
10:11–12	2.201		11:27–33	3.*278–280*
10:13–16	3.7, *241f*		12:1–12	3.*280–284*
10:14	1.3; 3.7		12:9	14.166
10:17–22	2.213; 3.*243–245*		12:10	14.194
10:18	2.213		12:13–17	3.*284–288*
10:21	3.7; 5.19; 6.145; 16.49; 17.107		12:14	14.62
			12:18–27	3.*288–292*
10:23–27	3.*246–248*		12:28–34	2.278; 3.*292–297*
10:23	**16.**49		12:28–31	15.102
10:24	3.6		12:35–37a	1.349; 3.*297–299*
10:25	7.2		12:37b–40	3.*299–301*
10:26	3.6		12:41–44	3.*301–303*
10:28–31	3.*248–250*		12:42	4.171
10:32–34	2.227; 3.*251–253*		13	3.*303*

13:1–2	**3.***306–309*		14:51–52	**3.***347f*
13:2	**3.**350		14:53	**3.***348–351*
13:3–6	**3.**306, *314–317*		14:54	**3.***351–353*
13:3	**14.**9		14:55–65	**3.***348–351*
13:6	**5.**199; **15.**64; **17.**61		14:58	**5.**116
13:7–8	**3.**306, *317–320*		14:61	**6.**245
13:8	**16.**7		14:62	**16.**36
13:9–13	**3.**306, *312–314*; **6.**182; **17.**10		14:66–72	**2.**345; **3.***351–353*
13:14–20	**3.**306, *309–311*		15:1–5	**3.***354f*
13:14	**15.**62; **17.**79		15:5	**6.**245
13:19	**17.**17, 29		15:6–15	**3.***356–358*; **6.**248
13:21–23	**3.**306, *314–317*		15:6	**4.**280
13:22	**5.**199; **12.**92, 131		15:16–20	**3.***358f*
13:24–27	**3.**306, *317–320*		15:21–28	**3.***359–362*
13:24	**17.**14		15:21	**2.**366; **4.**283; **8.**215
13:26	**16.**36		15:25	**2.**368
13:28–37	**3.**307, *320f*		15:29–32	**3.***362f*
13:29	**14.**121; **16.**146		15:33–41	**3.***363–365*
13:31	**17.**195		15:34	**2.**368; **3.**8
13:32	**7.**14; **11.**205; **14.**123		15:37	**2.**369; **4.**288; **6.**258
13:37	**16.**119		15:40	**2.**229; **6.**256; **14.**8, 16
14:1–2	**3.***322–325*		15:42–47	**3.***365–367*
14:3–9	**3.***325–327*		15:46	**2.**368
14:3	**6.**109		15:47	**2.**374
14:5	**2.**329; **6.**97		16:1–8	**3.***367–369*
14:10–11	**3.***328–330*		16:1	**5.**16
14:12–16	**3.***330–334*; **6.**292		16:5	**4.**291; **17.**121
14:17–21	**3.***334–336*		16:7	**9.**143
14:22–26	**3.***336–340*		16:8	**3.**5, 370; **6.**271
14:27–31	**3.***340–342*		16:9–20	**3.**5, *369–371*
14:27	**6.**54		16:9	**6.**256
14:32–42	**3.***342–345*		16:15	**6.**64
14:33	**4.**16; **14.**9			
14:36	**2.**349; **3.**8			
14:41	**5.**102			
14:43–50	**3.***345f*		*Luke*	
14:43	**3.**8		1:1–4	**4.***7f*
14:44	**14.**279		1:3	**7.**2

1:5–25	4.*8–11*	3:23	1.41; 3.139; 4.37, 41;
1:5	5.76		14.19
1:26–38	4.*11–13*	3:38	4.3
1:36	2.96; 5.82	4:1–13	4.*41–44*
1:39–45	4.*13f*	4:1	3.6
1:46–56	4.4, *14–16*	4:2–3, 5	17.82
1:46–47	12.18	4:6–7	16.33
1:47	15.207	4:13	2.148; 17.82
1:55	15.78	4:14–15	4.*44–46*
1:57–66	4.*16–18*	4:16–30	4.*46–49*
1:67–80	4.4, *18f*	4:16	16.26
1:80	17.143	4:18	14.66
2:1–7	4.*20f*	4:24	5.172
2:7	14.20	4:25–27	4.5
2:8–20	4.*22f*	4:25	14.132
2:21–24	4.*23–25*	4:31–37	4.*49–51*
2:24	4.5	4:35	7.2
2:25–35	4.*25–27*	4:38–39	4.*51–53*
2:29–32	4.4	4:38	4.187
2:36–40	4.*27f*	4:40–44	4.*53–55*
2:36	16.105	4:40	1.2
2:41–52	4.*28f*	4:43	1.210; 4.120
2:48	4.12	5:1–11	4.*55–57*
2:49	2.169; 4.120	5:7–10	5.16
3:1–6	4.*30–32*	5:8	3.80; 5.163; 10.102
3:1–2	4.3; 7.93	5:10	14.9
3:3–11	7.141	5:11	16.51
3:4, 6	4.6; 5.79	5:12–15	4.*57–59*
3:7–18	4.*32–35*	5:16–17	4.*59–61*
3:7–13	3.20	5:16	4.4
3:8	3.271; 6.26; 14.72	5:17–26	1.1; 3.2
3:16	5.85; 7.141; 15.109	5:18–26	4.*61–63*
3:18	5.2	5:27–32	1.333; 4.*63–65*, 234
3:19–20	4.*35f*	5:33–35	4.*65–67*
3:19	7.93	5:36–39	4.*67–69*
3:20	5.2	6:1–5	4.*69–71*
3:21–22	4.*37f*; 15.108	6:6–11	4.*71–73*
3:21	4.4	6:6	4.187
3:23–38	3.298; 4.12, *38–41*	6:7	2.19

6:12–19	4.*73–75*	8:14	**14**.99
6:12	**4**.4	8:16–18	**4**.*100–102*
6:13–19	**1**.84, 360	8:16	**1**.85
6:13	**1**.361	8:19–21	**4**.*102–104*
6:14	**14**.9	8:22–25	**4**.*104–106*
6:15	**4**.3; **14**.8	8:26–39	**4**.*106–109*
6:16	**1**.359; **14**.8; **15**.169	8:26	**1**.319
6:19	**1**.2	8:28	**1**.322
6:20–49	**1**.85	8:31	**17**.191
6:20–26	**4**.*75–77*; **14**.108	8:36	**8**.20
6:20	**4**.5; **14**.66; **16**.78	8:38–39	**4**.228
6:22	**6**.47	8:40–56	**6**.100
6:24	**14**.117	8:40–42	**1**.342; **4**.*109–112*
6:26	**16**.118	8:43–48	**4**.*112–114*
6:27–38	**4**.*77–80*	8:49–56	**1**.342; **4**.*109–112*
6:37–42	**1**.85	8:51	**14**.9
6:39–46	**4**.*80–82*	8:52	**16**.169
6:47–49	**5**.*82f*	9:1–9	**4**.*114–116*
7:1–10	**4**.*83–86*; **5**.174	9:10–17	**1**.1; **3**.2; **4**.*116–118*
7:3	**14**.263	9:18–22	**4**.7, *119f*
7:9	**4**.5	9:18	**4**.4; **5**.230
7:11–17	**4**.*86–88*; **6**.100	9:20	**2**.137
7:13	**1**.354f; **16**.169	9:22	**4**.120
7:15	**5**.9	9:23–27	**2**.151; **4**.*120–122*
7:18–29	**4**.*88–91*	9:24	**6**.124; **17**.84
7:18–22	**9**.261	9:26	**15**.119
7:22	**4**.5; **5**.196	9:27	**1**.381f; **14**.310
7:24	**15**.23	9:28–36	**4**.*123–125*; **14**.310
7:30–35	**4**.*91–93*	9:28	**14**.9
7:36–50	**2**.329; **4**.5, *93–95*;	9:29	**2**.157; **4**.4
	11.157	9:31	**2**.160
7:45	**14**.279	9:32	**2**.157; **11**.166; **14**.269
7:47	**14**.134	9:37–45	**4**.*125–127*
8:1–3	**4**.*96f*	9:37	**2**.157
8:1	**1**.210	9:38	**7**.2
8:2	**6**.256	9:46–48	**4**.*127f*
8:4–15	**4**.*98–100*	9:49–56	**4**.*129–131*
8:10	**6**.132	9:49	**5**.16
8:12	**17**.82	9:50	**2**.40

9:51–56	4.5; **14**.90	12:2–9	**6**.182
9:51	4.119; **8**.206	12:5	1.141; 3.231
9:54	**5**.16; **14**.9	12:6	1.389; **4**.171
9:57–62	4.*131f*	12:8–9	**16**.123
9:57–58	2.107; **6**.80, 155	12:13–34	4.*163–166*
9:59	**17**.108	12:16–21	**14**.113
10:1–19	3.23	12:19	9.154
10:1–16	4.*132–135*	12:24	**13**.29
10:7	**12**.116; **14**.118	12:32	**6**.54
10:12–13	1.371	12:35–48	4.*166–168*
10:12	**15**.185	12:36	**16**.146
10:17–20	4.*135f*	12:49–53	4.*169f*
10:18	**15**.78, 183	12:51–53	**6**.182
10:21–24	4.*136–138*	12:54–59	4.*170–172*
10:22	**15**.67	12:58–59	1.145
10:23–24	**14**.178	13:1–5	4.*172–174*
10:25–37	4.*138–141*	13:1–4	4.281
10:25	4.171	13:6–9	2.253, 271; 4.*174–176*
10:30–37	4.5	13:10–17	4.*176–178*
10:30	1.363	13:13	4.187
10:37	**6**.64	13:16	**17**.82
10:38–42	4.*141f*, 104; **6**.91	13:18–19	4.*178–180*
11:1–4	4.*143f*	13:20–21	4.*180–182*
11:1	1.198	13:22–30	4.*182–184*
11:5–13	4.4, *144–146*	13:27	**12**.177
11:9–13	1.85	13:28	1.210; 4.54
11:11	3.27	13:29	4.5; **6**.64
11:12	1.271	13:31–35	4.*184–186*
11:14–23	4.*147f*	13:31	4.94
11:22	**16**.180; **17**.190	13:33	4.120
11:24–28	4.*149f*	13:34	**5**.3
11:26	**14**.335	13:35	2.2
11:29–32	2.49; 4.*150–152*	14:1–6	4.*186–189*
11:30	2.49	14:7–11	4.*189f*
11:33–36	4.*152–154*	14:11	**11**.38; **14**.111
11:37–44	4.*154–157*	14:12–14	4.*190f*
11:41	**14**.134	14:14–24	1.333; 4.*192–195*
11:45–54	4.*157–159*	14:15	1.216
12:1–12	4.*159–162*	14:25–33	4.*195–197*

14:25–27	**2**.151	18:18	**2**.213
14:26	**1**.313	18:19	**2**.213
14:34–35	**4**.85, *197f*	18:24	**14**.117
15	**3**.316	18:25	**7**.2
15:1–7	**4**.*199–201*	18:31–34	**2**.227; **4**.*230f*
15:4–7	**14**.269	18:31	**3**.7
15:4	**6**.54	18:35–43	**4**.*231–233*
15:8–10	**4**.*201–203*	18:38–39	**4**.252
15:8	**4**.172	19:1–10	**4**.5, *233–236*
15:11–32	**4**.5, *203–206*	19:9	**2**.219
15:13	**12**.235	19:11–27	**4**.172, *236–238*
15:17–18	**3**.14	19:28–40	**4**.*238–240*
15:17	**16**.64	19:38	**2**.2
15:18	**16**.65	19:39–40	**2**.249
15:22	**16**.144	19:41–48	**4**.*240–242*
15:24	**16**.116	19:45–46	**5**.4, 107
16:1–13	**4**.*207–210*	19:46	**5**.111
16:14–18	**4**.*210–212*	20:1–8	**4**.*243f*
16:16	**2**.8	20:9–18	**4**.*244–247*
16:17	**1**.85	20:16	**2**.69; **14**.166
16:18	**2**.201; **9**.62	20:17	**14**.194
16:19–31	**4**.5, *212–214*; **6**.102	20:19–26	**4**.*247–249*
16:21	**11**.54	20:21	**14**.62
16:22–31	**6**.34	20:27–40	**4**.*249–251*
17:1–10	**4**.*215–217*	20:41–44	**4**.*252f*
17:6	**3**.275	20:45–47	**4**.*253f*
17:11–19	**4**.5, *217–219*	21:1–4	**4**.*254–256*
17:18–19	**4**.228; **6**.64	21:5–24	**4**.*256–260*
17:20–37	**4**.*219–221*	21:8	**17**.61
17:20–21	**4**.*220f*	21:12, 18	**17**.10
17:21	**1**.211; **4**.54	21:21–24	**4**.173
17:25	**4**.120	21:25–37	**4**.*260f*
17:29	**1**.371; **15**.185	21:38	**6**.291
17:33	**2**.151; **6**.124; **17**.84	22:1–6	**4**.*262–264*
18:1–8	**4**.4, *221–223*	22:3	**3**.23, 330
18:9–14	**2**.187; **4**.*223–225*	22:7–23	**4**.*264–267*
18:14	**11**.38	22:24–30	**4**.*267f*
18:15–17	**3**.7; **4**.*225–227*	22:24	**6**.138; **14**.190
18:18–30	**2**.213; **4**.*227–230*	22:28	**1**.65

22:31–38	4.*268–271*		24:34	9.143f
22:31–32	12.11		24:36–49	4.*297f*
22:31	17.82		24:39	6.270; 15.23
22:32	4.4		24:42	3.27
22:39–46	4.*271–273*		24:47	15.53
22:42–44	1.65		24:50–53	4.*299f*; 7.13
22:47–53	4.*273–275*		24:52	7.14
22:54–62	4.*268–271*			
22:61–62	14.269; 16.49			
22:61	14.155		*John*	
22:63–71	4.*275–277*			
23:1–12	4.*277–279*		1	5.26; 13.1
23:1–2	3.354		1:1–18	5.*25–37*
23:2	2.357		1:1–2	5.*37–40*
23:3	12.136		1:3	5.13, *40–42*; 16.141
23:6–12	4.173		1:4	5.*42–46*
23:7ff	7.93		1:5	5.45, *47–49*; 15.27
23:9	6.245		1:6–8	5.*49–53*
23:13–25	4.*279–281*		1:7–8	5.52
23:17–25	6.248		1:8	5.12, 50
23:24	7.62		1:9	5.9, *54–56*; 6.18; 13.56
23:26–31	4.*282–284*		1:10–11	5.*56–60*
23:26	7.99		1:10	6.18
23:30	17.16		1:11	7.161
23:32–38	4.*284–286*		1:12–13	5.*60–63*
23:39–43	4.*286f*		1:12	5.128
23:43	4.5; 16.71		1:13	14.171, 189
23:44–49	4.*287–289*		1:14	4.137; 5.13, *63–70*;
23:45	17.14			15.7, 23, 93; 16.180
23:46	2.369; 3.364; 4.4;		1:15–17	5.*70–73*
	6.258; 14.262		1:15	15.112
23:47	4.84		1:18	5.*73–75*; 15.114
23:50–56	4.*289f*		1:19–2:11	5.76
23:50f	2.373		1:19–34	5.75f
24:1–12	4.*290–293*		1:19–28	5.*75–80*
24:5	6.271		1:19–20	5.195
24:7	4.120		1:20	5.50
24:13–35	4.*293–296*		1:20ff	5.12
24:28	16.148		1:23	4.6

1:26	5.195	3:7–13	5.*130–133*
1:28	5.6	3:11	16.32, 140
1:29–31	5.*80–82*	3:14–15	5.*134–137*
1:29	5.195; 15.77; 16.170	3:16	5.13, 43, *137–138*;
1:32, 34	5.*82–85*; 15.108, 112		6.18; 12.19, 55;
1:35–39	5.75, *85–88*		15.40; 17.205
1:35–36	1.78; 5.195	3:17–21	5.*138–140*
1:36	16.170	3:17	6.18
1:40–42	5.75, *88–91*; 8.221	3:19–20	5.46, 47
1:40–41	5.5	3:19	15.27
1:41–51	5.76	3:21	5.68; 14.133; 15.29
1:41–42	14.292	3:22–30	5.2, *141–144*
1:43–51	5.76, *91–95*	3:25–30	5.50
1:43	17.107	3:28	5.12
1:44	5.6, 202	3:29	17.173
1:45	5.52	3:31–36	5.*144–146*
1:48	2.252; 6.82	3:36	5.44
1:51	16.140, 150	4	5.5
2:1–13	5.2	4:1–9	5.*146–151*
2:1–12	5.106, 232	4:1–4	5.172, 228
2:1–11	5.5, 76, *95–105*	4:1	5.50
2:1	5.6; 14.19	4:1–2	5.2, 12, 228
2:4	5.15, 231	4:4–42	1.363
2:6	5.5	4:5	5.6
2:11	5.9, 68, 75	4:6	5.14
2:12–16	5.*105–114*	4:9	4.5, 129; 5.6; 7.65
2:13–22	5.4	4:10–15a	5.*151–156*; 6.86
2:13–17	10.156	4:14	5.250; 17.37
2:13	3.263; 5.2, 4, 80	4:15b–21	5.*156–158*
2:15	5.14	4:16–17	5.15
2:16	5.111	4:21	5.116
2:17–22	5.*114–117*	4:22–26	5.*158–162*
2:20	5.6	4:26	6.72
2:23–25	5.*117–120*	4:27–30	5.*162–164*
2:23	5.228	4:29	9.132
3:1–15	5.5; 14.171	4:31–34	5.*164–166*
3:1–6	5.*120–130*	4:31	5.14
3:3–8	6.86	4:35–5:1	5.2
3:3, 5	16.140	4:35–38	5.*166–169*

4:39–42	*5.170f*	6:1–13	*5.200–205*, 232
4:39	**5**.53, 228	6:1	**4**.117; **5**.176
4:40	**6**.64	6:2	**5**.228
4:43–5:1	**5**.106	6:4	**5**.4, 106, 177, 208
4:43–45	*5.172–173*	6:5–7	**5**.5
4:46–54	*5.174–176*	6:5	**5**.14
4:46	**5**.6, 232	6:6	**5**.15
4:54	**5**.176	6:8–9	**5**.5, 89
5–7	**5**.176	6:8	**15**.175
5:1–9	*5.177–181*, 232	6:9	**3**.159; **5**.5
5:1	**3**.263; **5**.2, 106	6:14, 15	*5.206–207*
5:2	**5**.6	6:15	**2**.104
5:6	**5**.15	6:16–21	*5.207–210*
5:9	**4**.187	6:17	**5**.48
5:10–18	*5.181–184*	6:19	**5**.5
5:10	**5**.6, 176	6:20	**5**.14
5:19–29	*5.184–187*	6:22–27	*5.210–213*
5:19, 20	*5.187–189*	6:27	**5**.43
5:21–23	*5.189–190*	6:28, 29	*5.213–214*
5:22	**3**.51; **17**.194	6:30–34	*5.215–216*
5:24	**5**.43f; *190–191*	6:31–35	**16**.95
5:25–29	*5.191–193*	6:32	**5**.9
5:29	**5**.43	6:33–38	**5**.14
5:30–32	**15**.112	6:33–35	**1**.215
5:30	*5.193–194*	6:35–40	*5.216–218*
5:31–36	*5.194–196*	6:35	**17**.36, 230
5:33	**15**.112	6:38	**5**.166
5:36	**5**.12, 51, 166; **15**.112	6:39–40	**14**.175
5:37–43	*5.196–199*	6:40	**5**.43
5:37	**5**.51; **15**.112	6:41–51	*5.218–220*
5:39	**5**.52; **15**.112	6:42	**4**.13
5:40	**5**.43	6:44	**14**.175
5:41	**5**.69	6:47	**5**.44
5:43	**17**.61	6:51–59	*5.221–226*
5:44–47	*5.199–200*	6:54	**14**.175
5:46	**5**.52	6:59–65	*5.226–228*
5:47	**5**.238f	6:61–64	**5**.15
6:1–7:14	**5**.2, 106	6:66–71	*5.228–230*
6	**5**.10	6:70–71	**6**.111

11 Phil, Col, Thes
12 Tim, Tit, Phlm
13 Heb
14 Jas, Pet
15 John, Jude
16 Rev, v.1
17 Rev, v.2

7:1–9	5.*230–233*; 6.83
7:1–5	**14**.19
7:1	**5**.176
7:2	**5**.2, 106; **6**.10
7:3–9	**14**.9
7:5	**2**.52; **6**.257; **7**.96; **9**.144; **14**.9
7:6, 8	**5**.102
7:10–13	5.*233–238*
7:10	**3**.263; **5**.2, 15, 106
7:14	5.*242–245*
7:15–24	**5**.239
7:15–18	5.*238–240*
7:16	**16**.23
7:17	**12**.171
7:18	**5**.69
7:19–24	5.*241–242*
7:21–23	**5**.6
7:25–30	5.*242–245*
7:30	**5**.231
7:31–36	5.*245–247*
7:33	**6**.156
7:37–44	5.*247–252*
7:37	**6**.10; **17**.37
7:38–39	**17**.221
7:39	**6**.81
7:45–52	5.*253–254*
7:53–8:11	6.*1–9*
8:2–11	**6**.292f
8:12–20	6.*9–15*
8:12	**5**.45, 48; **6**.64; **15**.27; **17**.229
8:14	**5**.51
8:15	**6**.292
8:16	**5**.9
8:18	**5**.51; **15**.112
8:20	**5**.231
8:21–30	6.*15–20*
8:23	**6**.18
8:25	**6**.19
8:28	**5**.135; **16**.23
8:29	**5**.166
8:31–32	**5**.67; 6.*20–22*
8:33–36	6.*22–24*
8:33	**15**.78
8:37–41	6.*24–26*
8:37	**15**.78
8:39	**6**.64
8:40	**5**.67; **9**.146
8:41–45	6.*27–29*
8:44	**9**.147
8:45	**5**.68
8:46–50	6.*29–32*
8:48	**4**.140
8:50	**5**.69
8:51–55	6.*32–33*
8:54	**5**.69
8:56–59	6.*34–36*
8:58	**5**.14
9	**5**.10; **6**.50–52
9:1–5	6.*37–41*
9:3	**5**.9
9:4	**4**.168
9:5	**1**.122; **5**.45; **13**.56
9:6–12	6.*41–44*
9:6	**5**.6
9:13–16	6.*44–45*
9:14	**4**.187; **5**.6
9:17–35	6.*46–49*
9:25	**5**.53
9:35–41	6.*49–50*
9:35–38	**15**.68
9:37	**6**.72
9:38	**5**.53
9:39	**5**.139
9:41	**7**.35
10:1–18	**14**.215, 270
10:1–6	6.*52–57*

10:7–10	*6.58–60*
10:7, 9	**16.**129
10:10	**5.**43; **14.**298
10:11–15	*6.60–63*
10:11	**10.**148; **17.**38
10:12	**1.**281
10:14	**10.**148; **17.**38
10:16	*6.63–66*, 289
10:17, 18	*6.66–67*
10:18	**5.**15, 166
10:19–21	*6.68–69*
10:22–28	*6.69–73*
10:22	**5.**2, 106
10:23	**5.**6
10:25	**5.**52
10:28	**5.**43; **16.**61
10:29, 30	*6.74–76*
10:30	**4.**137
10:31–39	*6.76–78*
10:40, 41	*6.78–79*
10:41	**5.**12, 50
11	**5.**5, 10
11:1–44	*6.100–103*
11:1–5	*6.80–82*
11:3	**5.**19
11:4	**5.**9, 69
11:5	**5.**19
11:6–10	*6.82–85*
11:10	**5.**45
11:11–16	*6.86–88*
11:14	**5.**15
11:16	**5.**5; **6.**275
11:17–19	*6.88–90*
11:20–27	*6.90–96*
11:24	**14.**175
11:28–33	*6.96–98*
11:33	**5.**14
11:34–44	*6.98–100*
11:35	**5.**14
11:36	**6.**145
11:38	**5.**14
11:47–53	**6.**101, *103–106*
11:54–57	*6.106–108*
11:55	**5.**106
11:57	**3.**328; **4.**239; **6.**108
12:1–8	*6.108–113*
12:1, 3	**5.**6
12:4–5	**5.**5
12:5	**2.**329
12:6	**2.**331; **3.**173, 328
12:9–11	*6.113–114*
12:12–19	*6.115–119*
12:16	**6.**81
12:17	**5.**53
12:20–22	*6.119–120*
12:21	**5.**6
12:22	**5.**5, 89
12:23–26	*6.121–125*
12:23	**5.**102; **6.**81, 203
12:25	**2.**151; **17.**84
12:27–34	*6.125–130*
12:27	**5.**231
12:31	**9.**44, 196; **15.**78; **17.**82
12:32	**2.**371; **3.**29, 367; **5.**135; **6.**234, 264; **7.**28; **12.**55; **15.**40
12:35–36	*6.130–131*
12:35	**5.**48; **15.**27
12:36	**5.**45, 46
12:37–41	*6.131–133*
12:42, 43	*6.133–134*
12:42	**6.**47
12:44–50	*6.134–136*
12:44–45	**15.**67
12:46	**5.**45, 46, 48; **15.**27
12:48	**14.**175
12:49	**5.**239; **16.**23

11 Phil, Col, Thes
12 Tim, Tit, Phlm
13 Heb
14 Jas, Pet
15 John, Jude
16 Rev, v.1
17 Rev, v.2

13:1–17	5.5; 6.*136–142*		14:25–31	6.*170–171*
13:1	6.292		14:30	9.196; 17.82
13:2	17.82		15:1–10	6.*172–176*
13:4–5	14.270		15:1	5.9
13:18–20	6.*142–144*		15:7	15.115
13:21–30	6.*144–147*		15:10	6.75
13:23–25	5.19		15:11–17	6.*176–181*
13:27	3.330; 17.82		15:14	2.53
13:29	6.293		15:16	8.12; 11.103
13:30	3.348; 5.48; 6.85		15:18–21	6.*181–186*
13:31, 32	6.*147–149*		15:18–19	6.18; 14.87
13:33–35	6.*149–150*		15:19	15.4
13:34–35	14.227; 15.88, 141		15:22–25	6.*186–187*
13:34	6.75; 15.44		15:22	7.35
13:36–38	6.*151–152*		15:24	5.52
14–17	5.5		15:26, 27	6.*187–188*
14:1–3	6.*152–156*		15:26	5.53, 67; 15.112
14:4–6	6.*156–159*		15:27	5.53
14:5	5.5		16:1–4	6.*189–191*
14:6–9	15.67		16:2	6.47; 17.10
14:6	5.43, 66f		16:5–11	6.*191–194*
14:7–11	6.*159–163*		16:11	9.44, 196; 17.82
14:8–9	5.5		16:12–15	6.*194–196*
14:9	1.21; 2.15; 4.137, 288; 6.210; 9.197; 13.103; 14.197; 16.22		16:12–13	5.24
			16:13–14	14.133
			16:13	5.67
			16:16–24	6.*196–200*
14:10	5.239		16:22	1.89; 11.51; 16.97
14:11	5.52		16:25–28	6.*200–201*
14:12–14	6.*163–165*		16:29–33	6.*201–203*
14:14	15.115		16:33	6.18; 16.178
14:15–17	6.*166–168*		17:1–5	6.*204–209*
14:15	6.75; 15.141		17:1	5.102
14:17	5.67; 6.18; 14.87		17:2	5.43
14:18–24	6.*168–169*		17:4	4.167; 5.166
14:19	4.88; 16.53		17:5	5.14, 69
14:21	5.128; 6.75		17:6–8	6.*209–213*
14:22	14.87; 15.169		17:9–19	6.*213–217*
14:23–24	5.166; 6.75		17:11	6.75

17:14	**15**.4
17:15	**1**.287
17:20, 21	**6**.75, *217–218*
17:21–23	**14**.224
17:22–26	**6**.*219–220*
17:22	**5**.69
17:25	**6**.18
18:1–11	**6**.*220–224*
18:1	**5**.6
18:10	**2**.351; **3**.346; **5**.220
18:13	**4**.32, 242
18:12–14	**6**.*225–227*
18:15–18	**6**.*227–231*
18:15	**4**.270
18:19–24	**6**.*225–227*
18:25–27	**6**.*227–231*
18:28– 19:16	**6**.*231–249*
18:28	**6**.293
18:33–34	**2**.138
18:36	**14**.87
18:37	**5**.67; **12**.200; **14**.133; **16**.32
18:40	**3**.173
19:6–7	**4**.280
19:10–11	**6**.67
19:11	**5**.15
19:12	**4**.281
19:13	**5**.6
19:14	**6**.293
19:17–22	**6**.*249–252*
19:17	**4**.282; **5**.6
19:23, 24	**2**.367; **4**.285; **6**.*253– 255*
19:23	**3**.142; **5**.5
19:25–27	**5**.19; **6**.*255–257*
19:25	**14**.8, 16, 17
19:26–27	**14**.154; **15**.138
19:26	**5**.98; **14**.18
19:28–30	**6**.*257–259*
19:28	**5**.14
19:30	**2**.369; **3**.364; **4**.288
19:31–37	**6**.*260–262*
19:34	**5**.251
19:35	**5**.19, 53
19:38–42	**6**.*262–264*
19:39	**2**.219; **5**.5, 121
20:1–10	**6**.*264–268*
20:1	**5**.48
20:2	**5**.19
20:11–18	**6**.*268–272*
20:12	**4**.291
20:19–23	**6**.*272–274*
20:20	**6**.282
20:24–29	**5**.5; **6**.*275–279*
20:27	**6**.270
20:28	**14**.294
20:29	**14**.161, 179
20:30, 31	**6**.*279*
20:31	**5**.43
21	**6**.280
21:1–14	**6**.*280–284*
21:1	**2**.105; **5**.208
21:2	**5**.6, 94
21:6	**5**.220
21:11	**5**.220; **6**.284
21:15–19	**6**.54, *284–287*; **14**.269
21:16	**10**.148; **14**.215
21:18–19	**14**.287, 308
21:19–22	**17**.108
21:20–24	**6**.*287–288*
21:20	**5**.19
21:24	**5**.19, 53
21:25	**2**.11; **4**.134; **6**.*288–289*

Acts

1:1–6:7	**7**.5

1–5	7.6	2:40	8.20
1:1–5	*7.9–11*	2:41	2.145
1:1	7.2	2:42–47	*7.29–31*
1:5	15.109	3:1–10	5.16; *7.31–33*
1:6–8	*7.11–13*	3:1	1.195
1:7	11.205	3:2	6.37
1:8	7.4, 19, 193; **17**.170	3:11–16	*7.33–34*
1:9–11	*7.13–14*	3:12–26	9.17; **14**.140
1:9	17.78	3:13–14	14.141
1:12–20	*7.14–17*	3:13	7.27; **14**.141
1:13	5.16; **14**.8, 9; **15**.169	3:14	6.248; **14**.120
1:14	14.10, 14; **15**.171	3:15	9.78; **13**.25
1:15	12.91	3:17–26	*7.34–36*
1:16	7.18	3:17	4.285
1:21–26	*7.17–18*	3:18	7.26
1:21–22	10.3, 146	3:19–23	14.141
1:22	9.78, 115; **14**.155	4:1–13	5.16
1:25–26	16.133	4:1–4	*7.36–37*
1:26	14.267	4:5–12	*7.38–39*
2:1–13	*7.20–22*	4:5	14.263
2:4	15.109	4:8–12	9.17; **14**.140
2:13	7.22	4:10	7.27
2:14–39	9.17	4:11	3.283; 4.247; 8.135; 14.141
2:14–21	7.22, *24–25*; **14**.250		
2:14–16	14.140	4:12	16.94
2:17	14.175	4:13–22	*7.39–41*
2:18	14.293	4:13	5.239
2:19–20	14.148	4:16	7.32
2:20–31	14.141	4:19	14.206
2:22–36	*7.26–28*	4:23–31	*7.41–42*
2:22–26	14.141	4:28	7.26
2:24	2.143	4:31	7.19; **15**.24
2:27	2.143; **13**.83	4:32–37	*7.43*
2:31	5.117	4:32	14.224
2:32	9.178	4:33	9.78
2:33	5.135; 7.27; **15**.109	4:36–37	7.90, 99; **13**.8
2:37–41	*7.28–29*	5:1–11	*7.44–45*
2:37	6.192	5:3	17.82
2:38–39	14.141	5:5, 10	12.54

5:12–16	*7.45–46*	8:25	7.77; **15**.24
5:17–32	*7.46–48*	8:26–40	7.6, *67–69*
5:17	**14**.316	8:29	7.19
5:29	**14**.206	9:1–9	**6**.193; *7.69–71*
5:30–31	**14**.141	9:2	7.139; **9**.186
5:30	7.27	9:4	**17**.85
5:31	**5**.135; **13**.25; **14**.141	9:9	**9**.258
5:32	7.20	9:10–18	*7.71–72*; **12**.44
5:33–42	*7.48–50*	9:11	**15**.169
6:1–7	*7.50–52*	9:13	**11**.11
6:1	**12**.106	9:19–22	*7.72–73*
6:2	**15**.24	9:23–25	*7.74–75*; **9**.255
6:3	7.19	9:25	**3**.184
6:5	**16**.67	9:26–31	*7.75–76*
6:7	**15**.24	9:26–28	**12**.44
6:8–9:31	**7**.5	9:27, 30	7.90
6:8–15	*7.52–53*	9:31–	7.6
6:12	**14**.263	10:48	
6:14	**5**.115	9:32–	**7**.5
6:15	**14**.259	12:24)	
7:1–7	*7.53–55*	9:32–43	*7.76–78*
7:6	**14**.201	9:32	**11**.11
7:8–16	*7.55–57*	9:43	7.80
7:17–36	*7.57–59*	10	**2**.145; **11**.145; **14**.292
7:37–53	*7.59–61*	10:1–8	*7.78–80*
7:51	7.19	10:6	**14**.254
7:52	**14**.120	10:9–16	*7.80–81*
7:53	**10**.29; **13**.17; **16**.24	10:17–33	*7.81–83*
7:54–8:1	*7.61–63*	10:17	**1**.301
7:55	7.19	10:19	7.19
7:60	**4**.285; **6**.86; **8**.168	10:22–23	**1**.300; **4**.84
8:1–4	*7.63–64*	10:26	**1**.301
8:5–13	*7.64–65*	10:28	**4**.85
8:9, 11	**1**.26	10:34–43	*7.83–84*; **14**.140
8:14–25	*7.65–67*	10:34	**14**.62, 141
8:14–17	**10**.23	10:36–43	**9**.17
8:14	**5**.16	10:38	**15**.70, 108; **17**.82
8:17–18	**15**.89	10:39–42	**14**.141
8:17	**13**.55; **15**.70, 109	10:39	**14**.178

---

11 Phil, Col, Thes	**13** Heb	**15** John, Jude	**16** Rev, v.1
12 Tim, Tit, Phlm	**14** Jas, Pet		**17** Rev, v.2

c

10:42, 43	**14**.141	13:5	**11**.170; **12**.217; **15**.24
10:44–48	**7**.*84–85*	13:6–12	**9**.21
10:44–46	**7**.66	13:6	**1**.26
10:44–45	**15**.90	13:7	**15**.24
10:44	**10**.23; **15**.109	13:8	**1**.26
10:46	**7**.21	13:9	**7**.19
11:1–10	**7**.*85–86*	13:11	**12**.54
11:1	**15**.24	13:12	**7**.3
11:11–18	**7**.*86–87*	13:13	**3**.3; **7**.*100–102*;
11:12	**7**.19		**10**.39; **11**.170;
11:19–30	**7**.6		**12**.217; **14**.275
11:19–21	**7**.*87–89* —	⊦3:14–15	**7**.*102–103*
11:20	**8**.215f	13:15	**16**.26
11:22–26	**7**.*89–90*	13:16–41	**7**.*103–105*
11:24	**7**.19	13:26	**15**.24
11:27–30	**7**.*91–92*, 97	13:27	**4**.285
11:28	**7**.19	13:29	**7**.26
11:30	**14**.264	13:35	**5**.117; **13**.83; **15**.24
12:1–11	**7**.*92–94*	13:38	**15**.53
12:2	**2**.230; **3**.256; **7**.1, 101;	13:42–52	**7**.*105–107*
	14.15	13:44, 49	**15**.24
12:12–19	**7**.*94–96*	13:50	**12**.197; **14**.149; **16**.79
12:12	**3**.3, 347; **12**.217	14:1–7	**7**.*107–108*
12:15	**16**.54	14:2	**16**.79
12:17	**14**.10	14:3	**15**.24
12:20–25	**7**.*96–97*	14:4	**10**.145
12:24	**15**.24	14:5–6	**12**.197
12:25–16:5	**7**.5	14:5	**16**.79
		14:8–21	**12**.21
12:25–14:8	**7**.6	14:8–18	**7**.*108–109*
		14:8	**6**.37
12:25	**3**.3	14:14	**10**.145; **14**.17
13–14	**7**.97	14:15	**17**.10
13:1–3	**7**.*98–99*; **12**.49	14:17	**8**.27
13:1	**3**.361; **7**.91; **8**.219;	14:19, 20	**7**.*109–110*
	14.79; **17**.127	14:19	**12**.197; **16**.79
13:2	**7**.19, 101; **8**.13	14:21–28	**7**.*110–112*
13:4–12	**7**.*99–100*	14:21–23	**15**.137
13:4	**7**.19, 101	14:22	**12**.198; **16**.40

14:23	**12.**71, 234; **16.**264; **15.**133	16:6–10	**7.***121–122*; **11.**179
		16:6	**7.**19
14:27	**16.**129	16:10–17	**7.**6
15:16	**7.**6	16:11–15	**7.***122–123*
15	**2.**145; **7.**4; **14.**10, 292	16:13–14	**11.**73
15:1–5	**7.***112–113*	16:14	**16.**102
15:2	**14.**264	16:16–40	**11.**188
15:5	**14.**316	16:16–24	**7.***124–125*
15:6–12	**7.***114–115*	16:19	**5.**220; **11.**30; **14.**143
15:7	**15.**24	16:20–21	**11.**4
15:13–21	**7.***115–116*	16:25–40	**7.***125–127*
15:13	**14.**36	16:25–34	**11.**73
15:14	**2.**145; **14.**145, 292	16:25, 29	**14.**143, 275
15:17	**14.**23	16:31	**14.**73
15:22–35	**7.***116–118*	16:32	**15.**24
15:22	**14.**17, 143, 275; **15.**169	16:35ff	**7.**3
15:23	**14.**23, 36	16:36–40	**16.**15
15:24	**14.**80	16:37	**14.**143, 275
15:27	**14.**143, 275; **15.**169	17:1–14	**11.**47
15:28–29	**16.**67	17:1–9	**7.***127–128*; **11.**181
15:28	**7.**19	17:4	**2.**290; **9.**21, 73
15:29	**16.**107	17:5–9	**8.**220
15:32	**7.**91; **14.**143, 275; **15.**169	17:5	**16.**79
		17:6	**1.**376; **2.**83, 182
15:39	**15.**24	17:10–15	**7.***128–129*
15:36– 18:23	**7.**119	17:10–12	**11.**181
		17:12	**9.**21, 73
15:36–41	**7.***118–119*; **11.**170; **12.**218	17:14–15	**12.**22
		17:16–21	**7.***129–131*
15:37–40	**3.**3; **14.**143, 275	17:22–31	**7.***131–132*; **9.**23
15:38	**7.**101	17:31	**17.**195
16–28	**7.**6	17:32–34	**7.***132–133*; **9.**23
16	**11.**5, 47; **17.**93	17:32	**2.**236
16:1–5	**7.***119–120*	17:34	**9.**21
16:1–3	**12.**20	18	**17.**93
16:1	**11.**47, 22; **12.**119, 199	18:1–17	**9.**5, 6; **16.**15
16:4	**14.**264	18:1–11	**7.***133–136*
16:6– 19:20	**7.**5	18:2	**8.**7, 208f; **9.**167; **12.**222

18:5	**11.**47; **12.**22; **14.**143, 275	19:31	7.3, 140
		19:33	8.216
18:8	**9.**16	19:34	1.196
18:9–10	**11.**27, 215	19:37	7.4
18:11	**9.**31	20:1–6	7.*147–148*
18:12–17	7.*136–137*; **14.**146	20:4	**8.**220; **9.**169; **12.**22, 222; **15.**148
18:12	7.3		
18:14	7.4	20:5–16	7.6
18:18–23	7.*137–138*	20:5	**16.**28
18:18	**8.**8, 209	20:7–12	7.*148–150*
18:19	**16.**60	20:13–16	7.*150–151*
18:24–28	7.*138–141*	20:17–38	7.*151–152*; **16.**60
18:24–26	**8.**209; **13.**9	20:17	**16.**28
18:24	**9.**14; **12.**266; **16.**60	20:28–29	**14.**264; **15.**194
18:26	**11.**68; **13.**9; **16.**60	20:28	**10.**148
19	**9.**253; **16.**59; **17.**93	20:17–35	**10.**63
19:1–7	**5.**11; 7.*141–142*	20:17	**12.**71
19:3–4	**5.**50	20:23	7.19
19:6	**7.**21; **13.**55	20:28	**6.**54; **7.**19; **12.**71; **14.**161
19:8–12	7.*142–143*		
19:9	**7.**139	20:29–31	**16.**119
19:10	**8.**20; **11.**94	20:29–30	**15.**4, 64; **16.**63
19:13–41	**16.**15	20:29	**1.**281; **6.**61
19:13–20	7.*143–144*	20:31	**9.**31; **10.**63; **16.**60
19:13	**1.**289	20:32	**15.**24
19:19	**17.**206	20:33	**14.**116, 266
19:21– 28:31	7.5	21–22	**17.**93
		21:1–18	7.6
19:21–41	**14.**203	21:1–16	7.*153–154*
19:21ff	**15.**153	21:9–10	**7.**91; **12.**68
19:21, 22	7.*144*; **8.**2; **11.**47; **12.**22	21:9	**16.**105
		21:15–17	**14.**161
19:22	**12.**222	21:16	**14.**254
19:23–41	7.*145–147*	21:17–26	7.*154–156*
19:23	**7.**139	21:18–25	**14.**11, 14, 264
19:24–27	**1.**378	21:27–36	7.*156–157*
19:25	**12.**214	21:28–29	**10.**112
19:28	**12.**89	21:29	**12.**222
19:29	**11.**169; **15.**147	21:30–40	**16.**15

21:37–40	7.*158–159*	25:25	7.4
21:38	1.69	26:1–11	7.*175–177*
21:40	11.59	26:4–23	11.60
22:1–10	7.*159–160*	26:9–11	6.190
22:2–21	11.60	26:10	9.61; 10.173
22:3	11.59	26:11	9.106
22:4	7.139	26:12–18	7.*177–178*
22:11–21	7.*160–162*	26:18	9.44; 10.122; 11.111;
22:14	14.120		12.45
22:22–30	7.*162–163*	26:19–23	7.*178–179*
22:26	4.84	26:24–31	7.*179–180*
23:1–10	7.*163–165*	26:24	9.208; 11.188
23:2	9.251	27:1–	7.6
23:6–10	2.128	28:16	
23:6	11.59	27	12.215
23:8	9.137	27:1–8	7.*180–182*
23:11–24	7.*165–166*	27:2	11.169
23:11	8.2	27:9–20	7.*182–183*
23:12–31	16.15	27:21–26	7.*183–184*
23:17	4.84	27:27–38	7.*185–186*
23:23–24	1.301; 4.84	27:39–44	7.*186–187*
23:25–35	7.*166–168*	27:43	1.301; 4.84
23:26–30	14.23	28:1–6	7.*187–188*
23:26	14.36	28:2	9.229
23:29	7.4	28:7–10	7.*188–189*
24:1–9	7.*168–169*	28:11–15	7.*189–190*
24:1	14.263	28:16–29	7.*190–192*
24:5	14.316	28:16	7.193; 11.20
24:10–21	7.*169–170*	28:17–29	11.170
24:14	7.139	28:17, 20	11.21
24:17	9.162, 164	28:25	7.19
24:22–27	7.*170–171*	28:27	6.132
24:22	7.139	28:30–31	7.*192–193*; 12.10
24:23	1.301; 4.84	28:30	11.20; 12.283
24:26	12.283		
25:1–12	7.*171–173*	*Romans*	
25:10–11	16.15		
25:13–21	7.*173–174*	1–8	8.5f
25:22–27	7.*174–175*	1:1–7	8.*11–14*

1:1   **8**.xi; **14**.17, 35, 293; **15**.171, 176; **16**.25

1:3   **1**.15; **3**.298; **8**.101

1:7   **8**.xi, 10; **11**.12; **12**.23; **14**.36; **15**.176

1:8–15   **8**.*14–18*

1:8   **8**.xi

1:11   **8**.2

1:15   **8**.2, 10

1:16–17   **8**.*18–23*

1:18–23   **8**.*23–28*

1:19–20   **5**.56

1:20   **3**.89

1:24–25   **8**.*28–30*

1:26–27   **8**.*30–32*

1:28–32   **8**.*33–40*

1:30   **14**.111

2:1–11   **8**.*40–44*

2:4   **10**.51, 139; **14**.348

2:5   **16**.22

2:6   **14**.72

2:8   **15**.29

2:11   **14**.62

2:12–16   **8**.*44–46*

2:14–15   **11**.142; **14**.57

2:17–29   **8**.*46–50*; **14**.80

2:24   **14**.319

2:28–29   **17**.24

2:28   **8**.101

3:1–8   **8**.*50–54*

3:5   **8**.26

3:9–18   **8**.*54–56*

3:10   **14**.82

3:19–26   **8**.*56–59*

3:23   **14**.82

3:25   **14**.348; **17**.31

3:27–31   **8**.*60–61*

3:28   **14**.72

4:1–8   **8**.*61–65*

4:4   **12**.23

4:9–12   **8**.*65–67*

4:13–17   **8**.*67–69*

4:15   **8**.26; **14**.7

4:18–25   **8**.*70–71*

5:1–5   **8**.*71–75*

5:1   **13**.72

5:2   **14**.235

5:6–11   **8**.*75–77*

5:9   **8**.26; **17**.31

5:12–21   **8**.*77–82*

5:12   **14**.248

5:13   **6**.29

6   **3**.315; **10**.163; **12**.169, 174; **14**.247, 349; **15**.160

6:1–18   **5**.184

6:1–11   **5**.126; **8**.*82–86*

6:1–4   **7**.69

6:3ff   **10**.32

6:4   **12**.6, 169

6:8   **12**.169

6:10   **14**.233

6:12–14   **8**.*86–88*

6:13   **16**.116

6:15–23   **8**.*88–92*

6:17–20   **6**.23

6:23   **9**.12

7:1–6   **8**.*92–94*

7:5   **8**.101

7:7–13   **8**.*94–97*

7:10–11   **14**.7

7:14–25   **8**.*97–100*

7:15–24   **14**.51

7:22–23   **14**.50

8:1–4   **8**.*100–103*

8:4–5   **8**.101

8:5–11   **8**.*103–105*

8:6–8   **8**.101

8:7–8	14.103	10:4	1.126; 10.115; 14.59
8:9	8.102	10:9	11.39; 12.136
8:11	11.64	10:11, 13	8.121
8:12–17	8.*105–107*	10:14–21	8.*140–143*
8:12	8.102	10:14	5.170
8:13	11.150	10:19	8.122
8:14–17	15.74	11:1–12	8.*143–147*
8:15–16	15.101	11:2	14.343
8:15	4.143	11:6	12.23
8:17	14.258	11:8	6.132
8:18–25	8.*108–111*	11:11	16.133
8:23	10.79	11:13–24	8.*147–151*
8:26–30	8.*111–115*	11:25–32	8.*151–155*
8:28	14.272; 15.177	11:26	8.122
8:31–39	8.*115–119*	11:29	15.177
8:32	1.214; 6.153; 11.122; 14.272	11:33–36	8.*154f*
		11:36	17.205
8:34	15.38	12–15	8.5f
8:35–39	11.51	12	8.6; 14.22
8:38–39	4.299; 16.85	12:1–2	8.*155–158*
9–11	8.5, *119–123*, 136	12:1	11.16; 14.191, 197
9:1–6	8.*123–126*	12:2	14.87, 326; 16.109; 17.152
9:3	8.101		
9:6–9	16.130	12:3–8	8.*158–163*; 14.255
9:6–7	17.24	12:4	14.225
9:6	15.65	12:8	1.245
9:7–13	8.*127–129*	12:9–13	8.*163–167*
9:7–8	14.41	12:11	16.142
9:11	2.71	12:13	7.123; 12.81; 14.255; 15.149
9:14–18	8.*129–131*		
9:17	8.120	12:14–21	8.*167–170*
9:19–29	8.*131–133*	12:15	14.227
9:22	10.51; 14.348	12:16	14.225
9:25	8.121	12:19	8.26
9:27	8.120	13:1–7	8.*170–174*; 14.159, 205; 16.15; 17.63
9:29	1.371; 15.185		
9:30–33	8.*133–135*	13:1–6	17.93
9:32–33	3.283	13:5	3.26
10:1–13	8.*136–140*	13:6–7	14.206

13:8–10	8.*175–176*	16:3–5	9.167
13:11–14	8.*176–179*; **14**.123	16:3–4	8.*208–211*
13:11	**8**.21; **16**.118	16:3	**12**.222
13:12	**14**.73, 249; **15**.27	16:5–11	8.*211–213*
13:13	**10**.47	16:5	**11**.172; **13**.9; **14**.254
14:1	8.*179–181*	16:7	**10**.145; **14**.17
14:2–4	8.*182–183*	16:12–16	8.*214–217*
14:5, 6	8.*183–185*	16:12	**16**.62
14:7–9	8.*185–197*	16:13	**3**.249, 361; **4**.283
14:10–12	8.*187–189*	16:16	**14**.279
14:10	**17**.195	16:17–20	8.*217–219*
14:12	**14**.72	16:17	**8**.8
14:13–16	8.*189–190*	16:19	**11**.172
14:15–23	**8**.9	16:20	**11**.82
14:17–20	8.*190–193*	16:21–23	8.*219–220*
14:17	**10**.50; **13**.72	16:21	**11**.47; **12**.22
14:20	**12**.244	16:22	**8**.xii, 45; **11**.74
14:21–23	8.*193–194*	16:23	**9**.16, 21; **11**.103;
15:1–6	8.*195–197*		**12**.222; **15**.148
15:5	**11**.83	16:25–27	**8**.9, *220–222*
15:6	**9**.163	16:25	**15**.206; **16**.22; **17**.109
15:7–13	8.*197–200*	16:27	**15**.163
15:9	**12**.25; **14**.27		
15:13	**10**.50; **11**.82		
15:14–21	8.*200–203*	*1 Corinthians*	
15:14–15	**15**.66		
15:14	**10**.51	1–4	**9**.8
15:15	**10**.124; **12**.24	1:1–3	**8**.xi; 9.*9–11*
15:19	**7**.148	1:1	**11**.9, 103; **14**.17;
15:22–29	8.*204–205*		**15**.176
15:24	**8**.3; **12**.10, 12, 283	1:2	**15**.176
15:25–26	**7**.145; **8**.3; **9**.162	1:3	**14**.36
15:28	**8**.3; **12**.10, 283	1:4–9	9.*11–13*
15:30–33	**8**.*206*; **11**.25	1:4	**8**.xi; **12**.24
15:30–31	**8**.3; **11**.216	1:3	**8**.xi; **11**.12; **12**.23
15:33	**1**.109	1:9	**15**.74
16	**8**.xi, 5, 7, 9; **9**.186;	1:10–17	9.*13–16*
	12.68	1:10	**14**.225
16:1–2	8.*207–208*	1:11	**9**.6

1:12	13.9; **14.**145	5:5	8.21; **12.**54; **15.**118
1:14	8.220; **15.**148	5:6–8	2.79
1:18–25	*9.16–20*	5:7	5.81
1:18	**15.**25	5:9–13	9.42, *46–48*
1:20	14.87	5:9	9.5f, 221f
1:22	1.48	6:1–8	9.42, *48–51*
1:24	**16.**179	6:2	17.193
1:26–31	*9.20–23*	6:9–20	9.42
1:26–27	14.27, 66	6:9–11	7.134; *9.51–54*, 261
1:26	**15.**177	6:9–10	2.79; 9.4
2:1–5	*9.23–25*	6:11	12.262; 17.30
2:6–9	*9.25–27*	6:12–20	*9.54–58*
2:6	13.50	6:13ff	11.64
2:7–8	12.91	6:20	11.9; **16.**177
2:9	3.292	7:1–	9.57
2:10–16	*9.27–28*	15:58	
2:10	**16.**108	7	10.172; 12.76
2:14–15	14.313	7:1–2	9.57, *58–59*
2:14	**15.**188	7:1	9.6
3:1–9	*9.29–31*	7:2	10.172
3:1–2	5.126	7:3–7	9.57, *59–61*
3:2	13.50; **14.**192	7:8–16	*9.61–64*
3:3	14.225	7:8–9	9.57
3:4	13.9	7:9	10.52, 172
3:8	14.73	7:10–11	9.57
3:10–15	*9.31–33*	7:12–17	9.57f
3:11	2.141	7:13–16	14.219
3:16–22	*9.33–35*	7:17–24	*9.64–66*
3:16	17.68	7:18	9.58
3:22	**14.**145	7:20	**15.**177
4:1–5	*9.35–38*	7:22	14.293
4:6–13	*9.38–40*	7:23	14.317; **16.**177
4:7	11.48	7:24	9.58
4:14–21	*9.40–42*	7:25	9.58, *66–68*
4:17	7.120; 9.6; 11.47; 12.22	7:26–35	9.58, *68–70*
		7:32–33	10.172
4:19	14.114	7:36–38	·9.58, *66–68*
4:21	10.52	7:38–40	9.58
5:1–8	9.42, *43–46*	7:39–40	*9.70–74*, 172

8–10	**9.**71; **16.**106	11:32	**16.**145
8	**9.**73, *74–76*	12	**9.**95; **14.**255
8:6	**5.**41; **11.**100	12:1–3	**9.***106–107*
9	**9.**73	12:3	**15.**90
9:1–14	**9.***77–81*	12:4–11	**9.**12, *108–112*
9:1	**10.**146	12:9	**6.**164
9:5	**2.**175; **14.**145, 277; **15.**171	12:10	**15.**90
9:6–7	**12.**161; **14.**17	12:12–31	**9.***112–116*; **14.**225
9:12	**14.**266	12:12–27	**8.**159
9:15–23	**9.***81–84*	12:12	**6.**273
9:16	**14.**265	12:13	**12.**272
9:22	**16.**93	12:26	**14.**226
9:24–27	**9.***84–86*; **12.**161	12:28	**6.**164; **14.**79; **17.**127
9:24	**11.**45	12:30	**6.**164
9:25	**10.**52; **16.**83	13	**9.**95, *116–119*; **12.**201
9:26–27	**11.**45	13:4–7	**9.***119–125*
10:1–13	**9.**73, *87–90*	13:8–13	**9.***125–126*
10:4	**5.**251	13:11	**10.**34
10:5–11	**15.**182	13:12	**6.**220; **14.**179
10:11	**14.**250	14	**7.**21; **15.**90
10:14–22	**9.**73, *91–93*	14:1–23	**9.**96
10:17	**14.**225	14:1–19	**9.***126–130*
10:23–11:1	**9.***93–96*	14:2	**15.**90
		14:6	**16.**22
10:23–26, 27–28	**9.**73	14:15	**14.**127
10:29–11:1	**9.**74	14:20–25	**9.***131–133*
		14:20	**13.**50
10:31	**14.**214	14:22	**14.**124
11–14	**9.**95	14:23–33	**9.**96
11:2–16	**9.**95, *96–100*	14:23	**7.**22; **15.**90
11:10	**14.**322	14:24–36	**9.**96
11:17–22	**9.**95, *100–102*; **15.**192	14:26–33	**9.***133–135*
11:18–19	**14.**316	14:26–27	**15.**90
11:21	**15.**194	14:26	**14.**127
11:23–34	**9.***102–105*	14:29	**16.**63
11:24–34	**9.**95	14:33	**11.**82; **15.**90
11:30	**15.**118	14:34–40	**9.***135–137*
		14:34	**16.**105
		15	**9.***137–141*; **12.**30

1 Matt, v.1	**3** Mark	**5** John, v.1	**7** Acts	**9** Cor
2 Matt, v.2	**4** Luke	**6** John, v.2	**8** Rom	**10** Gal, Eph

15:1–11	9.*141–146*
15:3	14.233
15:5	14.145
15:6	6.86
15:7	7.96, 115; 10.145; 14.11
15:8–10	11.60
15:10	12.24; 16.62
15:12–19	9.*146–149*
15:14ff	11.64
15:17	8.21
15:18	17.114
15:20–28	9.*149–152*
15:21	8.78
15:23	14.122
15:24	8.118
15:28	11.40
15:29–34	9.*152–156*
15:35–49	9.*156–159*
15:50–58	9.*159–161*
15:51–52	11.27
15:52–53	17.42
15:52	16.43
16:1–12	9.*161–165*
16:1–2	7.145; 8.2
16:3	9.163
16:7	14.114
16:9	16.129
16:10–11	11.48; 12.22
16:12	11.103
16:13–21	9.*165–169*
16:13	16.118
16:14	14.124
16:15	9.16
16:17	9.6
16:19	8.xi, 8, 209; 12.222; 14.254
16:20	14.279
16:21	8.xii

2 Corinthians

1–9	9.7, 8
1:1–7	9.*169–171*
1:1	8.xi; 11.9; 12.22; 14.17
1:2	8.xi; 11.12; 12.23; 14.36
1:3	8.xi; 11.83
1:5	11.64
1:8–11	9.154, *171–173*
1:11	11.25
1:12–14	9.*173–175*
1:12	12.24
1:15–22	9.*175–177*
1:19	12.22; 14.143, 275
1:20	14.297
1:22	9.205
1:23–2:4	9.*178–180*
1:23	1.161
2:4	9.7, 237
2:5–11	9.*180–182*
2:11	17.82
2:12–17	9.*182–185*
2:12–13	9.224
2:12	16.28, 129
2:13	9.7; 12.219, 233
3:1–3	9.*185–197*
3:4–11	9.*187–191*
3:5	11.83
3:12–18	9.*191–194*
3:14	6.132
4:1–6	9.*194–197*
4:2	14.133
4:5	16.25
4:6	15.27
4:7–15	9.*197–201*
4:10–11	11.64
4:16–18	9.*201–203*

4:17	4.77	8:18	12.216, 233
5:1–10	9.*203–206*	8:20	9.164
5:4	14.308	8:23	12.233
5:7	8.21	9:1–5	7.145; 8.2; 9.*231–233*
5:10	14.73; 17.195	9:1	9.163
5:11–19	9.*206–209*	9:5	9.164
5:14	4.193; 14.265	9:6–15	9.*233–237*
5:17	4.90; 5.126; 17.204	9:11	1.245
5:18–19	12.55	9:12–13	9.163f
5:19	15.25	10–13	9.7, 8, 237
5:20–6:2	9.*209–212*	10:1–6	9.*237–241*
5:21	2.369	10:1	10.52
6:3–10	9.*212–218*	10:7–18	9.*241–245*
6:6	10.51	10:10	9.145, 257f; 10.38
6:7	15.25	11:1–6	9.*245–247*
6:10	16.78	11:1–2	14.102; 16.108
6:11–13	9.*218–220*	11:2	5.143; 17.76, 173
6:14–7:1	9.6, 8, 218, *220–223*	11:7–15	9.*247–250*
6:14–15	17.153	11:7–12	11.86
6:15	11.212; 17.59	11:9	7.136; 11.6
6:16	17.68	11:16–33	9.*250–255*
6:17	16.93	11:22	7.159
6:18	16.38; 17.173	12:1–10	2.256; 9.*255–260*
7:2–4	9.*218–220*	12:2	17.78
7:5–16	9.*223–227*	12:7–8	7.102; 10.38
7:5	9.7	12:7	17.82
7:6	12.219	12:11–18	9.*260–262*
7:8	9.7, 237	12:14	9.6; 14.266
7:13	9.7; 12.219	12:18	12.219, 233
8–9	9.162	12:19–21	9.*262–266*
8:1–15	9.*227–230*	12:20	14.111
8:1–5	9.232	12:21	10.47
8:1	12.24	13	9.*266–268*
8:4	9.163	13:1–2	9.6
8:6	12.232	13:1	5.195
8:9	1.191; 11.34; 16.179	13:5	8.21
8:10	12.232	13:11	1.109; 11.83; 14.225
8:16–24	9.*230–231*	13:12	14.279
8:16	12.232	13:13	8.xi

Galatians

1:1–5	10.*1–9*
1:1	8.xi; **11.9; 14.17**
1:3	8.xi; **11.12; 12.23; 14.36**
1:4	**14.233**
1:6–10	10.*9–11*
1:6	**12.24**
1:7	**7.73**
1:8–9	**17.230**
1:11–17	10.*11–13*; **12.13**
1:12	**16.22**
1:13	**11.60**
1:15–24	**7.73**
1:15	**8.12; 12.24**
1:17–18	**7.74**
1:18–25	10.*11–15*
1:18	**14.145**
1:19	**7.115; 10.145; 14.10, 15**
1:20	**1.161**
1:21	**7.73**
2:1–10	10.*15–17*
2:1	**12.232**
2:2	**16.21**
2:5	**3.25**
2:6–10	**10.4**
2:7	**10.124**
2:9	**5.16; 10.124; 14.10, 22, 145; 16.134**
2:10	**8.205; 9.162; 14.75**
2:11–13	10.*18–19*
2:11	**14.145**
2:14–17	10.*19–21*
2:14	**14.145; 15.29**
2:16	**14.72**
2:18–21	10.*21–23*
2:19–20	**1.137**
2:20	**11.149**
3:1–9	10.*23–25*
3:7	**15.29**
3:10–14	10.*25–27*
3:13	**9.106; 14.317; 16.34, 177**
3:15–18	10.*27–28*
3:16	**15.78**
3:19–22	10.*29–30*
3:19	**13.17, 89; 16.24**
3:23–29	10.*31–33*
3:23–24	**14.7**
3:24	**9.41**
3:26–27	**15.74**
3:28	**12.68, 272**
3:29	**15.78; 17.24**
4:1–7	10.*33–35*
4:4	**4.13**
4:5	**10.79; 16.34**
4:6–7	**15.74**
4:6	**4.143**
4:8–11	10.*36–37*
4:10	**8.184**
4:11	**16.62**
4:12–20	10.*37–40*
4:13	**7.102**
4:14–15	**9.258**
4:21–5:1a	10.*40–42*
4:26	**17.199**
5:1b–12	10.*42–44*
5:7	**14.133**
5:9	**2.79**
5:13–15	10.*44–46*
5:13	**5.183; 14.207, 335, 349; 16.68**
5:16–21	10.*46–49*
5:19–21	**8.102; 10.101; 14.200**
5:19	**10.47**
5:22–26	10.*49–52*

5:22–23	**14**.301; **17**.222
6:1–5	**10**.*52–53*
6:1	**10**.149
6:6–10	**10**.*53–55*
6:11–18	**10**.*55–57*
6:11	**9**.258
6:15	**5**.126
6:16	**14**.41, 166; **16**.130; **17**.24
6:17	**11**.64, 175

Ephesians

1:1–14	**10**.*73–74*
1:1–2	**10**.*74–76*
1:1	**8**.xi; **10**.63; **11**.9
1:2–3	**10**.129
1:2	**8**.xi; **11**.12; **12**.23; **14**.36
1:3–14	**10**.64, 76
1:3–4	**10**.*76–79*
1:3	**8**.xi; **14**.153
1:4	**14**.153; **17**.96, 108
1:5–6	**10**.*79–80*
1:7–8	**10**.*81–83*
1:7	**17**.31
1:9–10	**10**.66, *83–85*
1:11–14	**10**.*85–88*
1:13	**3**.25; **15**.25
1:15–23	**10**.64, *88–94*
1:15	**10**.63
1:17	**10**.129, 130; **16**.22
1:18	**15**.177
1:20, 21	**14**.153
1:21	**8**.118
1:23	**6**.273
2:1–10	**10**.*94–95*
2:1–9	**10**.64

2:1–3	**10**.*95–101*
2:1	**16**.116
2:2	**9**.192; **17**.80
2:4–10	**10**.*101–105*
2:5	**16**.116
2:11–12	**10**.*106–110*
2:11–13	**14**.291
2:11	**10**.62
2:12	**14**.172
2:13–18	**10**.*110–117*
2:13–14	**14**.225
2:18	**6**.58; **10**.129; **14**.235
2:19–22	**10**.*117–119*
2:20–21	**17**.68
2:20	**2**.141; **3**.283; **8**.135
3:1–13	**10**.*119–120*
3:1–7	**10**.64, 120–125
3:1	**10**.61; **11**.21, 174
3:2–13	**10**.119f
3:2	**10**.63
3:3	**16**.22
3:6	**3**.25
3:8–13	**10**.*125–127*
3:8	**16**.179
3:10	**8**.118
3:12	**10**.129; **14**.235
3:14–21	**10**.*127–128*
3:14–17	**10**.*128–132*
3:18–21	**10**.*132–133*
3:20	**15**.206
4	**10**.*133–134*
4:1–10	**10**.*134–145*
4:1–3	**10**.*134–140*
4:1	**10**.61; **11**.174; **15**.177
4:2	**10**.52
4:3–6	**14**.225
4:4–6	**10**.*140–143*
4:4	**15**.177
4:6	**10**.130; **17**.205

4:7–10	**10.***143–145*	6:11	**17.82**
4:9–10	**14.242**	6:12	**8.118; 15.28**
4:11–13	**10.***145–150*	6:14	**14.153**
4:11	**6.54; 14.79; 17.127**	6:15	**3.25**
4:13ff	**13.50**	6:17	**16.94**
4:14–16	**10.***150–151*	6:20	**10.61; 11.21, 174; 12.280**
4:15	**14.133**		
4:17–24	**10.***151–154*	6:21–24	**10.***184–185*
4:17	**10.63**	6:21	**7.192; 10.62; 11.169; 12.219, 265**
4:19	**8.29; 10.47**		
4:22–24	**5.126**	6:23	**10.129**
4:25–32	**10.***154–160*		
4:26	**4.168**		
4:32	**4.285; 14.228**	*Philippians*	
5:1–8	**10.***160–163*		
5:6	**8.26**	1:1–3:1	**11.7**
5:8	**15.27**	1:1, 2	**11.***9–12*
5:9–14	**10.***164–166*	1:1	**8.xi; 11.47; 12.22, 71; 14.35, 293; 15.171; 16.25**
5:9	**10.51**		
5:11	**15.28**		
5:15–21	**10.***166–167*	1:2	**7.120, 192; 11.9–12; 12.23; 14.36**
5:18	**4.149**		
5:19	**14.128**	1:3–11	**11.***13–19*
5:20	**10.130**	1:3	**8.xi**
5:21–23	**16.173**	1:4	**10.50**
5:22–32	**5.143; 17.106**	1:7	**11.5, 21**
5:22–26	**9.69**	1:12–14	**11.***19–22*
5:22–23	**10.***167–175*	1:12–13	**7.193**
5:24–28	**14.102; 16.108**	1:13–14	**11.21**
5:26	**12.262**	1:14	**15.24**
5:27	**17.108**	1:15–18	**11.***22–24*
6:1–9	**14.222**	1:18	**11.14**
6:1–4	**10.***175–178*	1:19–20	**11.***24–26*
6:4	**9.41**	1:21–26	**11.***26–29*
6:5–9	**10.***178–180*; **12.272**	1:21	**11.149**
6:5	**9.24**	1:25	**10.50; 11.14**
6:6	**14.293; 16.25**	1:27–30	**11.5, 7, ***29–31*
6:9	**14.62**	1:27	**14.225**
6:10–20	**10.***181–184*	2:1–11	**11.6**

2:1–4	**11**.*31–34*	3:17–21	**11**.*67–70*
2:2	**14**.225	3:20	**11**.4
2:5–11	**11**.*34–40*	4:1	**11**.7, 15, 45, *70–72*
2:5	**15**.83	4:2–3	**11**.*72–74*; **12**.68
2:9–11	**17**.179	4:2	**11**.7; **14**.225
2:9	**5**.135	4:3	**16**.123; **17**.196
2:10	**14**.242	4:4–23	**11**.7
2:11	**9**.107; **10**.141; **12**.136, 153; **14**.350; **15**.68; **16**.180	4:4–5	**11**.*74–76*
		4:5	**14**.124, 249
		4:6–7	**11**.*77–78*
2:12–18	**11**.*40–46*	4:8–9	**11**.*78–83*
2:12–13	**14**.300	4:10–18	**9**.248; **11**.6
2:15	**16**.53; **17**.209	4:10–13	**11**.*84–85*
2:16	**15**.25	4:10–11	**11**.6, 15
2:17	**11**.14; **17**.11	4:14–20	**11**.*85–87*
2:19–24	**11**.*46–48*	4:16	**11**.6
2:19–22	**3**.72	4:18	**7**.192
2:19–20	**7**.120; **8**.219; **12**.22	4:19	**4**.118
2:20, 22	**12**.22	4:21–23	**11**.87
2:24	**12**.10	4:21–22	**8**.xi
2:25–30	**9**.230; **11**.*48–50*	4:22	**8**.212
2:25	**12**.159		
2:28	**11**.15		
2:29–30	**11**.6, 15	*Colossians*	
3:1	**11**.7, 15, *50–53*; **14**.336	1:1	**7**.120, 192; **8**.xi; **11**.9, 47, *103–105*; **12**.22
3:2–4:3	**11**.7		
3:2–3	**11**.*53–56*	1:2–8	**11**.*105–107*
3:2	**3**.178; **11**.7	1:2	**8**.xi; **11**.12; **12**.23; **14**.36; **16**.28
3:3	**17**.24		
3:4–7	**11**.*57–61*	1:4	**11**.94
3:4–5	**7**.159	1:5	**3**.25; **15**.24, 25
3:5–6	**9**.252	1:6	**11**.94
3:5	**8**.13	1:7	**11**.94, 171
3:8–9	**11**.*61–63*	1:8	**11**.94
3:10–11	**11**.*63–65*	1:9–11	**11**.*107–110*
3:10	**14**.258; **17**.204	1:12–14	**11**.*111–112*, 136
3:12–16	**11**.*65–67*	1:12	**14**.267
3:14	**11**.45; **15**.177	1:13	**9**.44; **15**.27

1:14	10.65	3:6	8.26
1:15–23	11.*112–125*	3:8	1.139
1:15	11.95, 119; **16**.32, 141	3:9b–13	11.*154–157*
1:16	5.41; 11.95, 96, 114	3:9	14.73
1:17	11.95	3:11	11.179; **12**.272
1:18	**16**.141	3:14–17	11.*158–160*
1:19	5.71; 10.65; **11**.95	3:17	14.214
1:20	17.31	3:18–4:1	11.*160–165*
1:21	11.94	3:19	14.128
1:22	11.95, 115; **17**.108	3:20–4:1	14.222
1:23	3.25	3:22–4:1	12.272
1:24–29	11.*125–127*	3:25	14.62
1:24	11.64	4:2–4	11.*166–167*
1:27	11.94; **12**.19	4:3	11.21; **16**.129
1:28	11.97, 116	4:5–6	11.*167–168*
2:1	11.93, *127–128*	4:7–11	11.*168–170*
2:2–7	11.*129–132*	4:7	10.61; **12**.219, 265
2:2	11.95	4:9	12.274
2:3	10.65	4:10	3.4; 7.192; **12**.217
2:5	11.94	4:11–12	7.2
2:8–23	11.*133–135*	4:12–15	8.xi; 11.*171–172*
2:8–10	11.*135–138*	4:12–13	11.94
2:8	11.95, 96	4:12	14.293; **16**.25
2:9	5.71; 10.65; **11**.95, 115	4:13	12.273; **16**.28
2:10	8.118; **11**.96	4:14	4.1; 7.3; **12**.213, 216; 15.153
2:11–12	11.*138–140*	4:15–16	12.273
2:12	10.32	4:16	10.68, 70; 11.*172–174*; **12**.273
2:13–15	11.*140–143*		
2:14	12.283	4:17–18	11.*174–175*
2:15	8.118; 11.96; **15**.78	4:17	12.273; **16**.140
2:16–23	11.*143–146*	4:18	8.xii; **11**.21
2:16–17	8.184; **11**.96		
2:18	11.97		
2:20	11.95		
2:21	11.96		

1 Thessalonians

3:1–4	11.*147–149*	1	11.*185–187*
3:5–9a	11.*149–154*	1:1	8.xi; 11.12; **12**.22, 23; 14.36, 143
3:5–8	11.94, 97		

1:3	**8**.xi
1:5	**11**.190
1:8	**15**.24
1:10	**8**.26
2:1–12	**11**.*187–190*
2:3–12	**11**.183
2:5	**11**.182
2:6–7	**10**.145; **11**.182
2:7	**14**.192
2:9	**7**.136; **11**.182; **14**.266
2:11	**11**.182
2:13–16	**11**.*190–192*
2:13	**15**.24
2:14	**11**.182
2:17–20	**11**.*192–194*
2:17	**11**.181
2:19	**14**.124; **16**.83
2:20	**11**.182
3:1–10	**11**.*194–196*
3:1–2	**11**.181
3:2–6	**7**.120
3:2	**12**.22
3:4–6	**11**.182
3:4	**12**.198
3:5	**11**.181
3:6	**11**.48; **12**.22
3:11–13	**11**.*196–197*
3:13	**14**.122, 123
4:1–8	**11**.*198–200*
4:3–8	**11**.182
4:9–12	**11**.*200–202*
4:9–10	**11**.182
4:9	**15**.66
4:11	**11**.182
4:13–18	**11**.182, *202–203*
4:13	**6**.86
4:14, 16	**11**.27
4:15	**14**.122
4:16	**16**.43; **17**.42, 114

4:17	**17**.78
5:1–11	**11**.*204–206*
5:2	**2**.303; **4**.257; **7**.25; **11**.182; **14**.123
5:4–5	**15**.27
5:6	**11**.182; **16**.119
5:12–22	**11**.*206–208*
5:12–14	**11**.182
5:21	**16**.63
5:23–28	**11**.*208*
5:23	**1**.109; **11**.82; **14**.122f
5:25	**11**.25, 216; **15**.116
5:26	**8**.xi; **11**.189; **14**.279

2 Thessalonians

1	**11**.*208–211*
1:1	**8**.xi; **11**.12; **14**.143, 275
1:2	**8**.xi; **12**.23; **14**.36
1:3	**8**.xi
1:4	**8**.21
1:7–9	**16**.132
1:11	**10**.51; **15**.177
2:1–12	**11**.*211–213*
2:1	**14**.122
2:3–4	**15**.63
2:3	**3**.310; **12**.92; **17**.56
2:5	**17**.61
2:6–7	**17**.93
2:7	**16**.15; **17**.61
2:8	**16**.51
2:9	**14**.122
2:10	**14**.133
2:13–17	**11**.*214–215*
2:16	**12**.24
3:1–5	**11**.*215–216*
3:1–2	**11**.25

1 Matt, v.1	**3** Mark	**5** John, v.1	**7** Acts	**9** Cor
2 Matt, v.2	**4** Luke	**6** John, v.2	**8** Rom	**10** Gal, Eph

3:1	**15**.24
3:6–18	**11**.*217–219*
3:8	**7**.136
3:17	**8**.xii

1 Timothy

1:1–2	**12**.*17–25*
1:1	**15**.207
1:2	**3**.71
1:3–7	**12**.*25–34*
1:3	**16**.60
1:4	**12**.5, 6, 28, 29
1:6–7	**14**.80
1:7	**12**.6
1:8–11	**12**.*34–41*
1:12–17	**12**.*41–48*
1:15	**4**.95; **12**.13
1:16	**10**.51, 139
1:17	**12**.29; **15**.163
1:18–20	**12**.*48–54*
1:18	**3**.71; **12**.159
2:1–7	**12**.*54–64*
2:1–2	**8**.171
2:1	**15**.117; **17**.93
2:2	**14**.205
2:3	**15**.207
2:4	**12**.5, 29; **14**.343; **15**.40
2:5	**12**.29
2:6	**16**.177
2:8–15	**12**.*64–69*
2:8	**13**.83; **14**.107
2:13–17	**17**.93
3:1–7	**12**.3, *69–84*, 234
3:2	**8**.167; **14**.255; **15**.150
3:3	**14**.266
3:5	**12**.74
3:6	**17**.80

3:7	**12**.74
3:8–13	**12**.3
3:8–10	**12**.*84–86*
3:8	**14**.266
3:10	**12**.72
3:12–13	**12**.*84–86*
3:11	**12**.*86–87*
3:14–15	**12**.*88–89*
3:15	**13**.32
3:16	**12**.4, *89–91*
4:1–5	**12**.*91–95*
4:1–3	**15**.199
4:1	**12**.3
4:3	**12**.30
4:4–5	**12**.5, 30
4:4	**9**.12
4:6–10	**12**.*95–97*
4:6	**12**.3; **14**.134
4:7–8	**11**.46; **12**.29
4:10	**12**.29; **15**.207
4:11–16	**12**.*97–102*
5:1–2	**12**.*102–105*
5:3–16	**12**.3
5:3–8	**12**.*105–108*
5:6	**16**.116
5:9–10	**12**,*109–113*
5:9	**15**.149
5:10	**14**.255
5:11–16	**12**.*113–115*
5:17–22	**12**.*115–118*
5:17–19	**12**.3
5:17	**12**.73; **14**.264
5:18	**12**.73; **14**.118
5:19–22	**12**.73
5:19	**5**.195
5:22	**17**.152
5:23	**12**.13, *118–120*
5:24–25	**12**.*120–121*
6:1–2	**12**.*121–123*

6:3–5   **12.***123–128*
6:4   **12.**5, 29
6:5   **12.**6; **14.**315
6:6–8   **12.***128–131*
6:6   **15.**198
6:9–10   **12.***131–133*; **14.**117
6:10   **1.**252
6:11–16   **12.***133–136*
6:11   **14.**301
6:15   **15.**163
6:16   **16.**151
6:17–19   **12.***137–138*
6:20–21   **12.***138–141*
6:20   **12.**6, 28

2 Timothy

1:1–7   **12.***142–145*
1:2   **12.**23
1:5   **7.**120; **11.**147; **12.**21,
          68
1:8–11   **12.***145–150*
1:10   **3.**25; **16.**53
1:12–14   **12.***150–154*
1:12   **4.**120; **9.**78; **14.**296
1:13   **15.**25
1:14   **12.**4
1:15–18   **12.***154–157*
1:16   **12.**222
2:1–2   **12.***157–158*
2:3–4   **12.***159–160*
2:5   **11.**46; **12.***160–162*
2:6–7   **12.***162–163*
2:8–10   **12.***163–168*
2:8   **1.**15; **3.**298; **12.**4;
          15.25
2:11–13   **12.***168–170*

2:11–12   **6.**220
2:12   **14.**258; **16.**40
2:14   **12.***170–172*
2:15–18   **12.***172–176*
2:15   **15.**25
2:16   **12.**29
2:17   **12.**53
2:18   **12.**6, 30
2:19   **12.***176–178*
2:20–21   **12.***178–179*
2:22–26   **12.***179–181*
2:23   **12.**5, 29
2:24   **14.**293
3:1   **12.***182–183*; **14.**175
3:2–5   **12.***184–191*
3:5   **16.**118
3:6–7   **12.***191–193*
3:6   **12.**5, 30
3:8–9   **12.***193–195*
3:8   **12.**3; **15.**30
3:10–13   **12.***195–198*
3:14–17   **12.***198–202*
3:15   **12.**1
4:1–5   **12.***202–208*
4:1   **14.**122; **17.**195
4:3   **14.**80
4:4   **12.**29
4:5   **10.**147
4:6–8   **12.***308–312*
4:6   **17.**11
4:8   **11.**45; **14.**49; **16.**83
4:9–15   **12.***212–220*
4:10   **11.**171; **14.**103;
          15.153
4:11   **3.**4; **7.**1f, 101, 192;
          11.171
4:14   **12.**53
4:16–22   **12.***220–223*
4:18   **8.**21

4:19	**8.**8, 209
4:20	**12.**11

Titus

1:1–4	**12.***227–234*
1:1	**6.**178; **14.**293; **15.**171; **16.**25
1:3	**15.**207
1:4	**12.**23, 218, 233
1:5–7a	**12.***234–235*
1:5–6	**12.**3
1:5	**12.**9, 71, 72; **14.**264
1:6–9	**12.**71
1:7–16	**12.**3
1:7	**14.**266
1:7b	**12.***235–238*
1:8–9	**12.***238–240*
1:8	**8.**167; **13.**83; **14.**255; **15.**150
1:10–11	**12.***240–242*
1:10	**12.**6
1:11	**12.**6; **14.**266, 315
1:12	**12.***242–243*
1:13–16	**12.***244–246*
1:13	**12.**3
1:14	**12.**6, 29
1:15	**12.**5, 30
1:16	**12.**5, 30
2:1–2	**12.***246–248*
2:3–5	**12.***248–251*
2:3	**12.**68
2:4	**12.**5
2:5	**14.**319
2:6	**12.***251–252*
2:7–8	**12.***252–254*
2:7	**12.**233
2:9–10	**12.***254–256*

2:10	**15.**207
2:11–14	**12.***256–257*
2:11	**12.**5
2:13	**14.**122
2:15	**12.***257–258*
3:1–2	**12.***258–260*
3:1	**8.**171
3:3–7	**12.***260–263*
3:3	**14.**99
3:4	**15.**207
3:5	**5.**125
3:8–11	**12.***263–265*
3:9	**12.**5, 6
3:10	**14.**316
3:12–15	**12.***265–266*
3:12	**12.**9

Philemon

1–7	**12.***277–279*
1	**7.**120, 192; **12.**22
2	**11.**172; **12.**159, 273; **14.**254
3	**11.**12, 21; **12.**23; **14.**36
8–17	**12.***279–282*
9	**11.**174
10	**3.**249; **12.**269
11	**12.**271
12	**12.**281
13–14	**12.**274
13	**11.**21; **12.**270
15	**12.**271
16	**12.**271; **14.**213
18–25	**12.***282–283*
18–19	**12.**269
19–21	**12.**274f
22	**11.**25, 217; **12.**10

24   3.4; 7.1; 11.170, 171;
            12.213, 216; 15.153

Hebrews

1:1–3   13.*12–16*
1:2   5.41; 14.175
1:4–14   13.*16–20*
2:1–4   13.*20–22*
2:2   10.29
2:3   13.5, 6
2:4   16.32
2:5–9   13.*23–25*
2:10–18   13.*25–28*
2:18   4.271; 9.171; 16.132
3:1–6   13.*28–32*
3:1   15.177
3:7–19   13.*32–34*
3:12   13.35
3:18–4:2   15.182
4:1–10   13.*35–38*
4:2   15.24
4:11–13   13.*38–41*
4:12   16.51, 94; 17.182
4:14–16   13.*41–44*
4:14–15   15.93
4:14   6.154
4:16   14.106; 16.35
5:1–10   13.*44–48*, 64
5:1, 3   14.233
5:11–14   13.*49–51*
5:12–14   5.126
5:12   13.5–7; 14.192
5:13   15.25
6   13.64
6:1–3   13.*51–55*
6:2   14.192
6:4–8   13.*55–59*

6:4–6   15.119
6:9–12   13.*59–61*
6:10   13.6
6:13–20   13.*61–63*
6:18   13.59
6:20   6.155
7   13.*63–71*
7:1–3   13.69, *71–75*
7:3   13.68
7:4–10   13.*75–77*
7:8   13.70
7:11–20   13.*77–79*
7:11   13.70
7:15–19   13.70
7:19   14.106
7:21–25   13.*79–83*
7:25   10.133; 15.38
7:26–28   13.*83–85*
7:27   13.71; 14.233
8:1–6   13.*86–89*
8:5   17.10
8:7–13   13.*90–94*
9:1–5   13.*94–97*
9:4   16.94
9:6–10   13.*97–101*
9:11–14   13.*102–105*
9:14   17.31
9:15–22   13.*105–108*
9:23–28   13.*109–111*
9:23   17.10
9:24   15.38
9:28   14.233
10:1–10   13.*112–115*
10:4   13.59; 16.79
10:10   14.233
10:11–18   13.*116–118*
10:19–25   13.*118–123*
10:19–23   13.2; 15.114
10:19–22   16.35

10:20	6.58
10:24–25	14.124
10:26–31	13.*123–126*
10:26	13.45
10:32–39	13.*126–128*
10:32–34	13.6
10:32	13.5
10:37	2.2; **16**.133; **17**.55
11:1–3	13.*128–131*
11:4	13.*131–133*
11:5–6	13.*133–139*
11:6	13.59; **16**.145
11:7	13.*139–142*
11:8–10	13.*142–146*
11:8	3.62; 7.55; **8**.63; **16**.145
11:9	13.148; **14**.201
11:11–12	13.*146–147*
11:13–16	13.*147–150*
11:13	14.201
11:17–19	13.*150–153*
11:20–22	13.*153–154*
11:21	3.62
11:23–29	13.*154–159*
11:27	9.203
11:30–31	13.*160–162*
11:32–34	13.*162–165*
11:35–40	13.*165–171*
12:1–2	13.*171–173*; **16**.132
12:2	13.25; **14**.303
12:3–4	13.*174–175*
12:4	13.6
12:5–11	13.*175–179*
12:6	14.247
12:12–17	13.*179–185*
12:18–24	13.*185–187*
12:22	17.199
12:25–29	13.*187–189*
12:29	17.117

13:1–6	13.*189–194*
13:2	8.167; **14**.255; **15**.149
13:4	17.106
13:7–8	13.*194f*
13:7	13.5f; **15**.24
13:8	16.30
13:9–16	13.*195–199*
13:14	14.168
13:17–20	13.*199–200*
13:18	15.116
13:20–24	13.*200–202*
13:20	1.109; **6**.54; **10**.148; **17**.38
13:22	13.9
13:23	11.48
13:24	13.6

James

1:1	6.178; **14**.8, 21, 23, 31f, *35–41*, 137, 293; **15**.171; **16**.25
1:2–4	14.*42–44*
1:2	14.29
1:5–8	14.*44–46*
1:5	1.245
1:7	14.21
1:9–11	14.31, *47–48*
1:10	14.29
1:11	14.29
1:12	14.31, *48–49*; **16**.83
1:13–15	14.*50–53*
1:15	14.28
1:16–18	14.*53–54*
1:17	14.25, 29
1:18	5.125; **14**.21, 31, 171, 172; **15**.79
1:19–20	14.31, *54–56*

1:20	1.139	3:9–12	14.*89–90*
1:21	10.51; **14.***56–58*	3:11–13	14.22
1:22–24	14.*58–59*	3:11–12	14.28
1:25	14.7, 21, *59–60*	3:13–14	14.*91–93*
1:26–27	14.*61–62*	3:15–16	14.*93–94*
1:27	1.119; **16.**121	3:17–18	14.*94–98*
2:1–3	14.27	4:1–3	14.*98–101*
2:1	14.24, 31, *62–63*	4:1–2	14.31
2:2–4	14.*63–66*	4:1	14.28
2:2	14.21, 26	4:4–7	14.*101–106*
2:4	14.28	4:4	14.28, 29
2-5–7	14.*66–68*	4:6	3.175; 8.37; 12.186;
2:5	14.28; **16.**78		14.29
2:7	14.23	4:7	3.23
2:8–11	14.*68–70*	4:8–10	14.*106–110*
2:8	14.21, 111	4:10	14.21
2:12–14	14.*71–74*	4:11–12	14.*110–112*
2:12–13	14.22, *70–71*	4:12	14.29
2:12	13.7	4:13–17	14.*112–114*
2:13	1.102; **2.**194; **14.**28,	4:13	14.28
	29	4:15	14.21
2:14–26	14.22, 349	4:17	7.35
2:14–19	14.29	5:1–6	14.27, 29
2:14–17	14.28, *75–76*	5:1–3	14.*115–118*
2:14	14.28	5:3	14.28, 175
2:18–19	14.28, *76–78*	5:4–6	14.*118–121*
2:20–26	14.*78–79*	5:6	14.28
2:20	14.29	5:7–9	14.22, 26, *121–124*
2:21–23	14.29	5:7–8	14.21, 29, 31
2:24	14.22	5:8	14.249; **16.**133
2:25	13.161; **14.**29	5:9	**16.**146
2:26	14.29	5:10–11	14.21, *124–125*
3:1	14.26, *79–81*	5:11	14.29
3:2	9.175; **14.***81–83*	5:12	14.22, *126–127*
3:3–6	14.29	5:13–18	14.31
3:3–5a	14.*83–84*	5:13–15	14.*127–130*
3:5b–6	14.*85–88*	5:13–14	14.28
3:6	1.141; **3.**231; **14.**25	5:14	6.164; 9.110; **14.**21,
3:7–8	14.*88–89*		264; **15.**116

5:15	6.180; **14**.21
5:16–18	**14**.*130–132*
5:17	**14**.29
5:19–20	**12**.45; **14**.*133–134*
5:19	**15**.30
5:20	**14**.29, 31

1 Peter

1:1–2	**14**.159, *165–170*
1:1	**14**.137
1:2	**15**.140
1:3–4:11	**14**.160
1:3–5	**14**.*171–176*
1:3	5.125; **12**.25; **14**.140, 152, 172
1:5	8.21; **14**.139, 141
1:6–7	**14**.*176–178*
1:6	**14**.146, 158
1:7	**14**.122, 139, 141, 156; **16**.22, 143
1:8–9	**14**.*178–179*
1:8	**14**.141, 160
1:10–12	**14**.140, *180–182*
1:13–25	**14**.141
1:13	**14**.122, 139, 141, 142, 153, *182–183*; **16**.22
1:14–25	**14**.*184–189*
1:14	**14**.145
1:17	4.143
1:18	**14**.165
1:19–20	**17**.96
1:19	**14**.141; **16**.171, 177; **17**.31, 108
1:20–21	**14**.141
1:21	**14**.141, 142
1:22–23	5.125
1:23–25	**14**.191

1:23	**14**.172; **15**.79
2:1–3	**14**.141, *189–193*
2:1	**14**.111
2:2	**13**.50
2:4–10	**14**.*193–199*
2:4–8	2.141
2:4–6	8.135
2:4	3.283
2:5	8.32; **17**.68
2:7	3.283; 4.247; **14**.141
2:9–10	**14**.145; **15**.27
2:10	**14**.165, 291
2:11–12	**14**.*200–204*
2:12–17	**16**.15
2:12	**14**.139, 142, 158
2:13–17	8.171; **14**.159; **17**.63
2:13–15	**14**.*204–206*
2:15	**14**.158, 159
2:16	**14**.141, *207–208*, 335
2:17	2.274; **12**.59; **14**.*208–209*
2:18–3:7	**14**.160
2:18–25	**14**.*209–217*
2:21	**15**.83; **17**.108
2:22	**14**.142; **17**.108
2:23	**14**.120
2:24	**14**.141, 142
2:25	6.54; **10**.148; **17**.38
3:1–2	**14**.*217–219*
3:3–6	**14**.*220–222*
3:7	**14**.*222–224*
3:8–12	**14**.*224–228*
3:13–15a	**14**.*228–230*
3:14	**14**.146, 159
3:15b–16	**14**.*230–231*
3:15	5.160
3:16	**14**.146, 158
3:17–4:6	**14**.*231–232*
3:17–18a	**14**.*232–236*

3:17	**14.**159	5:1	**12.**71; **14.**139, 140, 141, 154, 161
3:18–22	**6.**35; **14.***243–245*		
3:18b–20	**14.***236–243*	5:2–3	**6.**54; **10.**148; **12.**71
3:18–20	**16.**52	5:2	**14.**161, 215
3:18	**14.**120	5:4	**10.**48; **14.**139, 141, 160; **16.**83
3:19	**14.**235		
3:20	**10.**51, 139	5:5	**8.**37; **12.**186; **14.**105, *270–271*
3:21	**14.**160		
3:22	**14.**141, 153, 235; **15.**78	5:6–11	**14.***271–274*
		5:8–9	**3.**23; **14.**106; **16.**118
4:1–5	**14.**141, *245–248*	5:9	**14.**146, 158
4:3–4	**14.**145	5:12–14	**14.**159
4:3	**10.**47; **14.**165	5:12	**14.**143, *274–276*
4:4	**14.**158	5:13	**3.**4, 72; **11.**170; **14.**160, *276–279*; **15.**18, 131, 138
4:5	**14.**141; **16.**132		
4:6	**6.**35; **14.**235, *236–243*, *248–249*		
		5:14	**14.**148, *279–281*
4:7a	**14.**123, 139, 140, *249–251*		
4:7b–8	**14.***251–253*		
4:8–9	**14.**124	**2 Peter**	
4:9–10	**14.***254–256*	1:1	**14.**145, *291–294*
4:9	**7.**123; **8.**167; **12.**81; **15.**149	1:2	**14.***294–296*
		1:3–7	**14.***296–305*
4:10	**14.**177	1:4, 5–8	**14.**283
4:11	**14.**159, *256–257*	1:8–11	**14.***305–307*
4:12–5:11	**14.**160	1:9	**14.**283
4:12–13	**14.***257–258*	1:10	**15.**177
4:12	**14.**146, 158	1:12–15	**14.***307–309*
4:13	**14.**139, 141, 159; **16.**22	1:16–18	**14.***309–311*
		1:16	**14.**122
4:14–16	**14.***258–260*	1:19–21	**14.***311–314*
4:14, 16	**9.**12; **14.**155, 158	1:20	**14.**283
4:17–19	**14.***260–262*	2	**15.**168f
4:17	**13.**32; **14.**139, 141	2:1	**14.***314–318*; **16.**177
4:18	**14.**141	2:2–3	**14.***318–319*
4:19	**14.**146	2:2, 3	**14.**283
5:1–4	**14.***262–270*	2:4–11	**14.***320–330*
5:1–3	**14.**160	2:4–5	**3.**34; **14.**237, 240, 283

2:6	1.371; **14**.283; **15**.185	1:8–10	**15**.10, 14, *32–34*, 80
2:9	**15**.28	1:8	**14**.82
2:10	**14**.283	2:1–2	**15**.*34–40*
2:12–14	**14**.288, *330–332*	2:1	**15**.13, 14, 52, 81
2:12	**14**.283	2:2	**14**.233; **15**.14
2:13	**14**.283; **15**.193	2:3–6	**15**.*40–43*
2:14–15	**14**.283	2:3–5	**15**.17
2:15–16	**14**.*332–333*	2:4–6	**15**.10
2:15	**14**.283	2:4	**15**.31
2:17–22	**14**.*334–335*	2:7–8	**15**.*43–46*
2:18	**10**.47; **14**.283	2:8	**15**.16, 27
2:19	**14**.207, 283	2:9–11	**15**.12, 16, 28, *46–49*
2:20–22	**14**.284	2:12–14	**15**.*49–55*
3:1–2	**14**.*336–337*	2:14	**15**.13
3:2	**14**.287	2:15–17	**15**.*55–59*
3:3–4	**14**.284, *337–339*	2:17	**15**.16
3:4	**14**.123, 287	2:18	**11**.213; **14**.175, 249;
3:5–7	**14**.284		**15**.*59–65*; **17**.62
3:5–6	**14**.*339–340*	2:19–21	**15**.*65–67*
3:7	**14**.*340–342*	2:19	**15**.5
3:8–9	**14**.284, *342–343*	2:22–23	**15**.*67–68*
3:8	**17**.188	2:22	**11**.213; **15**.6, 13, 32,
3:10	**4**.257; **6**.184, 198;		61, 68; **17**.62
	7.25; **14**.123, 284,	2:24–29	**15**.*68–72*
	343–345; **17**.195	2:26	**15**.6
3:11–14	**14**.284, *345–347*	2:28	**14**.122, 124; **15**.52
3:15–16	**14**.284f, 288, *347–349*	2:29	**14**.172; **15**.17
3:15	**10**.139	3:1–2	**15**.*72–76*
3:16	**14**.283	3:1	**15**.16
3:17–18	**14**.*350–351*	3:2–3	**12**.19
		3:2	**14**.179; **15**.43; **16**.84
		3:3–10	**15**.17
1 John		3:3–8	**15**.*76–78*
1:1–4	**15**.*21–25*	3:5	**15**.14
1:1, 4	**15**.13	3:7	**15**.52
1:5	**15**.10, 13, *25–28*	3:9	**14**.172; **15**.*78–81*
1:6–7	**15**.*28–32*	3:10–18	**15**.*81–85*
1:6	**15**.10	3:10–11,	**15**.17
1:7	**15**.12, 15, 16; **17**.31	11–17	

11 Phil, Col, Thes   **13** Heb   **15** John, Jude   **16** Rev, v.1
12 Tim, Tit, Phlm   **14** Jas, Pet   **17** Rev, v.2

3:13	**15**.16
3:14–17	**15**.12
3:14–15	**14**.227
3:16	**15**.14
3:19–24a	**15**.*85–88*
3:19	**14**.133
3:21	**15**.44
3:22	**15**.17, 115
3:23	**15**.12, 17
3:24	**15**.15
3:24b–4:1	**15**.*88–92*
4:1–7	**15**.91f
4:1–3	**16**.63
4:1	**15**.5, 44
4:2–3	**5**.13, 65, 223; **15**.7, 14, *92–94*
4:2	**15**.142
4:3	**11**.213; **15**.61, 119, 129; **17**.62
4:4–6	**15**.*94–96*
4:4–5	**15**.16, 52
4:7–21	**15**.*96–101*
4:7–12	**15**.17
4:7–10	**15**.13
4:7–8	**15**.12
4:7	**14**.173; **15**.44
4:9	**15**.15
4:10–12	**15**.12
4:10	**15**.14
4:11	**15**.139
4:13	**15**.15
4:14	**5**.171; **15**.15
4:15, 16	**15**.13
4:20–21	**15**.12, 17
4:20	**14**.227; **15**.32
5:1–2	**15**.*102–103*
5:1	**15**.13
5:2	**15**.17
5:3–4a	**15**.*103–105*

5:4	**14**.173; **15**.16
5:4b–5	**15**.*105–106*
5:5	**15**.13
5:6–8	**15**.*106–111*
5:6	**15**.9, 14
5:7	**5**.53; **15**.110
5:9–10	**5**.197; **15**.*111–112*
5:11–13	**15**.*113–114*
5:11–12	**15**.15
5:14–15	**15**.*114–116*
5:16–17	**15**.*116–121*
5:18–20	**15**.*121–123*
5:18	**14**.172; **15**.17
5:19	**15**.16
5:21	**15**.52, *123–125*

2 John

1–3	**15**.*137–140*
1	**5**.23; **15**.18, 138
4–6	**15**.*140–141*
4–5	**15**.130f
4	**15**.129f, 138
6	**15**.130
7–11	**15**.131
7–9	**15**.*141–144*
7	**15**.61, 129; **17**.62
8	**15**.130, 138
10–13	**15**.*144–145*
10	**15**.130, 138
12	**15**.129, 130, 138
13	**14**.160; **15**.130

3 John

1–4	**15**.*147–148*
1	**5**.23, 44

2	**15**.44
3–5	**15**.131
4	**11**.193; **13**.200; **15**.29
5–8	**15**.*148–151*
5	**15**.44
6–8	**15**.131
9–15	**15**.*151–154*
9, 10	**15**.132
11	**15**.44
12	**12**.214; **15**.132
13–14	**15**.129

Jude

1–2	**15**.*175–177*
1	**14**.293; **16**.25
2	**15**.140
3	**15**.158, 168, *177–179*
4	**10**.47; **15**.158, 160, 163, *179–181*
5–7	**15**.*181–186*
5, 6	**15**.158
7	**1**.371; **15**.158, 160
8–9	**15**.*186–188*
8	**15**.158, 160, 166
9	**14**.324; **15**.159, 166, 168
10	**3**.226; **15**.159f, *188–189*
11	**15**.159, *189–191*
12–16	**15**.*191–199*
12	**15**.161
13	**15**.28, 159
14–15	**15**.168
15	**15**.159
16	**15**.159, 161
17–19	**15**.*199–202*
17–18	**15**.168
18–19	**15**.159

18	**14**.175
19	**15**.165
20–21	**15**.159, *202–204*
22–23	**15**.160, *204–206*
24–25	**15**.160, *206–207*

Revelation

1:1–3	**16**.*21–27*
1:1	**16**.11, 24; **17**.228
1:2	**15**.24
1:3	**14**.249
1:4–6	**16**.*27–35*
1:4	**16**.11, 1i6, 155
1:5	**16**.92
1:7	**16**.*35–37*
1:8	**16**.*37–39*; **17**.173, 204
1:9	**15**.24; **16**.11, *39–42*
1:10–11	**16**.*42–44*
1:11	**16**.12
1:12–13	**16**.*44–46*
1:12	**16**.28
1:14–18	**16**.*46–53*
1:14	**17**.179
1:16	**16**.28; **17**.182
1:17	**17**.225
1:18	**2**.144
1:19	**16**.12
1:20	**16**.*53–55*
2–3	**16**.149
2:1–7	**16**.*57–71*
2:1	**16**.47
2:2	**17**.114
2:7	**16**.29, 84; **17**.229
2:8–11	**16**.*72–85*
2:8	**16**.47; **17**.225
2:10	**14**.162f; **16**.154
2:11	**16**.29; **17**.229

2:12–17	**16**.*86–99*	5:2–4	**16**.*166–168*
2:12	**16**.47	5:5	**16**.153, *168–170*
2:14	**15**.190	5:6–14	**17**.170
2:17	**11**.39; **16**.29, 176; **17**.229	5:6	**16**.28, 31, 157, *170–172*; **17**.170
2:18–29	**16**.*100–111*	5:7–14	**16**.*172–183*
2:18	**16**.47; **17**.179	5:8	**16**.152, 153, 154, *174–175*
2:19	**17**.114		
2:24	**15**.10	5:9–10	**16**.177–178
2:29	**16**.29; **17**.229	5:9	**14**.317; **16**.34, 98, 157, *175–176*; **17**.26
3:1–6	**16**.*112–123*		
3:1	**16**.31, 47, 155	5:11–12	**16**.*178–180*
3:4	**16**.154	5:11	**16**.152; **17**.168, 170
3:5	**16**.98; **17**.95, 196	5:13–14	**16**.*180–183*
3:6	**16**.29; **17**.229	5:13	**14**.242
3:7–13	**16**.*124–135*	5:14	**16**.152, 157; **17**.170
3:7	**2**.144; **16**.47	6:1–8	**17**.*1–9*
3:8	**16**.149	6:1–7	**17**.170
3:12	**11**.39; **16**.98, 176	6:1–2	**17**.*3–5*
3:13	**16**.29, **17**.229	6:1	**16**.157
3:14–22	**10**.69; **16**.*136–149*	6:3–4	**17**.*5–6*
3:14	**16**.92	6:5–6	**17**.*6–8*
3:15–16	**8**.165	6:7–8	**17**.*9*
3:16	**10**.69	6:7	**16**.157
3:17	**2**.218; **11**.91	6:9–11	**17**.*10–13*
3:20	**16**.150	6:9	**15**.24; **17**.40
3:22	**16**.29; **17**.229	6:10	**4**.220
4:1	**16**.*149–150*, 168	6:12–14	**17**.*13–15*
4:2–3	**16**.*150–152*	6:15–17	**17**.*15–17*
4:4	**16**.*152–154*; **17**.170	7	**17**.103
4:5–6a	**16**.*154–156*	7:1–3	**17**.*17–22*
4:5	**16**.28, 31	7:2–3	**17**.67
4:6–9	**17**.170	7:3	**17**.171
4:6b–8	**16**.*157–163*	7:4–8	**17**.*22–25*
4:6	**17**.117	7:9–10	**17**.*25–27*
4:7	**5**.1	7:9	**16**.98; **17**.168
4:9–11	**16**.*163–164*	7:11–12	**17**.*27–28*
4:10	**16**.152; **17**.170	7:11	**16**.152, 157; **17**.170
5:1	**16**.28, *164–166*	7:13–14	**17**.*29–34*

7:13	**16**.153	12:1–2	**17**.*75–76*
7:15	**17**.*34–36*	12:3–4	**17**.*77–78*
7:16–17	**17**.*36–39*	12:3	**17**.130
7:17	**5**.153; **17**.220	12:5	**17**.78
8–11	**17**.124	12:6	**17**.69, *79–80*
8:1–5	**17**.*39–41*	12:7–9	**17**.*80–83*
8:2, 6	**17**.*41–43*	12:9	**17**.58, 62, 130
8:5	**17**.10	12:10–12	**17**.*83–84*
8:7–12	**17**.*43–45*	12:13–17	**17**.*84–86*
8:7, 8, 10–11, 12	**17**.125	12:14	**17**.69
8:13	**17**.*45–46*	13	**17**.62f, *86–92*, 184
9:1–12	**17**.125	13:1–5	**17**.*92–94*
9:1–2	**17**.*46–48*	13:1	**15**.63; **17**.131, 138
9:3–12	**17**.*48–52*	13:3	**17**.138
9:11	**17**.47	13:5	**17**.69
9:13	**17**.40	13:6–9	**17**.*94–96*
9:13–21	**17**.*52–53*, 125	13:7	**17**.26
10:1–11:4	**17**.54	13:8	**17**.95, 196
10:1–4	**17**.*54–55*	13:10	**17**.*96–97*
10:1	**16**.167	13:11–17	**17**.*97–100*
10:3	**16**.28	13:12	**17**.138
10:5–7	**17**.*55–56*	13:13f	**17**.131
10:7	**17**.171	13:14	**17**.138
10:8–11	**17**.*56–64*	13:18	**17**.*100–102*
10:11	**16**.12	14:1	**17**.*102–104*
11	**17**.*64–66*	14:2–3	**17**.*104–105*
11:1–2	**17**.*66–69*	14:3	**16**.152, 176; **17**.118, 170
11:3–6	**17**.*69–71*		
11:7–13	**17**.*71–72*	14:4	**16**.157
11:7	**17**.47, 62	14:4a	**17**.*105–107*
11:8	**15**.185	14:4b–5	**17**.*107–109*
11:9	**17**.26	14:6–7	**17**.*109–110*
11:14–19	**17**.*72–74*	14:6	**17**.26
11:15	**17**.125	14:8	**17**.*110–111*
11:16	**16**.152; **17**.170	14:9–12	**17**.*111–113*
11:17	**17**.173	14:13	**16**.27; **17**.*113–114*
11:18	**17**.171	14:14–20	**17**.*114–116*
12	**17**.62, *74–75*	14:18	**17**.10, 19, 40
		15:1–2	**17**.*116–118*

11 Phil, Col, Thes
12 Tim, Tit, Phlm
13 Heb
14 Jas, Pet
15 John, Jude
16 Rev, v.1
17 Rev, v.2

15:3–4	**17.***118–120*	18:20	**17.***165*, 168
15:3	**17.**173	18:21–24	**17.***166–168*
15:4	**13.**83	18:21	**16.**167
15:5–7	**17.***121–122*	19:1–10	**17.**167
15:6–8	**16.**28	19:1–2	**17.***168–170*
15:7	**16.**157; **17.**170	19:2	**17.**171
15:8	**17.***122–123*	19:3–5	**17.***170–171*
16	**17.***123–126*	19:4	**16.**152, 157
16:1–11	**17.***126–128*	19:6–8	**17.***171–174*
16:2	**17.**125	19:6	**16.**39
16:5	**13.**83; **17.**19	19:7	**14.**102; **17.**76
16:7	**17.**173	19:8	**16.**98
16:12	**17.**126, *128–129*	19:9–10a	**17.***174–177*
16:13–16	**17.***129–133*	19:9	**16.**27
16:13	**15.**63	19:10	**16.**12; **17.**224
16:14	**17.**173	19:10b	**17.***176–177*
16:15	**16.**27	19:11–18	**17.**167
16:17–21	**17.**126, *133–134*	19:11–12	**17.**3
17–18	**14.**278; **17.***134–136*	19:11	**17.***177–178*
17	**3.**310; **17.***135–142*	19:12	**16.**135; **17.***179–180*
17:1–2	**17.***142*	19:13	**17.***180–182*
17:1	**17.**208	19:14–16	**17.***182–183*
17:3	**17.**63, *142–143*	19:14	**16.**98
17:4–5	**17.***143–145*	19:15	**17.**173
17:5–6	**16.**15	19:17–21	**17.***183–184*
17:5	**15.**19	19:19, 20–21	**17.**168
17:6	**17.***145–146*	19:20	**15.**63; **17.**131
17:7–11	**17.***146–147*	20	**17.***184–191*
17:8	**17.**95, 96	20:1–7	**14.**237
17:12–18	**17.***147–149*	20:1–3	**17.**168, *191–192*
17:15	**17.**26, 136	20:1, 3	**17.**47
18–22	**17.**167	20:4–6	**17.**168
18:1–3	**17.***149–151*	20:4–5	**17.***192–193*
18:4–5	**17.***151–152*	20:4	**15.**24
18:6–8	**17.***152–154*	20:6	**16.**27, 84; **17.***193*
18:9–10	**17.***154–157*	20:7–10	**17.**168, *193–194*
18:11–16	**17.***157–164*	20:10	**15.**63; **17.**47, 131
18:12–13	**7.**140; **12.**185; **16.**58	20:11–15	**17.***194–197*
18:17–19	**17.***164*		

1 Matt, v.1	**3** Mark	**5** John, v.1	**7** Acts	**9** Cor
2 Matt, v.2	**4** Luke	**6** John, v.2	**8** Rom	**10** Gal, Eph

20:11–14	17.168	21:19	16.151
20:11	16.98	21:22–23	17.*215–216*
20:12	17.95	21:22	17.173
20:14	16.84; 17.47	21:24–27	17.*216–219*
20:15	16.123; 17.47, 95	21:27	16.123; 17.95
21:1–22:5	17.168	22:1–2	17.*220–222*
21:1	2.179; 16.98, 176; 17.*197–199*	22:1	5.154
21:2	16.176; 17.*199–202*	22:3–5	17.*222–223*
21:3–4	17.*202–204*	22:6–9	17.*223–224*
21:5–6	17.*204–205*	22:6	16.12; 17.171
21:5	16.98, 176	22:7	16.12, 27
21:6	5.153; 17.220, 225	22:8	16.11
21:7–8	17.*205–206*	22:9	16.12
21:8	6.189; 16.84; 17.227	22:10–11	17.*224–225*
21:9–27	17.*207–208*	22:10	16.12
21:9–10	17.*208–209*	22:12–13	17.*225–226*
21:9	14.102; 17.76	22:14–15	17.*226–228*
21:11	17.*209*	22:14	16.27
21:12	17.*209–210*	22:15	3.178; 11.54
21:13	17.*210–211*	22:16	1.15; 16.111; 17.*228–229*
21:14	1.360; 16.13	22:17	17.*229–230*
21:15–17	17.*211–212*	22:18–19	16.12; 17.*230–232*
21:16	4.180	22:20–21	17.*232*
21:18–21	17.*212–215*	22:20	14.249

11 Phil, Col, Thes	**13** Heb	**15** John, Jude	**16** Rev, v.1
12 Tim, Tit, Phlm	**14** Jas, Pet		**17** Rev, v.2

D

INDEX OF SUBJECTS AND PLACES

Aaron's rod **13**.96

Abaddon **16**.181

Abiding, spiritual **6**.175; **15**.71f, 115

Abilene **4**.3

Abomination **12**.246

Abomination of desolation **2**.306; **3**.309f; **15**.62f

Absolution **2**.139

Absolutism **3**.286

Abstinence **2**.208; **12**.79f, 120

Abyss, The **17**.47f, 168, 191

Academics, The **12**.140

Acceptance, duty of **8**.113

Accuser, The **17**.83

Achaea **3**.12; **9**.3

Acre **1**.40; **3**.52

Acropolis **7**.134; **9**.3

Acts, *Book of*
'Gospel of the Resurrection' **7**.27; **14**.24
'Gospel of the Holy Spirit' **7**.18
Introduction to **7**.1–7
Purpose of **7**.193
Sermons of **14**.140f
Size of **16**.165
'We passages' **7**.6, 121

Adar **2**.169

Adoption
Roman law of **8**.105–107
Spiritual **8**.107, 110; **10**.79f; **12**.9; **15**.74

Adultery **1**.136, 139, 145, 152; **2**.199; **3**.173, 238f; **4**.211f;

6.2; **8**.176; **9**.51f; **14**.331
and divorce **2**.201f; **10**.168f
offerings for **5**.202
spiritual **6**.28; **14**.101f; **17**.105f

Adversary, The **2**.149; **3**.22–24

Adversity **3**.247

Afflictions **1**.355; **9**.170; **16**.78
spiritual **14**.108

Africa **1**.39, 73, 113; **3**.361; **5**.179

Aged, the **2**.80

Age to come, The **1**.373; **4**.257; **5**.168; **6**.122, 197; **15**.56, 80; **16**.10f; **17**.221

Agnosticism **5**.55; **15**.74

Agriculture **2**.21, 73; **3**.94–96, 157; **4**.34; **5**.167f; **17**.167

Air, Prince of the **17**.80

Akkar, Plain of **2**.76

Alexandria **1**.33; **2**.81; **3**.209; **14**.4, 39
and allegory **7**.139; **9**.15
and Christianity **3**.3; **7**.101; **11**.170
greatness of **7**.89
and Jews **1**.273; **7**.139; **9**.14f, 252; **11**.59; **16**.18
library of **16**.88
scholarship of **13**.107

Algiers **17**.50

Allegory **2**.55, 261; **3**.90, 281; **10**.41; **17**.85

Alms and almsgiving **1**.179, 185, 187, 233; **9**.164f

Greek **14**.75
Jewish **1**.335; **3**.30; **14**.75
Altars **2**.244
 heavenly **17**.10, 127
Amber **17**.159
Ambitions **1**.37, 90, 331, 396;
  2.86, 173, 175, 228f; **3**.147,
  222, 224, 253, 329; **11**.23, 31,
  147, 150; **12**.37; **14**.91, 318;
  15.57
America **1**.117
Amethyst **17**.159, 214
Amphipolis **7**.128
Amulets **7**.140; **15**.125; **16**.59,
  97
Anarchy **9**.265; **14**.205
Anchor, symbol of **13**.62
Ancyra **14**.144
Anemones **4**.165
Angels **1**.69; **3**.289; **10**.92;
  15.159, 166, 171; **16**.167,
  174f
 archangels **8**.17; **16**.31
 avenging **17**.121f
 of the churches **16**.53–55, 104
 contempt of **15**.186–188
 of death **2**.339; **3**.135; **13**.134,
  158
 of doom **17**.109f
 fallen **3**.34; **14**.240, 321–323;
  17.47
 and Gnostics **11**.119f
 guardian **1**.321; **2**.180; **3**.35;
  4.161; **13**.18; **16**.31, 54
 hosts of **13**.17
 immortality of **13**.18f
 and Jesus **3**.24; **12**.90f;
  13.16–19
 in Judaism **2**.128; **4**.250;

  8.117f; **15**.167
 and the Law **10**.29; **13**.17;
  16.24
 of the Lord **3**.22; **4**.291
 and lordships **8**.117
 and natural forces **17**.127
 of Peace **17**.40
 of the Presence **13**.18; **16**.31;
  17.41f, 202, 204
 of Punishment **17**.53
 ranks of **14**.323
 at resurrection **2**.376; **4**.291
 'of service' **17**.19
 sin of **1**.321; **14**.321f; **15**.183f
 worship of **11**.97, 135, 146;
  16.173; **17**.27f, 175f, 224
Anger **1**.96, 136, 137–139;
  2.47, 280; **3**.236; **8**.35;
  9.264; **10**.155, 159; **11**.153;
  12.65, 187, 236; **14**.56
Animals, in Judaism **4**.177
Anointed One, The **1**.24, 29,
  36; **2**.137, 241, 254; **3**.12,
  297; **4**.119, 252; **5**.115, 154,
  176, 237, 243, 245, 252; **6**.53,
  72f, 117f; **8**.126; **10**.86f,
  107; **15**.69f; **16**.169; **17**.60,
  84
 as King **4**.26, 239f; **5**.88f
Anointing of kings **15**.69–71
Anthropomorphisms **5**.29
Antichrist **5**.223; **11**.213; **15**.14,
  61–64, 119; **17**.25, 55f, 57–64,
  66, 70, 77, 90, 102, 118, 138f,
  184
 spirit of **5**.13, 65; **15**.64
Antinomianism **3**.315; **11**.66, 97,
  98; **14**.284, 297; **15**.160–163,
  172

Antioch in Pisidia 7.97, 101, 102,
106f, 119; 14.291
Antioch in Syria 3.209; 7.4, 5f,
88f, 97, 117, 119, 138; 10.18–
20; 14.39, 79
Antipatris 7.167
Antisemitism, ancient 2.290;
4.85; 8.208f; 14.38, 148, 202
Antitypes 14.243f
Antonia, castle of 2.346; 7.157f
tower of 3.324; 6.223
Anxiety 1.218, 255; 3.116f;
4.165; 9.213; 11.195; 12.132;
14.272
Apartheid 5.159
Apii Forum 7.190
Apocalypse, The See *Revelation,*
Book of
Apocalyptic 1.7; 3.194, 305;
16.6–11; 17.117
literature of 5.7; 16.2–4
and prophecy 16.5f
Apocrypha, The 5.32
Apollonia 7.128
Apostacy 15.119
Apostates 1.121; 2.49; 6.174;
9.106; 13.57, 124; 17.112
Apostles, The 1.359–362; 3.144;
4.74f; 7.91; 9.134; 11.49;
12.158, 196–198; 14.17, 179;
15.132; 16.12, 25, 154
definition of 10.3, 145f;
12.195–197; 14.154f; 15.176
in Early Church 9.115, 184;
15.90
and elders 14.154
false 9.247; 249
female 8.212
respect for 7.44, 67

and the resurrection 7.17f;
9.78, 115
and the Sanhedrin 7.38f, 47f;
10.74f
Statutes of See Index VI
'super-apostles' 9.246, 261
support of 9.79
Teaching of See Index VI
Appian Way 7.190
Arabia 1.82; 3.52; 4.48; 7.73;
10.41
Arabs 1.93; 8.128; 9.173;
12.104; 13.143
Aralu 17.133
Aramaic language 5.29; 7.51;
14.37; 17.175
Ara Maxima, The 14.147
Archer, sign of the 17.215
Areopagus 7.131
Aretas 2.96
Aridity 11.166; 12.119
Aristocracy 10.45
Armageddon 17.132f
Armour, spiritual 10.181–184
Arrest, Greek law of 1.144
Arrogance 2.288; 8.37; 12.62,
185–187; 14.91f
Artaban 3.65f
Asceticism 9.55, 58f; 11.96, 98f,
135, 144f, 150; 12.5f, 30, 93f,
119–121; 15.9
Asher, tribe of 1.73; 3.178;
14.31
Asia 7.19, 121; 8.8; 12.155;
14.137, 144f, 160, 166; 16.11,
17, 28f, 58, 87
Asia Minor 2.218; 3.209; 5.17,
26; 7.5, 119; 8.209; 12.184f;
14.39f, 145, 160f; 17.86

Asiarch   7.3, 140
Aspasia   1.155
Ass, symbol of   2.243; 3.264;
    4.240; 6.118
Associations, Roman   12.165f
Assos   7.150
Assyria   1.58; 3.193; 11.111;
    16.8; 17.136f
Assyrians   1.73, 75; 2.281;
    5.149; 6.120; 7.65; 9.131;
    13.164; 14.37; 16.3; 17.53
Astrology   1.26; 7.66; 8.118;
    9.47; 10.35; 11.95f, 134, 137;
    12.182
Astronomy   5.57
Atheism   1.207; 8.49; 11.197;
    16.80
Athenaeum   12.124
Athens   1.154, 333; 2.80; 3.279;
    7.119, 130–133; 8.19; 9.1,
    49f, 119, 132, 164; 10.162,
    174; 12.38, 88, 210; 13.89;
    14.298
  Stoa Poikile of   3.279
Athenians   6.119; 8.202; 10.34,
    108f; 12.106; 17.103
Atonement
  Day of   1.142, 146, 233; 2.243,
    391; 3.58, 365; 4.223, 288;
    6.210; 7.182; 10.129; 13.3,
    18, 84, 96, 97–101
  Jewish   1.52, 142, 187f, 233;
    3.258; 4.266; 12.9, 18f, 43,
    127; 13.98–101; 16.177f
Attalia   7.97
Attalus   16.28
Augustan cohort   7.181
'Authorities'   10.182; 15.166
Authority   1.75, 133–135; 4.243f;

    6.4f; 16.127f
Avarice   2.331f, 335
Azariyeh   6.102

Baal   1.58; 4.126; 8.120, 144;
    10.47
  prophets of   1.64; 4.48; 6.143;
    16.106
  worship of   2.134; 3.192;
    4.17; 16.105f
Baal-peor   16.67
Baaras   4.51
Babylon   1.13, 163; 5.149;
    14.277; 15.18–20, 131, 138;
    16.8, 36; 17.2, 88, 153, 161,
    211
  carpets of   9.2
  coverlets of   17.160
  deportation of Jews   11.93;
    14.37f
  doom song of   17.149, 150
  exile of Jews in   6.22, 117;
    11.111
  fall of   17.110, 128, 166
  symbolic use of   14.276–278;
    16.15; 17.63, 134, 136, 167,
    168, 209
Babylonians   2.281; 3.193;
    6.121; 7.11; 11.212; 14.37;
    16.3; 17.53, 80
  and astrology   16.153, 155
  and creation   17.58, 198
  empire of   5.185
  legends of   15.61; 17.77, 133
  religion of   16.153
Balaam   12.194
Balance, sign of   17.215
Balinas   3.192
Balsam   4.234; 9.2; 17.161

| 1 Matt, v.1 | 3 Mark | 5 John, v.1 | 7 Acts | 9 Cor |
| 2 Matt, v.2 | 4 Luke | 6 John, v.2 | 8 Rom | 10 Gal, Eph |

Ban, The 6.47; 8.124; 12.53
Banias 2.134; 3.192
Banishment 16.40–42
Baptism 5.84; 6.262; 7.69, 85;
    8.83f; 11.154f; 12.169;
    13.53f; 14.243–245, 247f;
    15.89, 109
  of adults 10.32; 12.135;
    14.306
  and anointing 15.70f
  and confession 3.14; 5.iii, 83;
    10.32
  for the dead 11.152f
  and enlightenment 15.119
  with fire 1.50f
  by immersion 8.208; 12.86
  of infants 8.83; 11.140; 13.53
  and instruction 8.89f
  'into Christ' 9.16; 14.67
  and kiss of peace 14.280f
  Jewish 1.59f; 3.14, 255; 5.79;
    7.69; 8.84; 10.31f
  of John 1.47, 50; 3.13, 15,
    17f
  new birth of 14.192
  oneness of 10.142
  ordained 2.278
  in Paul 10.174; 9.15; 11.139f
  and perfection 11.65
  and resurrection 12.174
  robes of 16.121
  and sealing 17.23
  sermon of 14.160
  symbolism of 5.180; 6.141f;
    13.56
Barbarians 10.113; 11.155
Barley 3.323; 9.80, 150; 17.7
Barley-bread 3.159; 5.5, 202
Barriers 10.113f; 11.155f;

    12.64f
Baskets 2.127; 3.158, 184; 5.203
Basket, The 7.51; 12.85
Batanaea 3.53
Baths, public 1.144
Bear, symbolism of 17.88
Beast, The 17.47, 86–95, 138–
    142, 147, 184
  number of 17.100–102
  second 17.97f
Beatitudes, The 1.88–118; 4.5,
    76f
Beds, eastern 5.180
Beggars 7.32
Behemoth 1.216, 303; 17.77
Belief 3.227; 15.112
  and action 11.105
  certainty of 1.75, 352f; 8.181;
    9.130; 10.183; 11.41, 210;
    12.241; 13.128; 15.121–123
  and confession 8.139
  disturbed 3.123f
  and the Gospel 3.26
  impossibility of 3.317
  'in Christ' 5.44f, 135, 213;
    6.153
  Pauline 8.21
  Protestant 2.139
  purity of 12.153f
  restatement of 5.7
  unchangeability of 14.350
  uniformity of 12.241
  variety of 4.179; 14.73
Beloved Disciple, The 5.18–20;
    6.145
Benedictine Order, The 14.257
Benedictus, The 4.4
Benefactor, The 4.267
Benevolence 1.173; 10.164

11 Phil, Col, Thes   13 Heb   15 John, Jude   16 Rev, v.1
12 Tim, Tit, Phlm   14 Jas, Pet   17 Rev, v.2

Benjamin, tribe of **11**.58; **14**.31

Beroea **7**.119, 129; **8**.19; **11**.47, 73, 86, 181; **12**.22

Beryl **17**.159, 214, 215

Bethany **2**.238, 329, 331, 338; **3**.263f, 269, 324; **4**.142; **6**.80, 102, 108f

Bethany beyond Jordan **5**.6

Bethel **6**.53, 79

Bethesda **5**.177

Bethlehem **1**.23–25, 31, 37; **3**.65, 149; **4**.21; **5**.243, 252; **7**.68

Beth-peor **2**.159

Bethphage **2**.238; **3**.263, 324

Bethsaida **2**.11–13; **3**.27; **4**.117; **5**.6, 201

Bethsaida Julias **5**.201, 206, 225

Bethulia **13**.164

Bethzatha **5**.177

Betrothal, Jewish **1**.19; **4**.12

Bible

  availability of **4**.151

  criticism of **1**.4; **10**.64

  divisions of **3**.299; **9**.6, 223

  honesty of **7**.44

  importance of **10**.90

  inspiration of **4**.8

  order of books **2**.298

  power of **3**.13; **8**.178

  revelation and **6**.195

  study of **8**.195f

  understanding of **4**.70f

  unity of **9**.192f

  use of **5**.198; **12**.100

Binding and loosing **2**.145f, 182, 189

Birmingham **15**.162

Birth, Jewish **4**.17

Bishops **12**.3, 69–72; **14**.139;

  16.54, 104

Bithynia **7**.19, 121; **12**.99; **14**.137, 144f, 160f, 166; **16**.17

Bitterness **1**.110, 145, 174f, 202, 247, 392; **2**.32, 119, 247f, 288, 340; **3**.236, 243, 277; **4**.27, 116, 168, 283, 285; **6**.49; **9**.34, 226, 239, 267; **10**.90, 140, 157, 159; **11**.80; **12**.65, 128, 154, 162, 188; **13**.132; **14**.91f, 97, 173; **15**.32

Black Sea **17**.161

Blamelessness **10**.78f; **11**.43

Blasphemy **1**.324; **2**.315, 355, 357; **3**.175, 279, 321, 351; **5**.244; **6**.76; **7**.50, 61f; **12**.187; **15**.112; **17**.89, 94

Blessings **1**.370; **12**.24; **16**.180; **17**.28

Blindness **1**.349; **3**.35, 189

Blood

  and covenants **2**.342

  and Jerusalem Covenant **7**.116

  sanctity of **2**.112; **3**.332; **17**.10

  shedding of **13**.107f

  sprinkling of **14**.169f

  symbolism of **5**.224; **13**.131

  uncleanness of **1**.346

Blood-feuds **1**.164

Boasting **8**.38; **12**.185–187; **14**.114

  in Christ **11**.56; **16**.83

Body **1**.217; **3**.42, 105, 315; **8**.156; **9**.55–57, 85f; **10**.162f; **12**.119

  Egyptian doctrine of **1**.321

  and Gnostics **11**.98; **12**.7, 30; **15**.11

---

and Greeks **5**.64; **9**.55, 58, 140, 204
intestines **11**.18
spiritual **9**.141, 157–159, 204f
temple of Holy Spirit **8**.156f; **9**.33f, 56; **12**.96
as a text **14**.308
Boils, plague of **17**.125
Booths **2**.169
Boredom **12**.259; **15**.100
Bottomless Pit, The **17**.47
Bounty, The **3**.13
Bow, sign of **17**.4
Boy's Brigade **6**.185
Branding **16**.135; **17**.99
Bread **1**.23, 199; **2**.79
  bond of **9**.91
  breaking of **4**.295; **7**.149
  daily **1**.390
  of God **2**.127; **3**.185; **5**.215f; **16**.95
  of heaven **3**.179
  of Last Supper **4**.265
  of life **1**.215; **2**.124–128; **5**.10, 216, 218
  of the Presence **4**.70
  unleavened **2**.79; **3**.332
Britain **1**.113; **2**.87; **3**.177; **9**.121; **12**.222; **17**.140
Brotherhood, Christian **3**.249; **9**.13; **11**.103f
Bull, sign of **17**.214
Burden, definition of **1**.310; **2**.22; **4**.60, 156; **10**.52f
Burial, eastern **1**.345; **17**.197
  of Gentiles **3**.337
  Jewish **1**.313f; **2**.372; **3**.323f, 366; **4**.289; **6**.88
  mistaken **4**.111

Buskins **16** 115

Caesar
  household of **8**.212; **11**.87
  symbolic use **3**.284; **4**.247
  worship of **1**.114, 391; **6**.182f; **16**.15–20, 90f; **17**.63, 89, 93, 95, 98–100, 131f, 141, 184
Caeserea **2**.135, 358, 363; **4**.2; **7**.138
Caesarea Philippi **1**.65; **2**.133–135, 157; **3**.191f, 209, 251, 262, 324; **4**.31, 112, 263, 280; **7**.171; **14**.5
  capital city **6**.238, 243
  church of **7**.6
  fortress of **2**.143
  and Paul **7**.73, 76
  Roman H.Q. **7**.79, 167
Calvary **2**.160; **4**.3; **6**.251
Camel **2**.217, 294; **4**.229
Cana **1**.41; **5**.5f, 9, 91, 95–99, 174
Canaanites **1**.73; **2**.121; **13**.90
Cannibalism **1**.113; **4**.258; **14**.203; **16**.80
Canon, The **14**.5, 249
Capernaum **1**.71, 74, 133, 301, 307f, 326, 331, 345; **2**.11–13; **3**.29, 39, 41, 46, 49, 52f; **3**.176f; **4**.49, 86; **5**.106, 174, 201, 208
Cappadocia **14**.137, 144, 160, 166
Cappadocians **12**.242
Caria **16**.28
Carmel, Mount **1**.64; **3**.52, 176; **4**.48, 126
Carnelian **16**.152; **17**.214, 215
Carolina, North **3**.13

11 Phil, Col, Thes   **13** Heb   **15** John, Jude   **16** Rev, v.1
12 Tim, Tit, Phlm   **14** Jas, Pet   **17** Rev, v.2

Carousing **10**.49

Carthage **2**.364; **11**.50; **13**.192
    Council of **12**.234

Carthaginians **6**.250

Caspis **13**.160

Cassia **17**.161

Casting lots **7**.17

Castration **10**.44; **13**.193

Catholic Epistles **14**.137

Cayster, river **7**.140; **12**.184

Celibacy **2**.208; **14**.20; **15**.9;
    17.106

Cenchraea **7**.133, 138; **9**.2, 186

Censoriousness **8**.182f

Censuses **4**.20f

Centurions **1**.300f; **4**.84; **7**.79

Chalcedon **17**.213

Chalcedony **17**.213, 215

Chamber of the Silent **1**.188

Chance **1**.89, 207; **7**.14

Character **1**.242; **8**.74; **17**.114

Chariots **17**.162

Charity **1**.170; **3**.229, 277; **4**.109,
    209; **9**.118; **10**.139; **13**.199

Charm **7**.56; **9**.121; **10**.9

Chastity **1**.155; **2**.208; **3**.237f;
    4.211; **7**.116; **8**.90; **9**.43;
    10.46, 161f; **11**.97, 150f;
    12.39, 76; **17**.106

Cheerfulness **2**.124

Cherubim **8**.117; **13**.17, 96f;
    16.157f; **17**.171

Cherubs **16**.157

Childbirth **1**.320; **4**.24f

Child exposure **10**.176

Childlessness **4**.10, 283; **9**.61;
    10.41

Children **2**.174–178; **10**.175–
    178; **11**.161f

and angels **3**.35

'of the bridechamber' **1**.335;
    3.59; **4**.64

care of **1**.399f; **2**.81

'of God' **1**.109; **15**.73, 81f

and Greeks **8**.39; **10**.34;
    12.110

and Jews **10**.33f; **12**.199

and Romans **10**.34

Chiliasm **17**.184

China **17**.160

Chios **7**.150

Chislew, Month of **6**.69

Choice **1**.277; **8**.29

Chorazin **2**.11–13; **4**.134

Chorus, Greek **8**.202

Chosen People, The **1**.15, 60;
    2.264; **4**.25; **5**.79; **6**.63;
    7.4, 52f; **8**.119, 145; **10**.18;
    11.156, 192; **14**.166, 167, 169,
    198f, 291; **17**.84

Christianity **1**.50, 88f, 111–115,
    120, 167f, 172f, 286, 357, 391;
    2.66, 77, 79–81, 138, 230f;
    267; **3**.64, 99f, 145, 244f,
    262, 316; **4**.15f, 43, 58, 101,
    120, 170, 208, 297; **6**.288;
    8.139, 167; **9**.32, 121; **11**.13f,
    40; **12**.40, 100; **14**.59, 296,
    298

adventure of **1**.374, 396f;
    2.323; **3**.77; **4**.194f, 270

apologetic of **5**.132f, 173

basis of **2**.219

the Christian **1**.30, 291; **3**.155;
    4.183, 295; **7**.161f; **8**.87;
    9.13f, 148–154; **12**.160–163,
    190–194, 246–256; **14**.173,
    267, 296; **16**.22

| **1** Matt, v.1 | **3** Mark | **5** John, v.1 | **7** Acts | **9** Cor |
| **2** Matt, v.2 | **4** Luke | **6** John, v.2 | **8** Rom | **10** Gal, Eph |

and the Cross 1.95, 214, 287,
395; 2.107, 151f, 220; 4.121;
9.170, 200
and democracy 9.265; 10.45;
13.200
foolishness of 5.49; 9.16–20
growth of 3.125, 208f; 5.26;
8.213; 10.151; 14.36f
immortality of 12.168
Jewish 2.170; 5.10; 10.19;
14.22, 41; 15.6
name of 7.90
neutrality of 4.148
purifying influence 3.12f
revolutionary 7.128
and society 2.81, 83
task of 4.181f
universality of 12.23f, 55–57;
13.92f; 15.40; 16.178; 17.16
'The Way' 7.139
Christmas tree 1.35; 17.159
Christmonger 11.190
Christology 2.138; 4.120, 137;
5.224; 11.100
Chrysolite 17.214f
Chrysoprase 17.214
Church 1.6, 7, 43f; 2.89f; 6.273;
14.286; 16.104, 173; 17.170
assembly of God 12.88
attendance at 1.107, 121;
2.270
as body of Christ 2.183;
8.159; 9.95, 108, 112–116;
10.67, 92–94, 141; 11.120
as bride of Christ 5.143;
9.246; 14.102, 276; 15.131;
16.108; 17.76, 172–174, 208,
229
and buildings 9.167; 11.171f;

17.216
as a building 2.141; 8.192;
10.119
catholicity of 17.210f
a democracy 9.265; 13.200
divisions of 9.8, 13–16, 30, 34;
10.48; 11.182; 12.265;
14.225f; 15.200
flock of God 6.62f
function of 14.198f
growth of 3.110–112; 5.7;
7.9ff; 12.91; 14.145
house churches 11.73
household of God 12.88;
13.32
inclusivism of 1.266f, 288;
8.197–200; 9.34f, 100f;
16.154
importance of 4.181
indestructibility of 2.144
and Jesus 2.139–146; 11.120–
122; 17.85
leadership of 7.91; 8.162;
9.116, 166; 10.145–150;
12.69–86, 98, 99f; 12.101–
104, 117f; 13.194f; 15.194
membership of 2.155; 3.191;
4.131, 221; 12.118
nature of 2.142; 7.30f; 9.21;
14.195–197
organization of 9.133f;
11.129, 131; 12.3; 14.26,
139f
and Paul 8.159; 11.104
and Peter 2.139–146; 14.154
pillars of 14.10
services of 12.100; 16.26
as temple of God 9.33
unity of 2.311; 3.83; 6.65,

11 Phil, Col, Thes
12 Tim, Tit, Phlm
13 Heb
14 Jas, Pet
15 John, Jude
16 Rev, v.1
17 Rev, v.2

75, 190, 215, 217f; 7.92, 145, 148; 8.3, 196f, 198, 205; 9.9, 108, 113, 116, 157, 162; 10.114f, 116f, 119, 141–143, 149; 11.7, 30, 31, 33f, 71; 12.272; 13.144; 14.224–226; 16.61

universality of 6.288; 7.145; 9.35; 16.174

weakness of 1.269; 2.166

and women 9.96–100

younger churches 12.2

Church of the Nativity 1.24f

Chuthites 5.150

Cilicia 7.73, 119; 9.2

Cilicians 12.242

Cinnamon 17.161f

Circumcision 4.24; 5.241f; 7.69; 8.65f; 10.107; 11.135

and the Church 7.112–118

Ishmaelite 11.57

and Paul 7.120; 9.251; 10.16f, 43, 56; 11.55f, 138–140

and proselytes 3.14

spiritual 11.55

symbolism of 8.125; 11.55, 139

Citizenship 2.170f, 273f; 3.287; 4.248; 8.173f; 11.69; 12.258–260; 14.159

dual 9.206

of the kingdom 11.29f; 14.201

Roman 9.4; 11.20

state and church 2.132; 3.287; 8.170–174; 14.205f

Citrus wood 17.160

City of the gods 17.214

City of Palms 4.234

Class-distinctions 8.212; 10.19; 14.47, 64f

Cleansing 2.110–117; 3.164; 10.47; 14.107f

spiritual 4.150; 6.19; 8.120; 15.30f; 17.31f

symbol of 7.69; 14.170

Cleopatra's Needle 14.250

Clothing

aprons 7.143

cloaks 1.167; 2.367; 3.142; 12.219

fine linen 1.239; 4.213; 16.143f; 17.160

girdles 1.367; 2.367; 3.142; 4.285; 7.143

leprous 3.144

Jewish 2.367; 3.141f, 362; 4.285; 6.253

rending of 1.342; 3.134

robes 3.130, 299f; 4.167, 205, 285; 16.45

shawls 4.113

tassels 1.346f; 2.286f; 3.299; 4.113

'travelling-dress' 6.89

turbans 2.367; 3.142; 4.202, 285

veils 9.97f

Clouds 2.161

Cocks 2.346; 6.229

cock-crow, the 2.346f; 3.352; 6.230

Coffins 4.62

Cohort 7.79

Coins

Jewish 1.389; 2.273; 3.286, 302; 4.171f, 241; 5.109

Roman 17.99

| 1 Matt, v.1 | 3 Mark | 5 John, v.1 | 7 Acts | 9 Cor |
| 2 Matt, v.2 | 4 Luke | 6 John, v.2 | 8 Rom | 10 Gal, Eph |

Collection, The 7.51, 145, 147;
8.2f, 205, 220; 9.162–165,
228–232, 237, 262; 12.22,
232; 14.14; 15.148
collecting-bags 3.143
collecting-boxes 4.254
Colosse 11.91f, 128, 171;
12.184, 274; 16.28
heresy of 11.92f, 94–97; 12.27
Letter to 3.4; 10.61f; 11.91–
101
Comas 1.345
Comfort 3.121f; 4.228, 254;
9.129, 170f
Coming One, The 2.2; 3.266
Communism 4.81
Compassion 2.121; 4.140;
11.34; 14.227
Compromise 1.70; 4.44; 7.156;
13.73f; 15.145; 16.93, 102
Conceit 9.264f; 10.53; 12.126,
191; 13.122
Conclusions 5.192
Condemnation 1.48; 4.135, 152;
5.43, 46, 52, 67; 8.41, 51,
69, 116; 11.112; 14.176
Roman 3.358f
Confession 1.57, 142; 3.14f, 133;
8.139; 14.131; 15.33, 68
confessors 17.192f
Confidence 2.1, 3; 3.189;
11.87f; 15.114
Conformity 14.326
Congregationalism 9.162
Conscience 2.96, 154; 3.48;
4.115, 249; 6.192; 8.189f,
194; 9.222; 10.131; 11.142;
12.245f; 14.57
branding of 12.93

cleansing of 13.104
good 12.34
of others 9.250
petrifying of 10.153
rejection of 12.53
weak 9.73, 75
Conscientiousness 1.119
Consecration 2.202; 6.216
Constantinople 12.127
Contempt 1.139f; 5.193; 8.37,
49f, 181; 10.122
Contention 8.179
Contentment 1.183; 11.84f;
12.128–131, 132; 13.194;
15.198
Contraception 11.200
Contracts 8.92f; 14.244
Convention 8.185; 9.99
Conversion 3.191; 6.41, 131;
12.44f
Coptic Church 2.359
Coptic Gospels, The 5.96
Corinth 1.154; 7.119, 133f;
9.1–4, 6, 58; 12.38
bronze of 2.244; 17.161
church of 9.7, 8, 13–16, 42,
51–54
gulf of 9.1
industry of 9.125
Letters to 9.5–8, 178, 237
and Paul 7.133–136; 8.19;
9.4f; 11.47
synagogue of 9.16
women of 9.99
Corn 17.6f
Corn-ships 7.184
Cornwall 2.373; 3.177
Costus 17.162
Courage 1.79, 229, 380, 390;

2.344–346; 3.341; 4.230, 234;
6.88; 7.19, 39; 8.206; 9.166;
11.30, 50, 129; 13.158;
14.301f, 303; 17.206
Courtesy 2.260; 3.182; 9.121;
10.17; 11.6
Courtship 2.204
Covenant 2.342; 3.339; 4.266;
9.104, 189; 10.109; 13.3f, 80,
90f, 106f; 15.74; 17.96
ark of 13.96; 17.73, 121
Book of the 9.189
definition of 8.125
new 3.339f; 4.266; 8.125;
9.189–191; 13.80f, 90–94,
185, 202; 16.161
people of 11.57
ratification of 14.170
types of 7.116; 10.28; 13.90,
92–94; 16.161
Covenanters, The 1.213
Coverdale version 2.294
Covetousness 3.173f, 328; 8.176;
14.99, 259, 318, 333; 15.190f
Cowardice 2.258
Crab, sign of 17.215
Creation 1.22, 49, 52, 390;
2.200; 3.182, 240; 4.291;
5.30, 34, 183; 6.18; 9.157;
11.44; 12.30, 94; 13.35;
14.21f; 15.27, 56, 99, 140;
17.188
animal 14.88
culmination of 11.117
and demons 3.34
and Gnostics 11.97f; 12.27
by Jesus See Jesus and
creation
myths of 15.61; 17.77, 133,

198
new 2.309; 4.90; 11.121;
14.172, 342; 17.197–199
out of nothing 5.41; 13.130
reconciliation of 11.123f
song of 16.180f
Creed, The 6.35, 9.137; 14.232,
236, 243
basis of 8.139; 9.107; 12.135f,
153
centre of 16.16
in Early Church 10.141f;
11.39
Creeds 1.290, 339; 4.140; 8.116;
12.3f; 13.120
in Judaism 3.295; 17.119
singing of 12.90
Crenides 7.122
Cretans 12.237, 242f, 258
Crete 7.182; 9.21; 12.9, 71, 233,
234, 240f
Crises 8.74
Criticism 1.265; 9.181; 12.97f
Crowns 11.70, 193f; 12.211;
14.48f; 16.163
of glory 16.83
of life 14.48f
of righteousness 16.83
of victory 12.161
Crucifixion 1.395f; 2.363f;
3.360; 4.282f; 6.250f, 276;
13.197
common death 2.165; 4.121
cross-shapes 4.284
origin of 6.250
Crumbs 4.213f
Cummin 2.293
Cup, symbol of 3.255
Curiosity 15.41

| 1 Matt, v.1 | 3 Mark | 5 John, v.1 | 7 Acts | 9 Cor |
| 2 Matt, v.2 | 4 Luke | 6 John, v.2 | 8 Rom | 10 Gal, Eph |

Cuthaeans **5**.150

Cynics **5**.46, 67f; **8**.199; **12**.241;
    14.27, 315

Cyprus **1**.89; **2**.251; **7**.3, 99f;
    8.215f
  Church in **7**.88, 97
  and Greek language **13**.8

Cyrene **2**.366; **3**.361; **4**.282;
    7.88, 98; **8**.215f; **14**.39

Dagger-bearers **7**.16, 158; **8**.173

Dalmatia **12**.265

Damascus **1**.39, 73, 81, 331;
    3.52, 124, 177; **4**.48; **7**.107;
    9.255
  and Christians **7**.70
  and Jews **14**.39

Dan, tribe of **14**.31; **17**.25

Dark, darkness **5**.45, 47–49;
    11.112; **15**.26f
  end of **17**.198, 219, 228
  pits of **14**.321
  plague of **17**.125

Darnel **2**.72f

Day, Jewish concept of **1**.310;
    2.223, 374; **3**.37, 331; **4**.289;
    7.32
  religious observance of **8**.180,
    183f; **10**.36

Day of the Lord **1**.373f, 393;
    2.302–304, 308f; **3**.304, 318f;
    4.257f; **6**.184, 197; **7**.25;
    8.25, 108; **9**.12, 37; **11**.182,
    204f, 212; **12**.92, 182; **13**.12,
    57; **14**.115, 343f; **15**.39, 60;
    16.3, 42; **17**.16, 42, 69f
  of the Lord Jesus **9**.12; **15**.118
  The Day **9**.32f

Day of Questions, The **4**.243

Deaconesses **8**.207f; **12**.86f

Deacons **1**.377; **9**.163; **12**.3, 84–
    86; **14**.139; **16**.12

Dead, Place of **2**.143
  uncleanness of **2**.295

Dead Sea **1**.63; **2**.157; **3**.16,
    149; **4**.36, 43, 138; **15**.195

Deafness **3**.181

Death
  and Christians **8**.117, 187;
    16.27; **17**.193
  conquest of **9**.151; **13**.153f;
    16.10f; **17**.197
  consequence of sin **8**.80, 105;
    14.248f
  in East **3**.326; **5**.55; **13**.103
  fear of **9**.140, 160; **11**.203
  finality of **8**.92f; **13**.110f
  'in the Lord' **17**.113f
  and Jesus **2**.144, 371
  mystery of **13**.135–138
  and Paul **11**.27f; **12**.209
  preparation for **9**.110
  second **16**.84f
  as sleep **1**.344f; **4**.110; **6**.86
  spiritual **1**.365; **5**.192; **10**.95f;
    11.141; **14**.248; **16**.116
  'with Christ' **5**.126; **11**.182

Debts **1**.170; **2**.194f
  moral **1**.221; **4**.173
  of love **8**.176

Decalogue, The See Ten
    Commandments

Decapolis **1**.82, 363; **2**.125f
    128; **3**.124f, 180, 184; **5**.26

Deceit **2**.292; **8**.35; **11**.96;
    14.190

Decisions **1**.315; **3**.19; **13**.30

Dedication, feast of **3**.267; **5**.2,

106; **6.**69f

Defilement **3.**171–175

Degeneration, spiritual **12.**213

Deism **3.**315

Deliverance **8.**59; **9.**23; **10.**81f

Delphic oracles **14.**349; **16.**105,
  114

Democracy **2.**278; **3.**227; **4.**177;
  9.265; **10.**45; **11.**182; **13.**200;
  14.206

Demons **1.**289, 319–321, 366;
  2.35, 112; **3.**32, 34f, 71, 117–
  120, 225; **4.**50, 54, 107f,
  125f; **5.**178; **9.**72, 75, 91f;
  10.92, 99; **11.**96; **12.**90f, 92;
  15.89; **17.**47, 176
  demon-possession **1.**289, 308,
  320–322; **2.**35; **3.**34–36, 71f,
  115, 118–120; **4.**50; **9.**258

Dependence, spiritual **2.**176;
  9.198

Deposit, spiritual **12.**4, 138f, 151–
  153

Depression **9.**85

'Depths' **8.**118

Derbe **7.**97, 119; **11.**47

Desert **1.**46; **3.**34; **17.**143

Desire **1.**136, 148, 272; **4.**233;
  8.28f; **10.**100, 153; **11.**84,
  150f; **12.**37; 53, 129, 189,
  256; **13.**40; **14.**52f, 99–101,
  187, 200, 329f; **15.**57

Despair **2.**61–63, 70; **3.**97, 108,
  136; **3.**209, 217; **4.**100;
  5.55, 169; **10.**109; **11.**70,
  82f

Destroyer, The **17.**52

Devastation, The **1.**63; **3.**16;
  4.43

Devil, The **1.**106, 226; **3.**22f,
  330; **6.**26–29, 147; **9.**76,
  195f; **10.**157; **12.**73f; **14.**94,
  106, 272; **15.**77; **17.**58, 80–
  82, 84, 186, 191f, 193f, 197
  devils **1.**294; **2.**35, 317; **3.**32;
  5.2; **9.**72; **12.**189
  Prince of devils **1.**351; **2.**36;
  6.31

Dialogue—form **14.**28

Diamonds **17.**159

Diaspora **5.**246; **14.**21, 36–40,
  166

Difficulties **2.**167; **3.**276; **9.**170;
  12.182

Dignity **12.**253

Diligence **7.**45

Dill **2.**293

Dion **3.**124

Dionysia **14.**299

Discipleship **1.**123, 199, 312, 361;
  2.151–155, 177, 249; **3.**75,
  101; **5.**74, 163, 196; **6.**11f,
  20–22, 133, 211f; **10.**124f;
  12.195

Discipline **1.**175, 280, 292; **2.**87,
  173f; **3.**59, 232, 234; **11.**67,
  150; **9.**225; **10.**177f; **12.**161,
  193; **13.**175–179; **16.**145f
  of Church **2.**183f, 187f; **9.**44–
  46, 96, 136, 267; **10.**149;
  11.131; **12.**1, 116f

Discouragement **2.**311

Diseass **3.**23, 44

Disloyalty **1.**388; **4.**121; **6.**142

Disobedience **1.**386; **8.**38, 53;
  9.193; **10.**100; **13.**33, 46

Disorder **9.**265

Dispersion, The See Diaspora

Disputations 1.380; 11.43;
  12.139f, 180
Dissension 8.218; 10.48
Divorce
  and Christianity 2.200–205;
    3.237–240; 9.62
  Gentile law of 2.201
  and Greeks 1.155; 2.81;
    10.170
  and Jews 1.18–19, 150–152;
    2.195–199; 3.237–240;
    4.211f, 283; 10.168f; 11.198f;
    12.76f
  and Romans 1.156f; 8.32;
    10.170f; 11.199; 12.77f
Doceticism 5.13, 65; 15.7, 23,
  180
Doctors, ancient 3.129; 7.3
Doctrine 1.20; 3.227, 314; 11.82
  categories of 14.241f
  development of 12.153
  false 2.129; 15.199–202
  in Paul 8.10, 15
  and Scripture 1.387; 9.33;
    11.136
Dogmatism 12.32f
Dogs 2.122; 3.178; 11.53f, 62;
  17.227
'Dominions' 10.92
Doom Songs 17.149
Doors 4.145; 6.58f; 16.128f
Doubt 2.2; 3.116; 5.54f; 6.130;
  8.181; 9.130; 12.65f; 15.86
Doves 2.245f; 3.273f; 5.110
  symbol of 3.20; 5.83
Dragon, The 17.58, 62, 77, 80,
  84–86, 98
Drugs 10.47
Drunkenness 5.97; 8.178; 9.53;

  10.48f; 12.79, 237; 17.162
Dualism 12.62
Duty 1.41f, 188f, 243, 262, 317,
  326, 353, 379; 2.277f; 4.109,
  216, 220, 237; 5.52; 8.29,
  161, 164, 190, 195, 221; 9.24,
  94f, 163, 182, 232; 10.165;
  11.80; 12.106, 171; 13.179–
  184; 14.204–211
  of children 10.177; 12.187
  civic 4.64
  to the future 12.139
  Greeks 8.202
  and love 9.118f
  parental 1.366; 10.177f;
    12.106f
  and privilege 8.161
  Stoic 8.113
Dyeing 11.92; 16.102, 115

Eagle, symbolism of 5.1; 16.159;
  17.45f, 85
Earnest, the 9.177; 10.87f
Earthquakes 17.13, 134
East Africa, Church of 3.15
Ebal, Mount 5.157
Ecclesiasticism 2.166
Eden, Garden of 1.388; 6.38;
  8.95f; 9.246; 14.50; 15.164;
  16.69, 70; 17.17, 98, 220, 221
Edessa 1.81; 14.4, 152
Edification 12.172
Edom 4.31; 17.150
Edomites 1.12; 8.128; 11.58
Education 3.17; 17.57
  Jewish 14.37, 55
Eels 1.271
Effectiveness 9.261
Egnatian Way 7.127; 11.180

11 Phil, Col, Thes   13 Heb   15 John, Jude   16 Rev, v.1
12 Tim, Tit, Phlm   14 Jas, Pet   17 Rev, v.2

Egypt   **1**.32–36, 39, 73, 329, 331;
   3.52, 91; **4**.20f, 48; **14**.38;
   16.8; **17**.2, 117, 160
   deliverance from   **1**.390; **2**.160
   and Early Church   **3**.3, 209
   'the granary of Italy'   **7**.181
   symbolic use of   **17**.71
Egyptians   **1**.321; **2**.112; **17**.198
Eighteen, The   **1**.192
Elder, The   **15**.127
Elders
   Christian   **1**.377; **5**.17; **17**.19,
      91, 111, 152; **9**.110; **10**.148;
      12.3, 69–84, 115f, 158, 234–
      240; **14**.21, 26, 129f, 140,
      154, 262–268; **15**.127, 133,
      137; **16**.12
   Greek   **12**.70; **14**.263
   Jewish   **1**.145; **2**.54, 143, 147;
      2.276, 281, 287, 362; **3**.163–
      167, 279, 346, 349; **4**.133,
      221, 243; **9**.49; **12**.70; **14**.21,
      26, 262f; **14**.154; **16**.153
   Twenty-four, the   **14**.263;
      16.152–154, 163f, 174;
      17.170
Elect, the   **14**.160, 165f
Elect Lady, the   **15**.19, 129f
Election   **8**.120, 122, 127, 131;
   14.169
Elements   **16**.31
Emanations   **5**.12, 40f; **11**.97,
   114; **12**.6, 27f; **15**.164
Emancipation, spiritual   **15**.121;
   16.177
Emeralds   **16**.151f; **17**.159, 213,
   215
Emmaus   **4**.294
Emotions   **2**.60; **4**.150; **11**.84;

   14.75f
   seat of   **9**.218f
Emperor's Day, The   **16**.43
Encouragement   **8**.161; **13**.122
End, The   See Last Things
Endor   **4**.86
Endurance   **9**.123, 170, 212f;
   11.210; **12**.135, 169, 197;
   13.173; **14**.176–178; **16**.39f,
   62, 131f
Engannim   **5**.147
England   **2**.372
Enlightenment   **13**.56; **15**.119
Enmity   **10**.47
Enthusiasm   **1**.313
Envy   **2**.288; **3**.175; **8**.35, 179;
   9.120, 263f; **10**.48; **13**.132;
   14.190
Ephesians, *Letter to*   **10**.61–71;
   11.172, 174; **14**.139
   and *1 Peter*   **14**.152–154
   and *Revelation*   **16**.57–71
Ephesus   **1**.378; **7**.3, 146f; **9**.6;
   10.148; **11**.91; **12**.33, 71,
   92f, 170, 184f; **16**.28, 58–61;
   17.206
   and Andrew   **5**.21
   and Apollos   **8**.209
   Bishop of   **12**.275
   Capital of Asia   **12**.155
   'Ephesian Letters'   See amulets
   'Highway of the Martyrs'   **16**.58
   and John the Apostle   **2**.231;
      5.6f, 17, 20, 22, 27
   and John the Elder   **5**.23
   Market of Asia   **16**.58
   and Paul   **5**.50; **7**.119, 121,
      138, 140–144; **9**.4; **11**.47
   provenance of John's *Gospel*

| **1** Matt, v.1 | **3** Mark | **5** John, v.1 | **7** Acts | **9** Cor |
| **2** Matt, v.2 | **4** Luke | **6** John, v.2 | **8** Rom | **10** Gal, Eph |

and *Letters* **14.**161; **15.**18f, 123f, 137
and Roma **16.**17
and Timothy **12.**89, 143, 184
Ephraim **6.**106
Epicureans **3.**125; **7.**130, 132; **13.**42f; **16.**84
Epilepsy **1.**321; **4.**125; **9.**258; **10.**38
Epirus **12.**9, 265
Equality **12.**116
Escapism **2.**167; **13.**72f
Esdraelon, Plain of **1.**71; **4.**47; **17.**132
E.S.P. **1.**306
Essenes **1.**161, 359; **8.**182; **14.**127
Eternal life **2.**214, 216; **5.**43f, 127–129, 136f; **6.**207–209; **12.**228; **15.**113f
Ethics **1.**118, 123, 163, 272–277; **2.**172, 206, 310; **3.**29; **4.**79f; **6.**26; **9.**14, 64, 68; **11.**29f, **12.**40, 88f, 108; **14.**72, 201f; **15.**17f, 82, 88; **17.**107
  Greek **9.**37; **11.**84
  O.T. **1.**165
  of reciprocal obligation **1.**274; **11.**160f; **14.**222f
Ethiopia **7.**69
  church of **14.**64
  eunuch of **7.**19, 63, 68f
Eunuchs **2.**207
Euphrates **1.**113; **5.**178; **17.**52f, 128, 134
  valley of **12.**184
Europe **7.**5, 19, 119
Evangelicals **11.**23f
Evangelism **2.**173; **3.**191; **5.**173;

9.64, 84; **11.**15, 24; **12.**204, 229; **16.**142
Evangelists **10.**147
Evasion **2.**291–293; **13.**73
Evil **1.**70, 245f; **2.**118–120; **3.**174; **4.**150; **8.**38, 98; **13.**83; **14.**50, 86f, 189f
  and Belial **17.**59
  definition of **8.**34
  fascination of **14.**297; **17.**147
  influence of **6.**37f
  Man of **14.**328–330
  origin of **1.**226; **6.**216
  power of **1.**225, 351, 366; **11.**212f; **15.**89
  root of **12.**131–133
Evil One, The **1.**225; **3.**174, 330; **6.**216; **9.**196; **15.**51, 55, 122; **17.**82
Evolution **4.**137f, 175
Example **1.**124
Excellence **11.**80f; **14.**301
Exclusivism, Jewish **1.**266; **9.**48
Excommunication
  Christian **9.**44–46, 48; **15.**118
  Jewish **3.**165; **6.**45, 47; **9.**61; **12.**53
Exhortation **8.**161
Exile **1.**13, 73; **2.**136
'Exiles of Eternity' **14.**167f
Exorcism **1.**289; **2.**37–39, 166; **3.**35, 37, 78, 225; **4.**50f, 129, 147; **7.**144
  gift of **9.**110f
  and prayer **3.**219
Exorcists, Order of **3.**35
Expediency **2.**258
Experience **5.**173; **12.**32
Eyes **1.**351; **3.**231

generous **1.**245–248
evil **6.**42; **10.**24
Eye-salve **16.**138f

Factiousness **9.**264
Failure **3.**218f
Fair Havens **7.**182f
Faith **1.**69, 303, 340, 342; **2.**75,
　120–123, 167f; **3.**140, 216–
　218, 261f; **4.**112; **9.**143, 157;
　10.26, 183, 185; **11.**171, 186;
　12.3, 52, 134, 154, 180;
　13.53, 147; **14.**301; **17.**34,
　210
　aristocracy of **1.**304
　defence of **15.**177–179
　definition of **9.**78; **13.**128–130
　gift of **9.**109
　and love **9.**118
　and miracles **1.**350
　in Paul **8.**21f, 61–64, 140f;
　　10.23, 43; **14.**349
　and prayer **3.**276f; **6.**180
　quaternion of **14.**287
　and thought **12.**33
　vicarious **1.**326; **2.**166; **4.**63
　victory of **15.**105
　and works **1.**290; **14.**22, 71–
　　74, 76–79
Faith, The **8.**21; **9.**25f; **10.**141f;
　11.5; **12.**157f, 162; **13.**49, 53–
　55; **14.**182f
Falsehood **1.**286–290; **10.**155;
　12.194f
Family **1.**393; **3.**289f; **4.**145f,
　212; **8.**39; **12.**241
Famine **17.**6–8
Fasting **1.**44, 179, 185, 232–238
　Jewish **1.**233–236, 335; **3.**58f;

　4.66, 223; **13.**98
　pre-baptismal **13.**54
Fatalism **11.**96, 137
Fate **4.**250; **6.**212; **7.**49; **16.**167
'Father' **2.**287, 361; **8.**126
Fatherhood **10.**129f
Favouritism **14.**63
Fear **1.**386, 388; **2.**60; **5.**45;
　6.130; **8.**119; **9.**207; **11.**42f;
　12.127; **13.**38, 121; **17.**206
Fearlessness **4.**160f
Feasts **1.**111; **3.**300, 322–324;
　4.192f, 267; **5.**177, 203; **9.**100
Feet-washing **6.**137
Fellowship **1.**384; **2.**53, 142,
　146, 174, 189, 221; **3.**73,
　316; **4.**296; **7.**30, 111, 149;
　8.161, 195–198; **9.**10, 34, 99f;
　10.133; **11.**14, 64, 157;
　12.118, 278; **14.**195f, 208,
　281; **15.**17f, 21, 30
　apostolic **9.**145, 163
　with Christ **8.**81f, 93f, 105;
　　15.35
　with God **5.**129; **13.**1, 106;
　　15.29, 39; **17.**202–204
　with unbelievers **9.**221–223
Fight, Christian **12.**210–212
Fig trees **2.**251f; **4.**174f; **9.**80
　symbolism of **2.**251; **5.**93
Fig-mulberry tree **4.**234
Fire **1.**200f; **3.**234
　symbolism of **4.**169; **17.**117
Firkin **5.**98
Firmament **16.**155; **17.**14
Firstborn **4.**24; **8.**84; **11.**119;
　13.187
　slaying of **17.**125
First-fruits **2.**371; **4.**155; **9.**149–

151; **17**.108
'of the seven kinds' **9**.80
Fish **3**.27; **5**.202
Fishermen **1**.78f, 332; **3**.27
Fishes, sign of **17**.215
Fishing **1**.77f; **2**.88f; **3**.27; **6**.281
Five Rolls, The **1**.127
Flaccus **14**.38
Flattery **11**.189
Flavia **16**.126, 135
Flesh **8**.93, 101–103; **9**.29f, 239f; **10**.100; **14**.200; **15**.57
Flood, The **2**.73; **14**.339f
Flowers **1**.257
Flute players **1**.344; **3**.134
Folly **3**.175
Food **2**.27; **3**.158, 325
    fat **2**.113
    heavenly **16**.95
    and idolatry **9**.71–76, 87–94
    meals **6**.145; **8**.178, 202; **9**.53; **12**.209; **16**.147
    pork **1**.379
Food laws **2**.113, 118; **7**.81; **8**.137, 149, 179; **10**.20; **11**.144, 146; **12**.5, 244; **13**.196; **17**.95
Fools **1**.140
Forbearance **8**.42; **9**.75, 158, **14**.124
Foreigners **10**.118
Forgiveness **1**.52, 59, 95, 102, 104, 199, 219–244; **2**.173f; **3**.51; **4**.19, 95, 226, 285f; **5**.71; **6**.19; **7**.29; **8**.58f, 163; **10**.82; **11**.112, 115, 158; **12**.263; **13**.93, 105–108, 184; **14**.74, 134, 228; **15**.53, 119

and confession **1**.143
God's will **5**.135
and health **1**.327f; **4**.62
and humiliation **3**.15
Jewish **1**.187; **2**.193; **3**.49
and others **1**.222f; **2**.193–195; **4**.216; **12**.65
and repentance **2**.44f; **3**.81; **4**.298
Formalism **1**.194; **12**.65
Fornication **3**.173; **7**.116; **9**.47f, 51f, 56, 89, 265; **10**.46; **11**.150f; **12**.38; **16**.107–109; **17**.111
Fortitude **3**.341; **8**.73, 166, 196; **9**.124; **11**.109; **12**.248; **13**.127
Forty days **3**.21f
Forty, The **9**.49
Four,
    horses **17**.1–9
    living creatures **16**.157–161
Fox, symbolism of **4**.186
Frankincense **1**.32, 391; **2**.366; **17**.161f
Freedom **1**.65, 97; **2**.27, 263; **3**.287, 335; **5**.67; **6**.21–24; **8**.180, 190–194; **9**.14, 55–57, 73, 78, 93–95, 215; **10**.45, 46; **11**.96, 112, 146, 189; **12**.9, 87; **14**.207, 349
Free-will **1**.14; **2**.333; **4**.91, 295; **6**.73, 212; **7**.105; **8**.29f, 121, 143; **9**.193; **11**.216; **15**.99
    in Judaism **4**.250; **7**.49
Friendship **1**.227, 302; **2**.53; **6**.178; **8**.168; **11**.193
    See Guest Friendships

'Friends of the Bridegroom'
5.143; 9.246
Fruits, spiritual 1.283–285;
3.271; 6.174; 10.164; 11.107
Fundamentalism 11.136
Funerals, Jewish 4.86f; 6.88f
Futility 14.187

Gabbatha 5.6; 6.245
Gad, tribe of 14.31
Gadara 1.319; 3.124f
Galatae 16.88
Galatia 4.31; 7.5, 138; 10.44;
12.184; 14.137, 144f, 160, 166
Galatians, *Letter to* 10.3–6
Galbanum 17.161
Galilee 1.39, 71–74, 80, 363f,
395; 2.12, 95, 98f, 127, 194,
343; 3.27, 37, 52, 53, 160,
176, 210; 4.3, 31, 45, 129;
7.5, 70; 8.173
revolts in 2.180; 3.229; 4.45,
172f, 278
Sea of 1.72, 76f, 308, 316f;
2.78, 125, 180; 3.115, 118,
180, 184, 187; 4.56f, 105
Games
gladiatorial 3.204
Isthmian 7.134; 9.2, 20, 85;
11.45
Marathon, the 12.210
Olympian 7.134; 9.2, 85;
11.45; 12.211; 16.83
Pan-Ionian 7.140; 11.45
Roman 2.77
of Smyrna 16.83
Torch-races 8.202
Gate, Eastern 2.142f
Gaul 2.97; 3.153; 14.144;

16.89; 17.92
Gaulonites 3.53
Gaza 3.52; 7.68
Ge 3.175
Gehenna 1.47, 139, 140f, 304,
388; 2.182f; 3.231f; 6.90;
12.67; 17.12, 47
Gehinnom 2.206; 5.162
Genealogies 1.12; 5.7; 12.6,
26, 264
General Epistles, The 14.137
Generosity 1.245–248; 8.161;
12.23, 278f
Geneva Version 1.245
Gennesaret 3.115; 4.56
Gentiles 1.6, 17, 73, 82, 363;
2.34, 114, 121f, 126f, 131,
187, 189, 224, 243f, 266, 270;
3.177; 4.6
conversion of 1.301–304; 2.71,
145; 3.283; 6.133, 283;
7.19, 88, 112–118; 8.53, 121–
123, 147–150; 10.126; 12.23f;
14.291f; 15.169; 17.216–218
and Jews 1.370; 2.80, 290;
3.178; 4.48, 140; 5.79;
10.107–110; 15.45; 16.7f
and Luke's Gospel 4.3
reception into Church 7.4,
62f; 14.10
uncleanness of 2.110, 295;
3.13f, 69, 143, 166; 6.235
Gentle, gentleness 1.98; 9.238;
10.51, 137; 11.19, 75, 158;
12.83, 135, 181, 259; 14.58,
231
Gerasa 1.320; 3.124; 4.107
Gerasenes 3.184
Gergesa 1.320

Gergesenes 1.319

Gerizim 2.359; 5.116, 157
  temple of 5.150

Germany 1.113; 14.221

Giants, The 3.175

Gibeonites 13.90

Gifts (talents) 1.66f; 2.67, 91;
    3.219; 4.97; 8.91, 159f;
    9.12, 116, 127; 10.81–83;
    11.127; 12.60–62, 94f;
    14.255f; 17.219
  Spiritual 9.95, 108–112, 117,
    133f, 136; 10.143–145; 14.45;
    15.90

Gifts, giving 1.169–172, 187–
    191, 357, 366; 3.302f; 4.178,
    191, 255; 5.161; 9.164,
    228–230, 232f, 234–237, 261f;
    14.44f; 15.151

Gihon 6.43

Glass 16.156

Glastonbury Thorn 2.372, 289f

Glory 5.68–70; 15.166
  crown of 16.83
  'to give glory to' 6.48

Gluttony 17.157

Gnat 2.294

Gnosticism 5.12f, 18, 40f;
    6.257f; 10.163; 11.68f, 97–
    99, 113–120, 130, 134f, 136,
    144–146; 12.6–8, 27–31, 119,
    192f, 244; 13.197; 14.284;
    15.5–12, 66, 76f, 78f, 93, 108,
    163, 171, 180; 17.106
  dualism of 12.62
  and matter 5.12, 40; 6.259;
    11.97, 114, 144; 12.6, 27
  scriptures of 12.199
  and sin 15.164

and spirit 11.97, 114; 12.30

Goat, sign of 17.215

God
  access to 10.117, 127; 13.1f,
    102
  almighty, the 16.38, 162;
    17.173
  alpha & omega 17.204
  arms of 17.85
  army of 13.17
  assembly of 12.88f
  authority of 6.6
  the beginning 17.204, 226
  the Blessed One 14.90
  breath of 7.20
  calling of 10.77; 15.177
  care of 1.217, 389f; 2.99, 173;
    4.161; 6.161
  children of 5.60–63
  city of 17.207–216
  comfort of 2.224; 11.83
  compassion of 2.127, 225;
    6.98
  consuming fire 14.188f;
    17.117
  council of 16.153
  creator 1.97; 7.132; 8.27;
    11.158; 12.94; 16.141, 164;
    17.110
  decree of 17.97
  the end 17.204f
  existence of 1.206–208
  eternity of 14.38, 163
  family of 3.112; 8.107, 124;
    10.117f; 13.17; 15.78, 102
  fatherhood of 1.200, 202–204;
    2.176, 349f; 3.249, 344; 4.74,
    143, 222, 226; 5.51, 73, 138;
    6.27, 64f; 8.107, 113f, 132f,

164; **10.**35, 128–131, 142; **11.**162; **12.**261; **13.**42; **15.**73f

fear of **6.**212

forbearance of **8.**41f

foreknowledge of **14.**169

forgiveness of **3.**51f; **4.**205; **10.**54

foundation of **12.**176

friend of **6.**178

fullness of **10.**65; **11.**118f, 137

generosity of **1.**247; **2.**225; **3.**282; **10.**25, 76, 77

glory of **2.**161, 191, 196; **3.**238; **5.**9, 68–70; **6.**39, 100; **7.**164; **8.**125; **11.**41; **17.**35f, 72f, 122f, 169, 202f

grace of **1.**198, 287, 300; **2.**31, 268; **5.**62; **6.**39; **7.**114; **8.**5, 13, 27, 139; **9.**160, 174, 211; **10.**30, 94f, 127, 163; **11.**17, 19, 53, 63; **12.**24; **13.**93, 182; **14.**177; **15.**96, 180, 206

greatness of **17.**120

hand of **14.**271

holiness of **1.**62, 203, 208, 388; **2.**6; **3.**315; **4.**225; **5.**112, 214; **8.**25; **9.**89, 132, 174; **10.**130; **13.**42; **15.**26, 33, 127; **16.**152, 156, 162; **17.**123

of hope **11.**82

house of **16.**153

household of **12.**88; **13.**119

image of **11.**116–118

infinite **13.**51

initiative of **5.**86; **11.**214

of Israel **2.**126

jealousy of **14.**104

joy of **4.**202

judge, the **1.**137, 146; **2.**75, 263, 309, 324–326; **3.**250; **4.**220, 246; **5.**187; **8.**33; **9.**190, 193; **11.**149, 197; **12.**121, 179; **13.**187; **14.**112, 115; **15.**176, 185; **17.**2, 16, 44, 57, 169, 194

justice of **1.**55, 208; **2.**6; **3.**282, 316; **8.**52, 138; **13.**93

kindness of **4.**201; **8.**41f

kingship of **1.**202, 388; **2.**100, 169; **8.**73, 222; **10.**108; **12.**17; **14.**166; **15.**24; **17.**119

knowledge of **6.**208f; **8.**114; **10.**91; **14.**294f; **15.**17, 40–43, 54

life-giver **1.**256; **2.**144; **5.**44, 64; **9.**140; **15.**113

the light **6.**13; **15.**25f; **16.**151

'the living God' **5.**43; **17.**21f

Lord of hosts **16.**39

Lord Sabaoth **16.**39

love of **1.**208, 214; **2.**6, 185f, 278, 367; **3.**277, 316; **4.**6, 114, 203, 205, 272, 288; **5.**73, 137, 214; **6.**55, 85, 201; **8.**75–77, 112, 115–119, 153–155; **9.**12, 147, 160, 190, 193; **10.**9, 10, 82, 119, 124, 130, 163; **11.**51, 78, 122f, 125, 187, 216; **12.**29, 36, 148, 230, 261; **13.**13, 58f, 93, 117, 119, 146; **14.**216, 253; **15.**24f, 97, 203, 207; **17.**97, 142, 169

is love **9.**34; **10.**104; **15.**17, 98

of love **11.**83

loyalty of **9**.199

majesty of **13**.186; **16**.151; **17**.28

mercy of **1**.14, 54f, 56, 309; **4**.90; **6**.24, 274; **7**.35; **8**.41f, 57, 85, 107, 138, 151–153; **9**.33, 89, 193; **10**.22, 43; **11**.56, 142; **12**.24f; **13**.43; **14**.240, 307; **16**.152, 176

names of **1**.205f; **5**.30, 60f; **6**.210–211; **16**.97, 135; **17**.138, 169, 180

nature of **5**.161; **13**.27; **15**.13, 25

omnipotence of **1**.390; **16**.162

omniscience of **16**.172

oracles of **8**.52; **13**.188

patience of **2**.263, 299; **3**.282; **4**.246; **8**.41f; **10**.51, 139; **11**.83; **14**.348

of patriarchs **3**.290

of peace **8**.219; **11**.82f, **13**.201

peace of **4**.182; **7**.72, 206; **11**.77f, 159; **13**.35

people of **5**.59; **8**.133; **12**.257; **14**.197, 267f

perfection of **10**.28, 104, 136

power of **1**.49, 69, 204; **4**.44, 182, 233; **5**.37, 180; **6**.39; **7**.42; **8**.199; **9**.200; **10**.91f; **11**.78; **16**.179; **17**.54, 128, 169

praise of **4**.4

presence of **1**.208; **3**.210; **5**.69f; **9**.132f; **10**.142; **13**.18, 66, 78, 119; **16**.155; **17**.215f

promises of **8**.68; **9**.176f; **13**.154; **17**.29, 205f

purposes of **1**.14, 16–17; **2**.70, 351; **3**.11; **5**.190, 231; **6**.73, 132, 211f; **7**.14, 23, 26f, 104; **8**.12, 112f, 114, 120f, 127, 129f, 132f, 152; **10**.13, 31; 73f, 77, 79, 86, 126; **11**.66, 191, 213; **12**.148, 229–231; **14**.124, 185, 194; **15**.177; **16**.167; **17**.13, 56, 109, 123, 147–149

reason of **5**.30f

rest of **13**.35f

the rock **2**.140

saviour **12**.18f, 29, 230; **15**.207; **17**.169

seed of **15**.78f

the seeker **16**.147

self-sufficiency of **3**.226; **9**.188; **11**.85

servant of **3**.281; **6**.177f; **11**.10

the shepherd **6**.53f; **14**.215f; **17**.37f

sorrow of **4**.91

sovereignty of **8**.129–131; **9**.144; **11**.213

spirit **5**.161

splendour of **15**.26

suffering of **9**.18

sympathy of **13**.42f

terrors of **17**.126–128

throne of **1**.52; **16**.150f

titles of **2**.277; **9**.188; **11**.82

transcendence of **5**.29; **13**.16; **16**.24, 175; **17**.175

treasure of **5**.59

triumph of **11**.213; **12**.183; **15**.59; **17**.147, 194

trust of **12**.153

trustworthiness of **12**.170

11 Phil, Col, Thes
12 Tim, Tit, Phlm
13 Heb
14 Jas, Pet
15 John, Jude
16 Rev, v.1
17 Rev, v.2

true **16**.127
unchangeableness of **14**.54; **16**.30
unity of **8**.60; **10**.142f; **12**.62; **15**.165; **17**.195
vengeance of **17**.165
vision of **1**.105, 184f; **9**.193 256; **14**.179; **15**.75; **17**.222
voice of **3**.20; **6**.126; **13**.188; **16**.44, 50; **17**.104, 126
'seven voices of' **17**.55
will of **1**.211–214; **2**.70, 87, 348, 369; **4**.271f; **5**.165f; **6**.104, 180; **8**.28; **10**.75, 76, 83f; **11**.78, 85, 108, 139; **12**.164; **13**.74; **14**.36, 69, 252; **15**.115
wisdom of **1**.213; **5**.33, 214; **11**.78; **13**.141; **16**.179; **17**.28
work of **5**.9, 183; **11**.41
wrath of **1**.46; **2**.251; **3**.48; **4**.49, 89, 186; **8**.21, 23–27, 41, 69, 153; **9**.193; **10**.101; **11**.60, 152; **16**.152, 157; **17**.3, 53, 111, 117, 122, 123–128, 134, 182f
God-fearers **2**.290; **7**.69, 79, 106f; **16**.79f
God-haters **8**.36f
Godlessness **12**.189–191
Godliness **11**.168; **12**.61, 97, 134
Gog **17**.133
Gold **1**.32
street of **16**.74
Golden Age **1**.373; **3**.24; **4**.257; **5**.185; **6**.59, 122; **9**.18; **17**.1, 221
Golden calf **7**.60

Golden Rule **1**.273, 275f; **4**.77–80
Golgotha **2**.366; **3**.366; **4**.3; **5**.6; **6**.251
Goodness **1**.21, 100–102, 124–126, 180, 181, 399; **2**.43f, 118–120, 297; **3**.25, 169, 213, 243, 245; **4**.160; **6**.62; **8**.15, 29, 42, 65, 164; **10**.9, 51; **11**.19, 157; **12**.35f, 179, 186, 260f; **13**.83, 142; **14**.229; **15**.202f
gospel of **2**.377
haunting **3**.152f; **4**.269; **8**.99, 146; **12**.44
inadequacy of **1**.137; **3**.107; **4**.184, 208
and rabbis **4**.227
triumph of **9**.147
Good Samaritan **4**.5, 138–140; **12**.201
Goodwill **1**.173
Gospel, The **2**.6; **3**.9, 24–26; **5**.137; **7**.23f; **8**.10, 13f, 18ff, 22; **10**.3f, 10; **11**.17, 20, 41, 107, 190; **12**.143, 145–150, 164f; **15**.24f
commands of **16**.120
everlasting **17**.109
and Law **1**.131–133
social gospel **3**.42; **4**.34; **14**.130
truth of **3**.25
universality of **5**.151; **11**.116
word of **15**.24f
Gospels, the
early forms of **1**.1–4; **3**.5; **4**.2f; **12**.219
importance of **12**.200

| **1** Matt, v.1 | **3** Mark | **5** John, v.1 | **7** Acts | **9** Cor |
| **2** Matt, v.2 | **4** Luke | **6** John, v.2 | **8** Rom | **10** Gal, Eph |

symbolism of **16**.160f
synoptic **1**.1–4; **2**.299; **3**.1f;
  5.3, 10
Gossip **1**.141; **12**.86f; **14**.111,
  190f
Goths **3**.204
Grace **2**.214; **4**.137; **5**.66, 71f;
  7.56f; **8**.67f, 73; **8**.82f;
  9.121, 259; **10**.9, 21, 36, 57,
  75f, 91, 104f, 163, 185; **11**.12,
  103, 107, 175; **12**.23, 95, 223,
  266; **14**.105, 294; **16**.29;
  17.232
  free grace **8**.88, 180; **9**.39;
    10.10
  gospel of **12**.147
  means of **17**.34
  word of **15**.24
Grace, mealtime **1**.192; **2**.100,
  270; **3**.338; **4**.118, 218
Gratitude **2**.100; **4**.191, 217;
  5.206; **11**.132; **13**.198;
  17.169
Great Harlot, The **17**.143–145
Great-heartedness **9**.40
Greatness **1**.278, 398f; **2**.230,
  232f; **3**.222, 254–257; **4**.127f;
  6.139
Great Road to the East **4**.48
Great Way of the Sea **4**.48
Greece **3**.209; **5**.26; **7**.133, 147;
  16.36
Greed **9**.47f; **12**.237
Greeks **1**.17, 172; **2**.122, 290;
  3.194; **5**.7f; **6**.119f, 252;
  7.11, 52; **8**.15, 17f, 19;
  10.86; **11**.45, 155; **12**.96,
  140; **16**.3
  language **1**.87, 101, 173, 272;

  3.8; **4**.7; **5**.27, 39; **6**.271;
  8.22; **10**.39; **11**.35; **12**.9,
  230f; **14**.28; **15**.34, 50f, 171;
  16.30, 34
  tragedy of **10**.54
Greetings, eastern **1**.369f
Grief **1**.93
Grumbling **9**.89; **15**.197f
Guest Friendships **12**.82; **13**.191;
  15.149
Guidance **1**.213; **7**.19; **9**.28;
  15.26
Guile **3**.174
Guilt **10**.102

Habit **1**.237; **10**.98; **11**.42;
  13.61
Hades **2**.142–144; **6**.35; **14**.236f,
  321; **16**.70, 181; **17**.197
Hallel, the **2**.342; **5**.249; **17**.169
  The Great **2**.342; **3**.338
Hallelujah Chorus **6**.195
Halley's Comet **1**.26
Halo **16**.84
Hammurabi, code of **1**.163
Hand-washing **1**.126; **2**.114,
  362; **3**.164, 337f; **4**.155;
  5.98f; **14**.107
Hanukah, feast of **3**.267; **17**.69
Happiness **1**.89; **4**.103; **10**.166;
  11.72; **12**.129f
Hardening, spiritual **4**.153;
  8.121, 132f, 145f, 152;
  10.152–154
Harlotry, spiritual **17**.142
Harps **16**.174
Harvests **2**.222f; **3**.323; **9**.150
  spiritual **1**.47f, 356f; **2**.62, 71;
  3.94, 108; **4**.100, 132f; **5**.166–

169; **17**.114–116
Thanksgiving **5**.248; **7**.21
Hate, chapel of **10**.89f
Hatred **8**.35; **12**.188; **15**.32, 48f
Hauron, Mount **3**.115
Head of Days **16**.167
Healing **1**.325, 345; **4**.115f; **6**.164; **9**.109f; **14**.129f
  Jewish **1**.129; **2**.30; **3**.67; **4**.60, 177; **6**.45
Health **1**.236; **2**.31; **11**.24
Heart **1**.242; **2**.50f; **3**.35, 231; **4**.153; **5**.250
  new **5**.131
Heaven **1**.203; **2**.277; **3**.291; **4**.224, 251, 299; **6**.152–156; **7**.13; **9**.177; **11**.215; **13**.186; **16**.71, 150, 154–156; **17**.180
  court of **16**.149
  Jewish **1**.225f; **2**.179; **3**.20
  in N.T. **13**.41
  primaeval war of **17**.80
  seventh **6**.38
Heavens, the **9**.256; **17**.15
Hebrew **9**.252
  language **1**.8–9; **5**.27; **11**.59
  parallelism **1**.211, 267; **3**.232; **4**.54; **5**.128; **7**.12
Hebrews, *Letter to* **13**.1–9, 59, 63
Hebron **1**.68; **6**.53; **7**.68
Heifer, red **2**.239; **13**.103
'Heights' **8**.118
Helios **2**.369
Hell **1**.52, 140f; **3**.231f, 315; **6**.35, 91; **9**.137; **10**.167; **14**.236, 321
  everlasting **2**.182

Hellenists **3**.267; **5**.7; **7**.76; **14**.40
Helplessness **1**.91
Herbs **2**.293, 340; **3**.333, 338; **4**.147
Heresy **3**.314f; **5**.11; **9**.120; **11**.123; **10**.48; **12**.4f, 26, 31, 92; **13**.190; **14**.316; **15**.92–94; **16**.66–68, 117; **17**.62
Heretics **12**.3, 31f, 178, 195, 265, 310; **15**.63, 204
Hermetic mysteries **5**.126, 222
Hermits **1**.149
Hermon, Mount **1**.77; **2**.157; **3**.115, 210; **7**.71
Herodians **2**.273; **3**.69, 229, 285
Heroism **1**.379f
Hierapolis **5**.23; **11**.91f, 128, 171; **12**.274; **14**.162; **16**.28, 139, 142
High priesthood **1**.29; **2**.243, 247, 327, 371; **4**.32; **7**.39; **13**.84f, 97–103, 116
  clothing of **2**.168; **4**.213; **6**.254; **13**.98f; **17**.121, 211, 214
  pronouncements of **6**.105
  and Sanhedrin **2**.353; **4**.276
Hinnom, valley of **2**.182f; **3**.231
Hippos **3**.124
History **1**.16, 260; **4**.7f; **8**.153; **9**.88; **14**.340f; **15**.144
  facts of **4**.297; **9**.130
  and Jesus **4**.137f; **8**.222; **12**.230; **15**.93
  purpose in **2**.312f; **3**.11, 322; **4**.261; **6**.155f; **7**.23f, 104, 132; **8**.222; **10**.83–85, 107f; **16**.24; **17**.13, 56, 143

1 Matt, v.1	**3** Mark	**5** John, v.1	**7** Acts	**9** Cor
2 Matt, v.2	**4** Luke	**6** John, v.2	**8** Rom	**10** Gal, Eph

Hobbies 13.73
Holiness 2.270; 4.44; 8.89;
    9.10; 10.154; 11.124; 12.146;
    13.181f; 14.188, 189f, 199
    beauty of 17.222
    spirit of 9.216
    way of 6.157
Holy 8.94; 10.77f; 11.10;
    12.65; 15.176f
Holy City, The 2.225; 4.180
Holy Grail, The 2.372; 4.290
Holy Land, The 5.59
Holy Spirit, The 1.20–23, 48–50,
    201; 2.39, 41–44, 83, 156;
    3.6, 17, 140; 4.8, 13, 26, 68,
    82, 145, 286; 5.154, 227;
    7.5, 66, 141f; 8.101–104, 110;
    9.106; 10.23, 141; 13.55f;
    14.141, 313; 15.15, 89, 101,
    108; 16.43f
    Comforter 1.200; 5.5; 6.166f;
        7.10
    coming of 5.82–85; 7.10, 12,
        18f; 9.205; 14.175, 250;
        15.70f
    and Docetics 5.13
    earnest of 9.177
    eternal 13.105
    filling of 10.166
    fruit of 10.49–52
    gifts of 6.284; 16.31f, 116
    grieving of 10.158; 13.125
    and Jesus 3.20f, 79f; 5.5, 52,
        53, 250; 6.273f; 7.29, 42;
        9.17, 157; 10.145; 11.25;
        12.90; 15.108f
    Jewish doctrine of 1.48f;
        4.161; 5.83f; 6.30; 13.166
    liberty of 9.194

    personal 5.252
    power of 12.262f
    and prayer 8.111; 15.203
    revealer 9.27f
    and Scripture 5.22f, 24, 185;
        14.180, 313f
    sealing of 10.87; 17.23
    sevenfold 16.31f, 116, 155
    sin against 2.41–45; 3.80f;
        4.161; 16.12
    symbolism of 16.160
    teacher 6.170
    temple of 8.156f; 9.33f, 56;
        12.96
    of Truth 4.161; 5.24, 53, 67;
        6.18, 194–196
    and unity 11.33f
    of wisdom 10.90
    witness of 6.188; 8.107
    work of 6.192–194; 7.19f,
        142; 9.189f; 10.35; 14.169,
        171; 16.22; 17.222
    and worship 11.56
Home-life 1.112; 5.100f; 9.70;
    11.199; 12.250
Honesty 1.119; 14.202
Homosexuality 8.32; 9.53;
    12.38, 97; 15.42, 185; 17.140
Honey 3.16; 9.80
Hope 2.63; 3.108, 136; 4.27f,
    57, 190, 287; 8.108–111, 166,
    196, 198f; 9.124, 169; 10.91,
    110; 11.25f, 83, 106, 125,
    186f; 12.19–21, 154, 263;
    13.61–63, 127, 128–131, 149f;
    14.172, 183; 17.26
    and character 8.74f
    and faith 2.124; 8.21
    gospel of 3.25

and love **9**.124
oneness of **10**.141
and religion **5**.160
Horeb, Mount **2**.159
Horns **16**.171; **17**.60, 94, 138
Horses **2**.243; **3**.264; **4**.240
white **5**.178; **17**.167, 179
Hosea, *Book of* **13**.13
Hospitality **1**.261, 397f; **3**.143,
326; **4**.145, 265; **8**.220; **9**.15;
12.81f; **13**.161; **14**.254
duty of **7**.123; **8**.167; **12**.238;
13.190f; **15**.148–150
laws of **1**.371; **4**.94; **5**.97, 101
See Guest Friendships
'Hospitals', ancient **16**.89
Houses **1**.122, 239f; **2**.46f;
3.44, 47, 331; **4**.62, 145f, 202,
264f; **7**.81, 149; **14**.89
Households **1**.383; **8**.213
Humble, The **1**.91
Humility **1**.97, 297; **2**.173, 175f,
283f, 297; **3**.219, 242; **4**.136,
185, 189; **6**.110; **8**.17, 164;
10.135–137; **11**.158; **14**.35,
105f, 109f, 228, 270f
Hunger **1**.99, 355; **5**.212
Husbands **10**.173f; **14**.222–224
Hybca **14**.221
Hymns, early **10**.164; **12**.89–91,
169f
Hymns of the faith **1**.274
Hypocrisy **1**.197; **2**.46; **3**.168;
4.160; **12**.85f; **14**.190
Hypocrites **1**.158, 188; **2**.288
Hyssop **3**.337; **6**.259

Iconium **7**.97, 107f, 119;
12.232

Idealism **10**.98, 103; **12**.180;
17.200
platonic **13**.88; **16**.55
Idleness **2**.51f; **12**.113f
Idolatry **1**.397; **3**.238; **4**.211;
5.161; **7**.116; **8**.28; **9**.47f,
52, 71–76, 89, 92; **10**.47;
11.152; **15**.123f; **16**.106f;
17.25, 44, 53
Idumaea **2**.194; **3**.70; **12**.156
Ignorance **3**.57; **8**.142; **14**.186f
wilful **5**.48, 194; **9**.136
Illumination **1**.50
Illyricum **7**.148
Imitation, spiritual **10**.160f;
15.35
Immorality **1**.324; **8**.178; **9**.47;
11.182, 199; **12**.5; **13**.182;
14.319; **15**.180
Immortality **3**.25, 289; **4**.287;
7.9f; **9**.125; **12**.148, 175;
13.55
conditional **1**.387
Impatience **2**.3; **8**.180; **11**.180
Impiety **12**.37
Impurity **10**.47; **11**.188; **12**.245;
14.43
Inaction **2**.13; **4**.214
Incendiarism **1**.113, 376; **16**.81
Indecency **2**.198; **3**.239; **4**.211f
Incense **4**.10; **16**.174; **17**.40,
99, 161f, 211
Incest **9**.42, 43–46; **12**.54
Independence **3**.330; **9**.235;
11.84
India **14**.221; **17**.161
Indian's Tomb, The **9**.119
Indifference **2**.12; **5**.232, 235;
6.254; **16**.142

Indiscipline **12.**37

Individualism **2.**174; **9.**139

Indulgences **3.**99

Infidelity, spiritual **1.**386; **2.**49; **16.**108

Infirmity **9.**198

Influence **13.**182

Ingathering, festival of **5.**248

Ingratitude **2.**108, 237; **4.**218; **12.**188; **17.**28

Innocence **10.**97, 102; **11.**43f; **12.**20, 245; **15.**53

Inns, ancient **4.**21; **12.**82, 110, 238; **14.**254; **15.**149

Insanity **2.**199; **4.**107

Insecurity **12.**20

Insincerity **4.**160

Insolence **8.**37; **9.**265f

Inspiration **6.**195; **14.**180

  biblical **4.**8

Instincts **15.**188f

Insults **1.**118, 139–141, 166f, 179; **2.**122; **9.**251; **10.**159; **12.**187

Intellectualism **11.**23f; **12.**4f, 127

Intemperance **12.**80

Intercession **15.**116f

Inter-testamental literature **14.**30f

Intolerance **3.**226; **5.**193; **11.**191

Invalids **1.**351

Iron **17.**161

Irony **14.**29

Irreverence **12.**37

Irritability **4.**188; **10.**155

Isauria **14.**144

Ishmaelites **11.**57

Islam **9.**118

Isles of the Sea **4.**48

Israel **1.**13, 176; **2.**142; **3.**214; **8.**124–126; **11.**58, 119; **15.**181f

  bride of God **2.**49; **5.**143; **6.**28; **9.**246; **14.**101f; **16.**108; **17.**76, 172

  new **14.**21, 41, 166, 286; **17.**24

  of God **14.**41, 166

  son of God **3.**71; **8.**124

  ten tribes of **3.**193

  true **3.**178; **8.**122

  vine of God **6.**172

Israelites **9.**252; **11.**58

Issacher, tribe of **14.**31

Italy **13.**6; **14.**145

Ituraea **2.**95; **4.**3, 31

Ivory **9.**2; **17.**161

Jacinth **17.**214

Jacob's Well **5.**147

James, *Letter of* **14.**1–33

Jamnites **12.**157

Japan, church of **16.**147

Jaspar **16.**151f; **17.**159, 213, 215

Jealousy **1.**244; **2.**93; **3.**328; **5.**193; **8.**35; **10.**47

Jehoshaphat, valley of **17.**116

Jeremiah, *book of* **3.**134

Jericho **1.**29; **2.**219; **3.**259f; **4.**138f, 234, 239; **5.**250; **13.**160f

Jerusalem **1.**15, 29, 37, 45, 58, 63, 69, 122; **2.**346, 348, 358; **3.**27, 175, 197, 231, 343; **4.**4, 8, 129, 138f, 172f, 239, 271, 296; **5.**6, 120, 178; **6.**43, 221, 239; **7.**12, 119, 138;

14.40; **17**.116, 142

church of **3**.4; **7**.5, 6, 95, 101; **7**.145; **8**.2; **9**.228, 236

conquests of **2**.281; **3**.193

council of **2**.145; **7**.19, 112–118; **14**.10, 23, 264, 292; **15**.169; **16**.67

fall of **1**.383; **2**.28, 267, 300, 302, 305–308; **3**.68, 306, 309–311, 321; **4**.173, 241, 258; **13**.167; **14**.38

gate of **4**.229

mountains of **2**.182

new **3**.197; **13**.145, 186; **16**.8f, 98, 128, 135, 176; **17**.199–202, 212

at Passover **2**.238; **3**.324

and the prophets **2**.299

Jeshimmon **1**.63; **3**.16; **4**.43

Jesse, stump of **1**.40

Jews

defined **7**.51; **8**.47, 66, 127

dispersion of **1**.383

and Gentile **1**.17; **4**.133; **5**.55; **7**.52f, 80, 82, 107; **8**.41, 137; **9**.49; **10**.4f, 18, 85f, 92; **11**.54; **12**.32; **14**.26, 62

and Gnosticism **10**.99

history of **2**.134

ingathering of **16**.8; **17**.18f

pride of **11**.155

problem of **8**.5, 6, 119–123

rebelliousness of **8**.173

religious genius of **10**.86

sins of **11**.191f

Jezreel, plain of **4**.47

Job, *book of* **1**.181; **3**.134

John, *Letters of* **5**.23f; **14**.137; **15**.3–20, 123, 127–136; **16**.165

John, *gospel of*

authorship **5**.15–24, 53

and crucifixion **6**.292f

discourses of **5**.164f, 185; **6**.16, 86

and Ephesus **5**.6

and Gnosticism **12**.27

introduction **5**.1–24, 42, 51, 66, 76, 107, 185; **16**.165

and Jews **5**.76

judgement in **5**.43, 138–140; **6**.193f

and life **5**.42–46

and light **5**.42, 45f, 48, 54

and love **6**.85, 169, 177; **15**.44

and miracles **6**.39

oral preaching **5**.3

order of **5**.176; **6**.108

paradoxes of **5**.138

prologue of **5**.1–75

and resurrection **5**.43

size of **16**.165

symbolism **4**.2; **5**.1; **16**.160f

and truth **5**.1, 9, 53f, 66–68

'witness' in **5**.19, 51–53, 76

words of Jesus **5**.133, 185

and the world **6**.18

Jordan, river **1**.58, 69, 82, 308; **2**.11, 134; **3**.52, 192; **5**.201

and Jewish hopes **3**.185

Jordan valley **1**.76, 316; **2**.157

Jotapata **3**.134

Joy **1**.89f, 95, 116, 337; **2**.267, 376; **3**.60; **4**.66, 103, 230; **6**.177, 198, 214, 220; **7**.65; **8**.192; **10**.50; **11**.13f, 50–52, 71, 75, 109f, 189, 195; **12**.163; **14**.48f, 174; **15**.13, 21; **16**.10

The Epistle of **11**.8

1 Matt, v.1   **3** Mark   **5** John, v.1   **7** Acts   **9** Cor
2 Matt, v.2   **4** Luke   **6** John, v.2   **8** Rom   **10** Gal, Eph

and wine **5**.97
Judaea **1**.39, 73; **2**.95, 194;
   3.16, 52f; **4**.31; **6**.53
  church of **7**.5
  and Pilate **2**.358f; **4**.3
  and Syria **4**.20
Judah
  and Benjamin **11**.58
  Lion of **2**.234; **5**.1
  tribe of **2**.49; **17**.25
Judaism **6**.157; **8**.48f, 50, 136f;
   12.7, 244; **14**.146, 156f
Judaizers **10**.4, 16; **14**.26
Jude, *Letter of* **15**.157–73
Judgement, The **1**.7, 137, 287;
   2.74f, 155; **3**.108, 304; **4**.26,
   89, 108, 169; **7**.132; **8**.187;
   11.24, 213; **13**.55, 110;
   14.71, 345; **16**.7, 22, 132;
   17.66, 114–116, 168, 192f
  Books of **17**.196
  certainty of **2**.309; **6**.85; **8**.21,
   29, 42; **9**.12, 132, 206;
   13.125f; **17**.123
  final **9**.37; **14**.175; **16**.85;
   17.194–197
  a fire **4**.169
  of love **15**.175
  and Messiah **1**.322; **6**.135
  seat of **8**.188
  second chance **4**.174f, 287;
   6.7
  standards of **3**.250; **4**.175;
   8.45f
  threefold **9**.35–38
Judgement Court, The **1**.138
Judgement of others **1**.246, 261–
   265, 334; **2**.74f, 188; **9**.48;
   14.110–112

Jupiter **1**.26
Jupiter Capitolinus **2**.170, 273
Justice **1**.131, 158, 164; **2**.83;
   8.22, 34; **11**.79f; **12**.117, 239,
   257; **14**.116–118; **17**.178
  'at the gate' **2**.143
  Greek **8**.94f; **9**.206, 238;
   11.75f
  Roman **4**.246, 280; **7**.172;
   8.188
  social **4**.242
Justification **8**.22f, 57, 72; **17**.31
  by faith **8**.58
  and James **14**.7
  and sanctification **8**.77
Just One, The **7**.161

Kanatha **3**.124
Katakekaumene, plain of **16**.125
Kavella **7**.122
Keys **2**.144–146; **16**.48
Khan Minyeh **1**.74
Kidneys **5**.250; **16**.110
Kidron,
  brook of **5**.6; **6**.221
  valley of **1**.68; **4**.44; **6**.43
Kindness **1**.103, 241; **3**.113, 228;
   4.142; **8**.42, 170; **9**.120, 165,
   216; **10**.51, 159f; **11**.157;
   12.259
Kingdom of God **1**.8, 67, 92,
   162, 210–214, 258, 304, 360;
   2.8, 39, 41, 74, 78f, 81f, 83,
   156, 207, 223–226, 266, 289,
   342f; **3**.106f, 177, 232, 242,
   246, 248, 255; **4**.5, 54, 103,
   122, 135, 148, 165, 179, 184,
   227; **6**.64; **7**.111, 127, 134;
   9.159f, 217; **11**.15, 112;

12.36, 198; **14.**347; **15.**56;
16.40, 94, 123, 129; **17.**187,
196
and children **2.**174–178
citizens of **2.**289; **11.**29f
consummation of **1.**212
entry into **2.**84; **4.**229
feast of **4.**195
imminence of **1.**364, 381f;
2.137, 155f, 315; **3.**208
and Jewish hope **3.**17, 188
and love **4.**193
mystery of **3.**91f
proclamation of **1.**370; **7.**5,11
and repentance **1.**352
signs of **4.**220
sons of **1.**304
stewards of **2.**145
word of **15.**24
yoke of **2.**17
Kingdom of heaven **1.**92; **2.**7f,
76, 87ff, 139–146, 169, 173,
217–219; **3.**111, 241; **4.**179,
181f, 228; **5.**127; **8.**192
Kingdom of priests **16.**35, 178
King's College **12.**176
King's Highway **1.**45
Kingship **3.**71; **4.**267; **11.**58;
15.69
spiritual **3.**82f
Knowledge **1.**291; **3.**104f;
8.100; **9.**109, 215; **10.**35, 82;
11.63, 99, 130; **14.**302; **15.**10
gift of **9.**118
and Greeks **5.**55; **8.**159; **9.**37
growth in **13.**50
O.T. **8.**114
responsibility of **6.**186
self-knowledge **8.**159; **9.**132

sexual **6.**209; **15.**185
way of **5.**197; **11.**18
Kranion **4.**3
Krenides **11.**3

Lake of Fire **17.**47
Lambeth Conference **1.**392
Lamentations, *Book of* **3.**135
Lamps **1.**85; **4.**167
Lamp of Israel **1.**122
Lampstand **1.**122; **2.**244
Landlords **4.**208
Language, eastern **4.**216; **11.**155
Laodicaea **3.**320; **11.**91, 93;
12.184; **16.**28, 47, 137–139
Church of **2.**218; **10.**68f;
11.127f, 171; **12.**273
and Jews **16.**139
Letter to **16.**136–148
Lost letter to **10.**172–174;
12.273, 274
Last days, The **3.**306; **14.**174;
15.59f; **16.**7, 22; **17.**5, 17
Last hour, The **15.**59f
Last Supper, The **1.**113; **2.**128,
338–343, 348, 372; **3.**347;
4.264–267; **5.**1, 19, 48, 204;
6.272, 292; **7.**95; **10.**84
Last Things, The **1.**8; **8.**151;
14.250; **16.**167; **17.**13, 29, 55
as Terror **17.**15–17
Last Trumpet, The **10.**165
Laughter **4.**66, 195
Lausanne **2.**359
Law, and Greeks **1.**144; **12.**35
Law, Jewish **1.**6, 47, 52, 80, 126–
131, 134, 166, 208, 268, 284,
337, 356; **2.**8f; **3.**31, 163,
293, **4.**59–61; **5.**120f, 197;

8.126; 13.66; 14.69
books of 1.347
burden of 2.17; 10.6
ceremonial 1.286; 2.290;
    4.250
of freedom 14.7
function of 10.29
and Gospel 1.131–133
homes of 1.242
inadequacy of 1.366–368;
    10.20f, 26; 11.61–63
and the Kingdom 3.17
oral 1.127, 129; 2.114, 128;
    3.32, 164, 289; 4.250; 8.44–
    46
personified 1.52
and religion 10.36
royal 14.68
scribal 1.127; 2.128; 3.57
simplicity of 2.117
son of 4.29; 10.33f
study of 5.124
tables of 13.96
use of 8.57
and wisdom 5.154
written 2.114
yoke of 2.17
Law, moral 1.201, 208; 10.55
Law, Roman 2.74, 372
Lawlessness 1.221; 8.90; 12.37
Lawless One, The 11.212
Laying-on of hands 7.66f;
    12.117f; 13.54f
Lazar-houses 3.45
Learning 1.97; 3.114; 4.29;
    13.48
    discipline of 17.224
Leaven 1.7; 2.79, 130–132, 339;
    3.187f, 225, 332; 4.50, 180–

182, 262; 9.45; 10.44
Lechaeum 7.133; 9.2
Legalism 1.128, 311f; 2.132,
    189, 209f; 3.32, 168; 4.157,
    159, 178; 5.121; 8.64; 9.160;
    10.24, 37, 42; 11.96, 189;
    12.6, 7
    and Jesus 8.138, 140f; 10.26,
    115
Legalists 2.282, 292; 8.180;
    9.15
Leontopolis 14.39
Leopard, symbolism of 17.88, 93
Lepers 1.293, 296, 365; 3.238
    cleansing of 1.299f; 14.170
Leprosy 1.295–299; 3.35, 43–46;
    4.217f
Lesbos 7.150
Letters, ancient 8.x–xi; 10.62;
    11.12
    of commendation 8.207;
    9.185
    of credit 16.138
Leviathan 1.216, 303; 4.192;
    17.58, 77
Levi, tribe of 14.31
Levites 1.26; 2.293; 4.155, 224;
    5.76f; 6.36; 9.80; 13.8, 76;
    17.34
Libations 1.111f; 11.46
Liberality 1.245
Liberation 8.59; 10.81f
Liberty 1.117, 168; 7.105;
    8.179, 192f; 9.76, 134, 214;
    11.68f, 189; 12.192; 13.196;
    14.207; 16.68
    of conscience 3.287
    law of 14.60, 70
    of speech 3.227; 11.26;

11 Phil, Col, Thes   13 Heb   15 John, Jude   16 Rev, v.1
12 Tim, Tit, Phlm   14 Jas, Pet   17 Rev, v.2

15.114
of truth **14**.133
and vigilance **12**.51
Licentiousness **10**.47
Life **1**.22, 160, 182; **2**.91;
    3.314; **5**.216–218; **14**.87f
Book of **16**.123; **17**.95, 147,
    186, 196
crown of **1**.183; **16**.83f
development of **9**.157
fountain of **17**.220f
from God **1**.49
laws of **2**.66f
natural **8**.24–40, 104, 178f
necessities of **9**.213
storms of **1**.318f; **2**.105f
symbolism of **6**.89
tree of **16**.69; **17**.221f
uncertainty of **14**.113
value of **1**.396f; **2**.152–154
word of **15**.25
Life after death **2**.275; **6**.91f
Life to come **1**.47; **3**.288, 290;
    6.95; **9**.155; **11**.64; **15**.99f
Light, The **1**.122–125, 243; **2**.7;
    3.97; **11**.112; **15**.28–30;
    17.209
Lilies **4**.165
Lion, symbolism of **5**.1; **16**.159;
    17.88, 215
Litany, river **1**.71
Liturgies, Greek **8**.202f
Locusts **3**.16; **17**.48–52
plague of **17**.125
Loneliness **1**.117, 350, 355;
    3.251f; **6**.190; **8**.119
Lord's Day **1**.286; **7**.27; **8**.184;
    16.42f
Lord's Prayer **1**.92, 102, 198–

232; **2**.86; **3**.232; **4**.54f, 143f;
    5.127f; **7**.11; **8**.16, 175;
    9.182, 196; **17**.82
Lord's Supper **1**.215, 266f;
    2.66; **5**.225; **6**.262; **7**.149;
    9.95; **14**.148; **15**.109; **16**.95
in *Didache* **7**.91
institution of **9**.103–105
name of **9**.102
symbols of **9**.104f
Lord's Table **1**.215, 266; **2**.103,
    291; **9**.73, 105; **11**.156;
    14.280; **15**.109
fencing of **1**.266; **10**.118
Lost, The **4**.235
Lots, casting of **7**.17
Louisiana **3**.13
Love **1**.124f, 172–178, 182, 224,
    302, 354, 400; **2**.4, 123, 330;
    3.292–296, 327; **4**.124, 189;
    8.190, 218; **10**.49f, 88, 139f;
    11.129f, 159, 186; **12**.98, 134,
    180; **13**.190; **14**.172f, 188,
    209, 227, 252f; **15**.82, 92,
    97f; **16**.64
brotherly **8**.164; **14**.304f
claims of **4**.217
debt of **8**.176
extravagance of **2**.329
& family **12**.188
Hymn of **9**.95, 116–126
immortal **3**.292
in Judaism **1**.388
kiss of **14**.279–281
and Law **1**.131; **9**.238f
law of **14**.60
motivation of **1**.132f; **8**.163;
    9.76, 166; **14**.102f
and obedience **2**.53

and tolerance 4.130f; 5.18; 9.116; 12.33
triumph of 9.147
Love Feasts 1.113, 166, 376; 6.184; 7.149; 9.95, 99f; 10.18; 11.189; 14.148, 203; 15.192f, 194; 16.80
Loving-kindness 1.171; 12.24
Loyalty 1.111, 392, 395; 2.310; 3.235; 4.103, 121, 162; 6.50; 7.41; 8.21; 10.51, 88; 11.46, 131; 12.99, 134, 154, 160; 13.127, 151, 189; 14.35; 16.82, 131; 17.97, 98, 102, 173, 205
conflict of 3.287f
Lucerne 2.359
Luck 9.47
Luke, *Gospel of*
introduction to 3.2; 4.1–6, 120; 5.22; 7.161; 16.165
symbol of 5.1; 16.160f
universalism of 4.179
Luna 14.147
Lust 1.147; 2.119; 8.34; 12.180; 14.51
Luxury, ancient 9.2; 14.119, 221f
Lycaonia 9.2; 11.92; 14.144
Lycia 14.145; 16.28
Lycus Valley 11.91, 128; 16.137
Lydda 7.77
Lydia 11.93; 16.125
and Jews 14.40
King of 16.113
Lying 1.158; 12.39
Lyons, Bishop of 5.20
Lystra 7.97, 109, 110, 119; 11.47; 12.21; 17.110

Maccabees 3.124, 172; 4.248; 5.150; 7.94; 12.149; 13.174; 16.171; 17.11, 26, 60
coins of 6.172
wars of 2.136f; 3.68; 5.82; 13.164, 166
Mace 17.162
Macedonia 4.4; 7.138, 147; 11.179
Empire of 5.186
'Man of' 7.121f
Machaerus 1.71; 2.1, 38, 93; 3.149; 4.36, 89
Maeander, river 7.150
valley 12.184
Maecenas 12.166
Magi 1.25–27
Magic 2.37f; 3.37; 7.66
Magistrates, Roman 4.222; 8.106
Magnesia 16.28
Magnificat, The 4.4, 15f
Magog 17.133
Magus 1.26
Makaria 7.99
Malaria 1.308
Malea, Cape of 9.1
Malice 11.153
Malignity 8.36
Malta 7.187f
fever of 1.307f
Mammon 12.138
Man 1.13–14, 21, 97, 100f, 136, 178, 378; 2.40, 278; 3.25, 108; 8.33, 55, 99, 110, 185f; 9.29f, 47; 13.39f
brotherhood of 1.202; 11.71; 12.63
glory of 1.225; 13.23

11 Phil, Col, Thes
12 Tim, Tit, Phlm
13 Heb
14 Jas, Pet
15 John, Jude
16 Rev, v.1
17 Rev, v.2

Greek belief **12**.175; **14**.93; **15**.201

Heavenly Man **6**.244

image of God **3**.287; **15**.75

Jewish belief **8**.98f; **14**.50

needs of **5**.71

perversity of **2**.9; **3**.152f

soul of **1**.217; **3**.42; **6**.38; **9**.28, 55, 120, 137–140, 201; **13**.39; **14**.93; **15**.11, 201

spirit of **5**.161; **6**.99; **9**.55; **11**.163; **13**.39, 129; **15**.11, 201

supremacy of **9**.28; **16**.159

symbolism of **5**.1

true **3**.139; **13**.84

will of **3**.140; **10**.98, 103f, 131

Manger **4**.21

Man of God **12**.134

Man of Lawlessness **3**.310

Man of Sin **11**.212; **15**.63; **17**.61

Manna **1**.67, 218; **4**.144; **5**.215f; **9**.88, 230; **13**.96

hidden **16**.94

Manuscripts, uncial **2**.27

Marazion **2**.373

Marble **17**.161

Mark, *Gospel of*

Earliest Gospel, 3.1; **9**.115

Introduction to 3.1–9, 192, 251, 253, 328, 345; **5**.1; **16**.165

and Peter **2**.345; **3**.4–5, 7–9, 136, 157, 353; **5**.10; **6**.101; **11**.170; **14**.278, 308f

realism of **3**.6; **5**.22

and Rome **3**.361; **4**.283; **8**.215

symbol of **4**.2; **5**.1; **16**.161

Market days **1**.235; **4**.223

Market-place **2**.223

Markings **17**.102–104

Marriage, Christian **1**.157, 377; **2**.203, 206, 209f; **10**.168, 174f; **11**.162f

desertion in **2**.199

fidelity **1**.155; **4**.211; **8**.178; **10**.171

infidelity **3**.240

and Jesus **1**.150; **2**.201f; **17**.106

love **10**.173f

mixed **9**.63, 71

and Paul **9**.57–64, 69–71; **10**.171–173

re-marriage **9**.71

symbolism of **17**.172f

Marriage, Greek **1**.153; **3**.289; **10**.174

Marriage, Jewish **1**.18–19, 150–152, 320; **2**.196f, 202f; **3**.237f, 240; **4**.211; **11**.198f

a civic duty **2**.196; **9**.60f

dowry **12**.77

inter-marriage **5**.149

levirate **2**.276f; **3**.289; **4**.41, 249

made in heaven **12**.76f

mixed **12**.237

Marriage, Roman **1**.156f, 377

Mars Hill **7**.131; **9**.23

Martyrs **1**.116, 378f; **2**.230; **7**.13; **11**.66; **12**.169; **16**.70; **17**.10–13, 25–27, 118, 171, 192f

Materialism **2**.132, 154; **4**.116; **9**.28, 47

Matthew, *Gospel of*

date of **1**.382; **2**.68, 153, 170,

214, 229, 267, 273
introduction to 1.1–9, 324;
2.207; 3.2, 55; 5.3, 22
Jewishness of 1.127
symbolism of 4.2; 5.1;
16.160f
use of O.T. 1.36, 39, 40, 75;
2.337; 4.3, 137
Meanness 9.182; 14.265f
Mecca. 3.274
Medes 1.25; 6.121
Media 5.156; 17.88
Empire of 5.186
Mediators 10.30; 12.62f
Medicine 1.26
Mediterranean Sea 1.7; 4.48
Meekness 1.96; 10.137
Megiddo 17.132f
Melancholy 9.219
Mercenaries 14.39
Mercy 1.103–105, 131, 163, 165;
2.295; 8.162f; 11.157; 12.23–
25; 14.70f, 198
personified 14.28
and wisdom 14.96
Merit
doctrine of 1.187; 8.67
treasure of 1.47
Meshech 17.194
Mesopotamia 11.93; 14.38
Messiah 1.5, 44, 58, 60, 67;
2.33, 147, 241f, 279; 3.72;
5.26; 7.23; 17.228
age of 14.140; 17.187f, 199
banquet of 1.67, 216, 303f;
4.192; 17.174f
community of 16.129
false 1.69; 2.33; 3.185;
5.115; 9.18

forerunner 2.136f, 159
Jewish doctrine of 1.267, 216,
303f, 322, 349; 2.6, 48, 129,
164f, 235, 279f, 303; 3.24,
147, 188, 193–199, 210, 222,
265–268, 297–299, 310;
4.18f, 26, 38, 54, 169f, 250;
5.7, 52, 77, 108, 114f, 155,
206f, 215, 243; 6.117f, 197,
210; 10.86; 14.178, 347;
16.2f, 6–11, 33, 69, 94, 110,
169; 17.13, 177f, 181, 206
as judge 9.50
kingdom of 16.9
and living water 5.251
mother of 17.75f
names of 1.52; 3.267, 297
at Passover 2.136; 3.338
as Shepherd 17.38
suffering 2.148; 7.27, 37, 129;
9.17f; 17.188
titles of 2.2; 3.196, 261; 298,
6.13; 11.119
travail of 3.194f; 16.6; 17.75
Methodists 4.56, 130
Middle age 12.214
Midianites 9.88
'Mights' 8.117; 10.92
Miletus 7.138, 150; 16.28
Military Service 4.20
Millenarianism 17.184, 189–191
Millenium 17.73, 186, 188–191
Millstones 2.179; 3.229
Mind, the 3.124; 11.79–81;
14.84
adventurous 1.337–340; 3.61,
67f; 4.270
and the body 3.48
and prayer 9.129

questioning 2.102; 4.124;
10.90; 16.117
shut 1.361; 2.59f, 323; 4.68,
100; 5.131, 192, 198; 6.21,
170, 245; 12.101; 13.49
and truth 1.338–340
and universe 1.207
Ministry, Christian 1.121; 4.115;
9.84; 10.90; 12.100f, 128, 217
in Early Church 9.134;
10.146f; 11.171; 15.132–
136; 16.12
Mint 2.293
Miracles 1.289, 300, 304–307,
350; 2.171, 237; 3.218;
4.57; 5.119; 6.100, 101;
7.32f, 193; 9.109f
Mirrors 9.125; 13.95; 14.59;
17.140, 159
Misenum 7.190
Missionary task 1.356f; 2.291;
6.67; 11.44; 16.129
Mites 3.302; 4.171
Mithradates 14.144
Mithraism 5.222; 17.33
Mitylene 7.150
Moab 2.159
Moabites 9.88
Mohammedans 1.194, 196, 233;
3.168, 291; 9.118
Molech 1.58, 141; 2.183; 3.231;
7.60
Monarchy 10.45
Money 1.252; 2.84; 4.164f
love of 3.328; 12.131–133,
184
money-changers 2.244f;
4.241; 5.109f
Monks 1.149

Monotheism 3.295; 6.161
Months, Jewish 2.169; 6.69;
10.36
Morality
of world 8.26f; 11.152;
13.108; 17.86
pollution 12.37f; 14.173
sexual 3.240; 15.199f
Moravian Church 14.131
Moriah, Mount 3.308
Morning Star, The 16.110f
Mote 1.85
Motherhood 12.68f
Motives 1.185, 342; 2.173;
9.37, 174f, 209; 12.120, 252f
Mourning 1.93, 233, 343f; 3.132–
135; 4.86f; 6.88f
spiritual 14.108f
Murder 1.135f, 379; 3.173, 238;
7.166; 8.35, 176; 12.38
and the Jews 2.297f; 4.211
Muslims See Mohammedans
Mustard 2.75f; 3.109f; 4.178f
Myra 7.181
Myrrh 1.32; 17.161f
Mysia 7.19; 16.28
Mystery 2.64, 66; 3.91; 5.226;
9.26, 94, 125, 170; 10.83;
16.53; 17.109, 143f
'Secret' 11.126, 130
Mystery Religions 2.65f; 3.91;
5.126f, 222; 8.84f; 10.113;
12.67f, 262; 14.25, 295f, 310f;
15.42, 70; 17.33
Mysticism 6.175; 9.256

Nablus 5.147
Nain 4.86
Names 6.5, 210; 13.60; 15.87

Jewish 1.205; 2.177; 3.225;
4.17, 24, 143; 5.62f, 90;
6.87; 7.100; 11.38; 15.53;
16.98f
New ones 16.95, 176
Roman 8.212
Naphtali, tribe of 1.73; 14.31
Nationalism, Jewish 1.330, 359;
2.332; 3.356
Nature 1.260; 7.109; 8.27, 45,
108f; 10.66f; 14.87f; 16.159,
162f, 173, 181; 17.19, 43f,
46, 86, 170f
Nazarenes 1.40; 7.169; 14.316
Nazareth 1.38–42, 73; 2.17, 78f,
91f; 3.18f, 128, 138–140,
177; 4.21, 46f; 5.92
Nazirites 7.138, 155; 12.119;
14.10
Neapolis 7.119, 122
Nebo 2.136, 159
Needle's Eye, The 2.217; 4.229
Nehardea 14.37
Neighbour 4.140
Nemesis 10.54, 82
Neocaesarea 16.126, 135
Neroneas See Caesarea Philippi
Neutrality 2.39–41
New Age, The 13.189; 15.16;
16.69
New Birth 4.130; 5.124–132;
9.145; 12.262; 14.21, 54,
171–173; 15.78f, 102f
of baptism 14.192
Greek 5.126; 8.85
Jewish 5.126
New heavens and earth 8.108f;
16.98, 176; 17.168, 197f
New song, the 16.98, 175f

New Temple 5.114; 17.212
New Things 16.176; 17.204f
New World 3.304; 5.154; 17.195
New Year, Jewish 13.98
Nicaea 16.17
Nicanor 2.136
Nicanor's Gate 2.244
Nicolaitans 16.66–68, 92f
Nicopolis 12.9, 265
Nile, river 2.65; 17.128, 198
Nineveh 2.129; 17.142, 150,
167, 211
Nirvana 9.204
Nisan 2.340; 4.262
Nisibis 14.37
North Africa 17.160, 162
Novelty 11.52; 12.31, 180
Nunc Dimittis 4.4, 26

Oaths 1.158–162; 2.116; 3.170;
14.126f
binding 2.292
Obedience 1.21, 92, 183, 209,
212, 289f, 292; 2.53, 153,
259; 3.233f, 242; 4.150, 226;
5.128, 217; 6.21, 169, 211;
7.48, 71; 8.93, 171–174;
9.194; 12.159f, 255; 13.33f,
114f, 199; 14.35, 100, 169f,
188, 199, 293, 347; 15.17f,
29, 35, 59, 77, 103f
Offerings 2.245; 9.80f; 13.116;
14.233; 15.37
of the poor 4.24
Oil 3.146; 15.70; 17.6f
Oligarchy 10.45
Olive tree 8.147–151; 9.80
Olives, Mount of 2.342, 348;
3.274, 339, 343; 4.241, 271;

5.14; 6.221
Olympus 17.133
Onycha 17.161
Opal 17.159
Ophites 15.164
Optimism 2.230; 3.304; 6.32
Opportunity 2.330; 6.40, 87;
    8.165; 11.24; 13.50; 16.149
Order 1.207; 5.57
Orontes 7.89, 97
Orphic religion 14.25, 87f;
    16.29f
Orthodoxy 3.316; 4.140; 11.105,
    113; 12.4, 31; 14.349;
    16.62–64, 117
   frozen 11.132
   Jewish 3.48; 4.140
Ostia 17.164
Ovens 1.121, 257; 4.165
Overseers See elders
Ox, symbolism of 5.1; 16.159

Pacifism 1.175
Pain 1.201, 354f; 2.39
Palaia Kaumene 17.45
Palestine 1.72, 298f, 307f; 3.37,
    46, 52, 53, 124, 208; 5.59,
    146f; 6.237f; 7.11, 15;
    17.5, 116
Palm, sign of 17.26f
Pamphylia 3.3; 7.97
Pan 2.134; 3.192
Panias 2.134; 3.192
Panium 2.134f
Pantheism 15.161
Papacy 2.139; 15.63; 17.100
Paphos 7.97, 100
Papyrus 1.330; 7.86; 8.x; 9.223;
    11.142; 15.127; 16.165f

Parables
  defined 2.54–56, 261; 3.85,
    90, 281; 4.146
  of dragnet 2.78; 12.179
  of the friend 4.4, 222
  of great feast 1.333
  of hidden treasure 2.79, 83–86
  of the Kingdom 2.79
  of last judgment 1.179f
  of the leaven 2.79
  of the lost sheep 4.200
  of the mustard seed 2.78
  of the pounds 4.172
  of the prodigal son 3.14; 4.5;
    16.116
  of the rich man 4.5
  of the sheep and goats 17.195
  of the sower 2.55–63, 78;
    4.98–102; 14.57, 189
  of the talents 1.184; 2.84,
    321–324; 4.172
  of the ten virgins 14.300
  of the unjust judge 4.4
  of the wheat and tares 2.78;
    12.179
  of the wicked husbandman
    2.69; 3.89f; 14.166, 194
Paradise 1.52; 4.286f; 6.34,
    153f; 9.257; 13.134; 16.69f,
    84, 122; 17.199, 220
Parchment 16.88
Parent-slayers 12.38
Parthia 15.63; 17.63, 147
Parthians 3.103, 320; 15.18;
    17.4, 53, 129, 141, 184
Partnership 11.17
Passion 1.137; 3.231; 4.106;
    9.158; 10.159; 11.151; 12.191
Passover 1.41; 2.79, 238f, 245,

| 1 Matt, v.1 | 3 Mark | 5 John, v.1 | 7 Acts | 9 Cor |
| 2 Matt, v.2 | 4 Luke | 6 John, v.2 | 8 Rom | 10 Gal, Eph |

296, 328, 339–342; 3.260, 270, 331–334, 336–339; 4.4, 9, 29, 232, 241, 262f, 265; 5.106, 108, 177, 201, 228; 6.115, 146f, 235; 7.21, 94, 148, 150; 9.149f; 10.36; 13.158; 14.185

and Bethany 3.264

Christian 9.44

and Elijah 2.136; 3.147

and Greeks 6.119

Lamb of 2.339, 341; 5.80f; 6.259, 261; 14.244

the Last 3.331–334

and Messiah 2.136; 3.338

and the Preparation 2.374

at spring-time 2.105, 252; 3.160f

and trials 2.353; 4.280; 6.241

Pastoral Epistles, the 12.1–13

Pastors 10.147f; 11.194–196

Paternity 10.129

Patience 1.78f; 2.63, 167; 3.108, 113; 4.220; 8.42; 9.119f, 216; 10.50, 138; 11.75, 83, 108, 158; 12.135, 196; 13.46, 144f; 14.43, 124f, 303

Patmos 5.17; 16.14, 40–42, 50, 156; 17.127

Patriarchs 8.149; 13.148; 16.154; 17.170

Testament of See Index VI

Paulinism 8.44; 9.204; 11.11; 13.1

paradox of 10.104f

pillars of 8.19–23

quintessence of 10.70f

Peace 1.97, 108, 112, 158; 3.213, 236; 4.230; 5.87, 93; 6.171; 7.114f; 8.169f, 191f, 199; 10.50, 76, 140, 185; 11.12, 206; 12.23f, 180; 13.72–74; 14.95, 294; 16.29; 17.5

angel of 17.40

Gospel of 3.25

King of 13.69

kiss of 1.113; 4.94; 8.169; 9.63, 168; 11.189; 14.148, 279–281

meaning of 4.19; 10.9

and Messiah 5.77

The Peace 9.168

and righteousness 13.72

way of 10.26

Peace-makers 1.108; 3.140f; 13.180f

Pearl 2.86f; 17.159

Pella 1.82; 3.124; 17.85

Peloponnese 9.1

Penitence 1.95, 142, 234; 6.274; 14.347; 17.34

and forgiveness 3.81

Pentateuch, The 1.127; 2.275f, 277, 281; 3.31, 163, 289

and Samaritans 5.159

Pentecost 2.42, 145, 156; 3.80; 5.83, 252; 6.115; 10.36; 15.109

Day of 7.18

Feast of 3.323; 4.9; 5.177; 7.21, 150f, 157

People, importance of 1.251; 2.173; 3.64; 4.174, 177; 8.12; 14.208

People of the land 3.56; 4.199; 5.253; 13.93

Peroea 1.82; 2.95; 4.31

Perfection, moral 1.177; 9.26;

11 Phil, Col, Thes
12 Tim, Tit, Phlm
13 Heb
14 Jas, Pet
15 John, Jude
16 Rev, v.1
17 Rev, v.2

10.79; **11**.65f, 69; **12**.204;
14.44
and martyrdom **11**.66
symbol of **17**.211
Perfectionism **15**.79–81
Perfume **2**.329; **6**.109
Perga **3**.3; **7**.97
Pergamum **16**.28, 58, 87–90
Letter to **16**.67, 86–99
library of **16**.88
Perjurers **12**.39
Persecution **1**.115–118, 179,
241f, 372–378, 382–384; **2**.8;
3.99, 250; **4**.193, 258;
8.167f; **9**.106f; **13**.6, 57;
14.247, 257f; **16**.40, 79;
17.127, 137, 145
courting of **9**.119
of Early Church **1**.112–114, 375,
376f, 393; **2**.153, 304, 310;
3.306, 312–314; **6**.181f;
7.62f; **9**.63; **11**.51; **12**.58f,
167; **14**.148, 156–158; **16**.80
salt of **3**.234
Perseverance **1**.79; **13**.127
Persia **2**.364; **16**.36; **17**.88
Empire of **1**.25f; **5**.186
Persians **1**.25f, 168; **2**.281;
3.193f; **6**.121; **7**.11; **15**.55;
16.3
beliefs of **3**.22f
and crucifixion **6**.250
Persistence **2**.123; **4**.222, 232
Personalism **13**.60
Pessimism **3**.108, 159, 189, 217,
304; **5**.55; **6**.213; **10**.91;
12.154
Pessinus **14**.144
Pestilence **17**.9

Peter, Letters of **14**.137–163,
275f, 283–289
and Ephesians **14**.154
Petra **1**.82
Phaeno **13**.192
Pharisees **1**.43, 129, 325, 351,
356, 359; **2**.30, 128f, 196,
200, 214, 261, 272f, 275–278,
279, 294, 374; **3**.63, 69, 73,
163, 185, 187, 237, 285, 288,
300, 349; **4**.4, 61, 65, 70, 73,
155f, 185f, 199, 206, 210, 244,
250, 275; **5**.77, 79, 120, 233f,
249, 253; **6**.45, 47–49, 93,
104, 212; **7**.49; **8**.13; **10**.114;
11.60
and the church **7**.113
and fasting **3**.59
heresies of **14**.316
origins of **2**.282
and religion **2**.132
and Sadducees **2**.128f, 131,
275; **4**.250; **7**.165; **12**.175
and the Scribes **2**.147
sin of **2**.291; **4**.223f
types of **2**.282–284; **4**.185
Philadelphia **3**.124; **16**.28
Letter to **16**.124–135
Philemon, Letter to **11**.172;
12.269–276; **16**.165
Philippi **2**.135; **7**.119, 122f,
128; **8**.19; **11**.3f, 9, 31, 73
Philippians, Letter to **11**.3–8
Philosophy **1**.26; **11**.96, 134
Mother of **15**.41
Philistines **3**.22
Phoenicia **3**.176; **9**.2; **17**.160
Phoenicians **1**.72f; **2**.121, 125
Phrygia **7**.138; **10**.44; **11**.93;

14.40, 144f; **16.**28, 125, 137, 139

Piety **1.**185, 325; **12.**239; **14.**303f

Phylacteries **2.**286; **3.**295; **4.**140; **17.**99

Pilatus, Mount **2.**359

Pilgrims **3.**273; **13.**149; **14.**144, 167; **16.**91
  Jewish **3.**324

Pillars **16.**134

Pisidia **14.**144

Pitiless **8.**39

Pity **1.**103, 354; **4.**214; **11.**157; **14.**96, 227

Plagues **2.**339; **17.**14, 44, 71, 124f, **17.**125–128, 130, 134

Platonism **8.**173f; **12.**2, 88; **16.**55; **17.**199

Pleasure **1.**94, 238, 240, 391; **2.**207; **4.**195; **6.**23; **8.**28f, 31, 96, 189; **9.**52, 76; **10.**100; **12.**161, 188, 191; **13.**129, 184; **14.**98–101, 331

Plutocracy **10.**45

Poetry **5.**22, 27

Polygamy **12.**76

Pomegranate **9.**80

Pompeii **3.**320, 359

Pontifical Letters, The **12.**1

Pontus **8.**209; **14.**137, 144, 160, 166

Poor, The **1.**90–92, 241; **3.**6, 326; **4.**5; **14.**61, 66f

Possessiuns **1.**239f, 249–254; **2.**215f; **3.**122, 244, 247f; **4.**164f, 194, 206, 228f; **9.**120, 235; **12.**129f, 185; **14.**255f

Postal system, Roman **10.**62; **16.**101, 129

Poverty **1.**90–92; **2.**208; **3.**122f; **12.**130; **14.**66f; **16.**78

Power **3.**219; **8.**200; **9.**110

Powers **8.**117f; **9.**92; **10.**92, 182; **11.**96

Praetorium **3.**359; **7.**167
  guard of **7.**193; **11.**20f

Praetor Urbanus **8.**188

Praise **8.**47, 197; **17.**169

Prayer **1.**179, 191–232, 270–272; 357; **2.**123f, 190f, 255–257, 350; **3.**38, 40f, 155, 275–278; **4.**5, 13, 53, 143f, 146; **6.**48; **8.**16, 111f; **9.**13, 173; **10.**184; **11.**13, 77f, 108f, 166f, 196; **12.**56–60, 64–66; **13.**199f; **14.**131f, 252, 279, 346f; **15.**115f, 203; **16.**129, 152f; **17.**34, 39–41
  constancy of **4.**221–223; **8.**166
  Jewish **1.**80, 185, 191–198, 261f, 335; **2.**80; **3.**104, 135f; **4.**64, 223f; **7.**123; **10.**32f, 128, 184; **12.**95, 156f; **13.**47f; **14.**89f, 131f
  laws of **6.**179–181
  morning **6.**176
  as sacrifice **17.**40f

Prayer-shawl **2.**287

Preaching **1.**75f, 79, 312, 352; **2.**69f, 108, 145; **3.**140, 245, 370; **4.**81, 134; **8.**137; **9.**39; **11.**53; **12.**31f; **14.**181f, 256, 307f, 336f, 347
  apostles' **7.**22–24, 33–36; **9.**17, 25, 32; **14.**140f
  defined **7.**67; **9.**176

equipment of **9**.216f
gift of **9**.111, 117f, 127–130
Greek **14**.27–29
and healing **4**.115f
Jewish **4**.81, 160; **14**.29f
the preacher **1**.44f, 106, 285,
   385; **2**.61, 91f, 289; **3**.131f;
   9.24, 117f, 179, 208; **13**.49;
   15.148
as proclamation **12**.258
and virtue **12**.52
Predestination **6**.73; **8**.114
Prefect **11**.21
Prejudice **1**.21, 50, 243, 338;
   2.60, 289; **3**.127; **4**.99, 124;
   5.193; **9**.33, 192
Presbyters See Elders
Prestige **1**.189, 285; **4**.128;
   11.32
Pride **1**.97, 137, 140; **2**.14, 60,
   119, 288; **3**.15, 128, 175,
   250, 330; **4**.15f, 27, 135f,
   190, 223f; **5**.193; **8**.37, 53f,
   169; **9**.34f, 38–40, 127, 182,
   197f, 232, 240, 244, 266;
   12.5, 73, 186f; **14**.105f;
   15.58, 184; **17**.80, 152–154
Priestesses **1**.154
Priests **1**.12; **2**.211; **5**.76f;
   6.104; **9**.81; **12**.109; **15**.69;
   16.153; **17**.34
chief **1**.29f; **2**.261, 275, 374;
   3.346, 349; **4**.243; **5**.233f,
   253; **7**.38; **14**.263
Priesthood, Christian **12**.1;
   14.199; **16**.35, 178; **17**.193
Jewish **2**.17, 217; **4**.9, 275;
   5.77; **11**.10; **13**.45–47, 68,
   74, 78; **14**.170

Principalities **8**.117; **9**.92; **10**.92;
   11.96
Privilege **1**.371, 383; **2**.12, 61,
   108, 224, 263; **4**.134, 151,
   245; **5**.200; **6**.186; **8**.43, 52,
   173; **9**.77, 122, 197; **10**.124f;
   14.199; **15**.72–74
Procurators **2**.357
Profanity **12**.37f
Profligacy **12**.235
Progress, spiritual **13**.50–55;
   14.299–307; **15**.46, 77;
   17.105
Promise **1**.48; **3**.25; **8**.126
and fulfilment **9**.176f
Promised Land, The **13**.33, 35–
   37, 153f; **14**.42, 173f
Property, Law of **4**.204
Prophecy **1**.5–6, 16, 36, 38, 43;
   2.8f; **3**.17; **5**.50, 157
and fulfilment **5**.115; **7**.23,
   27, 105; **9**.17; **10**.96
gift of **8**.161; **9**.111, 117f, 128
interpretation of **14**.311–314
personified **1**.52
symbolism of **2**.240–243, 253,
   341; **3**.264, 270, 339; **4**.239;
   7.154; **13**.13
Prophetesses **16**.105
Prophets **1**.20, 80, 116; **2**.5;
   3.16; **4**.51, 245; **5**.83, 145;
   8.12; **11**.10; **12**.227; **13**.12–
   14; **14**.180f, 293; **15**.132–135,
   170; **16**.25; **17**.143, 171
anointing **15**.69
clothing **1**.282
in Early Church **1**.282; **4**.134;
   7.91f, 98; **10**.146f; **12**.49,
   123; **14**.79; **15**.90; **16**.12f;

17.127

false 1.281–288; 2.258; 3.49; 4.220; 5.77; 6.48; 7.91f; 10.147; 14.312, 314–318; 17.47, 130–132, 184

and the Law 1.127; 2.282

Promised one, the 4.115; 5.78; 6.72; 9.18

Propitiation 8.58

Proportion, sense of 2.293f; 4.188f; 10.90f; 12.253; 14.58, 77, 329

Proselytes 1.59f, 273; 2.290, 359; 3.14; 5.79, 126; 7.69, 106; 8.65; 9.106; 10.31, 111; 12.194, 262; 14.38, 79, 149; 16.80

Prosperity 1.181; 2.251; 3.246; 4.210f; 9.173; 12.185; 13.126

Prostitution 1.154, 156; 3.152; 9.52; 10.169f; 12.67; 17.137, 144

Proverbs, Book of 5.31

Providence 10.142; 13.15; 15.99

Proxenos, The 15.149

Prudence 1.256, 379; 2.47, 330; 9.215; 12.80, 239, 247, 251, 257

Pseudonymous Writings 14.30f, 32, 288

Psoriasis 3.44

Psycho-analysis 9.86

Ptolemais 1.40

Ptolemies 14.39

Publicans 1.329f; 3.53

Punishment 1.138, 175, 180, 386; 2.179, 182, 323; 3.228–230; 4.214; 17.153

double 17.153

death-penalty 2.179, 357; 3.229; 6.233; 9.257; 16.90

everlasting 2.182

future 3.85f; 16.145

Jewish 3.113; 9.253

restorative 9.44–46, 182

Roman 2.179

and sin 2.98; 8.42

Purification 1.50f; 3.12, 234; 4.24f; 6.107; 14.246f

Purim, feast of 3.183; 9.228; 11.58

Puritans 2.372

Purity 1.119; 2.208; 3.236; 9.42, 174, 185, 215, 221; 11.19, 43, 80, 153f, 198–200; 12.99, 104; 13.102, 193; 14.61, 106–108; 15.75, 76–78; 17.105

of heart 1.51, 105–108; 2.16, 119; 9.193; 12.33f

symbolism of 16.122

Purple 14.221; 17.160

symbolism of 4.213

Purpose 1.177f; 5.35

Purses 1.367

Puteoli 7.190

Pythagoreans 8.182; 12.262; 13.197

Quakers 1.161; 2.52f

Quiet in the Land, The 4.26; 5.86

Quietness 17.143

Quiet Times 1.194; 3.123; 4.261, 298

Ra 3.71

Rabbis 1.86, 296f; 3.241, 279,

11 Phil, Col, Thes
12 Tim, Tit, Phlm
13 Heb
14 Jas, Pet
15 John, Jude
16 Rev, v.1
17 Rev, v.2

345; **4.**94, 96, 115, 140, 253f, 275; **9.**110, 251; **14.**80
authority **1.**134; **4.**243f
disciples of **2.**249; **4.**273, 276
and Messiah **2.**303
and sacrifice **13.**199
sayings of **1.**22, 52, 54, 56f, 110, 134, 139, 147, 151, 158, 159, 191, 236, 261, 268, 270, 304, 367, 379, 390, 393, 398; **2.**18, 26, 48, 84, 144, 145, 188, 206, 225, 269, 303, 330; **3.**17, 32, 47, 57, 104, 153, 231, 238; **4.**10, 70, 118, 191, 209, 211, 216, 227, 253; **5.**79, 83, 87, 97, 124, 126, 183, 213, 220, 243; **6.**2; **8.**70f, 187; **9.**125, 136, 235; **10.**168; **11.**54; **12.**76f, 129, 280f; **13.**18, 47; **14.**51, 69, 81, 85, 113, 127, 131, 134, 331, 347; **15.**37, 45; **16.**29, 48, 84, 95, 134; **17.**221, 227
teaching of **2.**236; **3.**52, 85, 222, 260, 278, 331; **4.**48, 81, 143, 230, 265; **8.**55; **9.**130; **10.**27f, 40f; **13.**67f; **14.**132
titles of **2.**287, 361; **3.**32, 300
trade of **1.**284, 366–368; **3.**300; **4.**254; **7.**135; **9.**79; **11.**218
Racial memory **1.**252
Rain **14.**121
Rainbow **8.**125
Ram, sign of **17.**214
Ramadan **1.**233
Ramah **1.**38
Ransom **3.**258; **8.**59; **10.**81; **16.**34

Ranters, The **15.**161f
Rapacity **8.**34f; **9.**53
Raphana **3.**124
Readers **16.**26
Reason **1.**137; **10.**131; **14.**337
Rebirth See New Births, Renatus
Rebukes **12.**102f
Received Text, The **15.**111
Rechabites **12.**119
Reciprocity, ethical **1.**274; **2.**160f; **14.**222f
Reconciliation **2.**189; **9.**211; **10.**67, 92, 117; **11.**12, 122–125; **13.**187
  word of **15.**25
Red Sea **2.**87
Redemption **3.**217; **4.**24; **5.**133; **8.**59; **9.**57, 65, 152; **11.**111, 115; **12.**30; **13.**104, 109; **15.**99; **16.**34; **17.**31
Reed **2.**5; **17.**66
Reformation, spiritual **12.**122
Reformation, The **1.**357, 385; **3.**61; **13.**39; **14.**77
  Scottish **12.**167
Reincarnation **8.**182; **12.**262; **14.**88; **17.**141
Religion **1.**97, 107, 286–288, 323, 325, 354, 359; **2.**4, 118f, 163, 166, 214, 278, 294, 296; **3.**40, 64, 69, 122f, 168f, 214, 271; **4.**8, 15, 156, 182; **8.**50, 100; **9.**46f; **10.**10, 36f, 90, 151; **11.**107; **13.**1, 66, 77f, 102, 112, 138; **14.**61f, 297, 304; **15.**31, 39, 203; **17.**110
  duties of **1.**187, 334f; **5.**160
  Jewish **1.**128f, 185; **2.**109, 115, 284–287; **3.**165

Negative 2.51f, 284f; 4.149f; 9.68
Prophetic 10.37
Remnant, The 8.53, 120, 122, 144f
'Removing mountains' 2.167; 3.276
Rents 4.208
Reparation 1.57
Repentance 1.51–58, 76, 95, 234, 352; 2.44f; 3.14, 17, 26, 144; 4.298; 7.28f, 35, 179; 8.42; 9.17, 227; 13.53, 134, 184; 14.141; 15.37; 16.65f, 120; 17.72
  baptism of 4.37
  'nine norms of' 1.54
Resolution 8.100
Respect 2.285; 14.62f
Respectability 3.244
Responsibility 1.252, 371; 2.12, 60, 108, 173, 178–181, 263; 3.105, 247f, 4.134, 151, 246; 5.200; 8.52; 9.122; 14.207, 254–256
Restitution 4.235
Restoration 1.143
Rest 13.33–40; 17.114
Resurrection 3.368; 5.193; 9.150; 11.203; 12.174; 13.55; 14.175; 16.9, 27, 110f; 17.168, 192
  of body 3.221, 290f; 9.137, 141; 12.6, 30f, 175; 16.123
  empty tomb, the 2.377; 4.291; 9.143
  Jewish 2.128, 275f; 3.289; 4.250f; 12.175; 13.111
Retaliation 1.165–169

Retribution 3.280
Reuben, tribe of 14.31
Revelation 2.130; 5.73–75, 156, 198; 6.169, 194–196; 7.35; 11.192; 12.41; 13.11f, 14, 20, 22; 15.42, 203; 16.21f, 23f, 45, 155; 17.26, 56f
  Book of 5.82; 16.1–20, 26, 28, 35, 41, 47, 97, 98, 165, 170, 176; 17.100f, 173, 195, 229, 230
Revelry 8.178
Reverence 1.131, 206–210, 297, 388; 2.163, 285; 5.112; 7.30; 9.207; 12.61f, 134; 14.188, 209, 231; 16.30, 51, 156; 17.138, 169
Revival 12.263; 15.157
Revolution, French 1.42
Rewards 1.179–185, 397–400; 2.317; 3.228–230; 16.82–84
Rhone 2.359
Riches 2.218f; 3.246; 12.137f; 14.27, 48, 66f
Rich young ruler 2.213; 5.19; 17.107
Ridicule 8.181
Righteousness 1.44, 101, 187; 8.5, 191; 9.22, 217; 10.164, 183; 11.54, 62; 15.84
  age of 16.11
  and almsgiving 9.164f
  of Christian 1.132; 12.178, 180; 14.172; 15.17f
  crown of 16.83
  and Greeks 8.91
  and Holy Spirit 6.193
  King of 13.69
  and Messiah 5.77

and peace 13.72
primary virtue 12.134
way of 13.74
and wisdom 14.45
word of 15.25
Rights 1.167f
Rings 4.205; 14.64; 17.23
Ritualism 1.43; 11.145
Roads 3.17; 5.79; 6.138f
  to the East 1.40, 73
  of the Sea 1.39; 3.52
  from the South 4.48
Robbery 9.52, 53
Rock 2.140; 5.251; 12.18
Rod 6.55; 17.66f
Roman Catholic Church 2.139;
    3.61, 99; 6.65
Romans, Letter to 8.1–10;
    10.44; 16.165
Rome 1.113; 2.135; 7.89; 8.1;
    14.159; 17.63, 139, 164
  army of 1.300f; 6.229; 8.49
  as 'Babylon' 14.277f; 15.19f;
    16.15; 17.63, 134, 136, 149–
    151, 166–168
  bishop of 2.139; 12.222
  Church of 1.120, 381f; 3.209;
    8.1, 15, 207, 211; 9.186;
    14.160
  citizens of 7.126, 163
  colonies of 7.123; 11.3f, 30,
    69
  doom of 17.110f
  emperor 1.114; 3.100
  empire of 1.25, 40; 3.100,
    287; 7.11; 12.231; 16.3,
    14–20, 36; 17.88, 101
  fear at 12.190, 219
  fever of 11.49

fire of 12.167
immorality of 8.32
and Jews 9.167; 11.59
laws of 6.252; 10.86; 17.219
luxury of 5.212; 8.31f;
    14.221; 17.154–157, 158f
people of 3.194
polytheism of 17.138
prisoners of 7.95
provinces of 3.284; 9.209f
as Restrainer 11.213
riots of 7.147, 169; 8.30f
sayings of 1.119
standard of 2.358; 4.280
Rust 1.239; 14.28

Sabbath 1.126, 128, 286; 2.19–
    23, 290, 374f; 3.31, 39, 63f,
    67–69; 4.70, 289, 291; 5.6,
    30, 181f, 238, 241f; 7.15;
    10.36; 16.93; 17.95
  and circumcision 4.24
  and Gentiles 8.48f
  and Jesus 2.26, 28; 4.187;
    6.44f
  journey on 3.263; 4.156
  law of 1.309f; 2.21–27, 30f,
    208, 372; 3.39; 4.60, 177;
    5.121f; 8.137, 180; 12.264;
    14.69; 17.19
  meals 3.37; 4.187, 213
  offerings 2.24
  rest of 17.188
  tyranny of 8.184
Sabbatic years 10.36f
Sacraments 2.103, 296, 342;
    4.265, 295; 6.262; 9.42, 91–
    93, 110, 168; 12.261; 13.198;
    14.130, 245; 17.34

| 1 Matt, v.1 | 3 Mark | 5 John, v.1 | 7 Acts | 9 Cor |
| 2 Matt, v.2 | 4 Luke | 6 John, v.2 | 8 Rom | 10 Gal, Eph |

Sacrifice
  and almsgiving 9.165
  Christian 1.115, 396; 2.87,
    151; 3.230f; 4.230; 8.58;
    10.25, 78, 117, 125, 161;
    11.16, 44, 46, 65, 86, 126;
    12.43f, 160, 208f; 13.151,
    195–199; 14.196f; 17.11, 31,
    108, 127
  heathen 9.71–76, 80, 91;
    13.197f
  Jewish 1.80, 119, 131, 142;
    2.245; 3.234; 5.112; 10.161;
    13.45, 78, 102, 113
  for proselytes 3.114
  Samaritan 5.157
  substitutionary 1.143
Sacrilege 13.125
Saddle, The 4.285
Sadducees 1.43, 355, 359;
    2.128f, 147, 211, 275–277,
    278; 3.288–291, 349; 4.249–
    251, 275; 5.86, 234, 249;
    6.93, 104, 113f; 7.37; 8.205;
    9.137; 16.84
  heresies of 14.316
Saffron 17.161
Sagan, The 4.273; 7.37
Saints 1.116, 354; 2.52; 7.77f;
    9.25; 10.150; 11.10; 12.45,
    83; 13.194; 15.4, 122, 176f;
    16.70
Salamis 7.97
Salt 1.85, 118–122; 3.234f;
    4.197f
  bond of 9.91
  and Christian life 3.233
  'of the covenant' 3.234
  at Passover 2.340; 3.333

Salvation 1.217; 3.25f, 213,
    226, 248, 256; 3.248; 4.220;
    5.7, 137, 190; 7.24; 8.13,
    19–21, 121, 134f; 9.39, 143;
    10.43; 11.40–44; 12.146;
    13.20f, 48; 14.174; 15.9,
    40, 100f; 17.28, 227
  chain of 1.398–400
  cost of 3.259; 6.161
  gift of 9.12; 10.56, 104;
    11.53
  and Gnostics 11.115f
  helmet of 10.183f
  the purpose of God 8.153;
    12.230; 14.180f
  universal 17.216
  wells of 5.249
  wholeness of 4.148; 7.178;
    10.163; 11.24f; 12.30f;
    14.175f
  word of 15.24
Salvation Army 3.54; 4.52;
    6.124; 9.208
Samaria 1.73; 2.95, 194; 4.31,
    129
  and Christianity 7.4f; 12.62f,
    64f, 88; 15.89
  and Dispersion 14.37
  and Pilate 2.359; 6.240
  Woman of 1.363; 5.5, 15,
    52f, 147–161; 9.132
Samaritans 1.363, 370; 4.5, 6,
    129, 139f, 217; 5.16; 7.4,
    62f, 64f; 14.37
  and Jews 5.6, 149, 157; 6.31
  Pentateuch of 5.159
Samos 7.150
Sanctification 2.202; 3.337;
    8.91

| **11** Phil, Col, Thes | **13** Heb | **15** John, Jude | **16** Rev, v.1 |
| **12** Tim, Tit, Phlm | **14** Jas, Pet | | **17** Rev, v.2 |

and justification **8**.77
Sandals **2**.367; **3**.17, 142; **4**.94,
  285; **5**.98; **6**.139; **10**.183
  symbolism of **4**.205
Sanhedrin **1**.12, 36, 140; **2**.258,
  343; **3**.279, 312; **4**.247f, 275–
  277; **5**.123; **6**.103f, 260;
  7.38; **9**.186
  administrators of **14**.263
  apostles of **7**.177; **13**.30
  composition of **2**.147, 353;
  3.346; **4**.133
  and divorce **3**.239
  local **3**.312
  and orthodoxy **5**.77; **17**.131
  police **3**.346; **7**.70
  procedure of **4**.276; **7**.164
  and Romans **3**.349; **7**.61
  trials in **2**.353f; **3**.348f
Sanity **14**.251
Sapphire **17**.213, 215
Saracens **4**.111
Sard **17**.214
Sardian **16**.151f
Sardis **9**.89f; **12**.184; **16**.28,
  113–115, 126; **17**.214
  Letter to **16**.112–123
Sardonyx **17**.159, 213, 215
Saronic Gulf **9**.1
Saturn **1**.26
Saturnalia **17**.159
Scapegoat, The **13**.100f; **14**.244
Scarlet **17**.160
Sceptics, The **8**.159
Schism **14**.316
Schoenus **9**.2
Scoffers **1**.158
Scorpion **1**.271, 17, 51
  Sign of **17**.215

Scourging **2**.363; **3**.358; **6**.244,
  250; **7**.163; **9**.253f
Scribes **1**.29f, 128, 133f, 294,
  328, 354; **2**.90f, 116, 165,
  227, 280–282; **3**.31, 164,
  279, 293, 299f, 346, 349;
  4.156f, 243, 275
Scribes and Pharisees **1**.6f, 8,
  46f, 132, 286, 333f, 337, 355;
  2.16, 18f, 22f, 27, 30, 32, 35f,
  44, 46, 50, 54, 109f, 113, 116–
  119, 121, 125, 147, 211, 280–
  284, 298, 323; **3**.56, 58, 76,
  79, 165–167, 177; **4**.65, 91,
  100, 161, 187f, 199; **5**.86,
  122, 199; **6**.1f, 4f, 15, 165,
  169; **14**.263; **15**.104
  woes against **2**.288–299
Scripture **12**.198–202; **14**.337;
  17.34
  and Jesus **2**.118; **15**.112
  and Jews **1**.127; **10**.40f;
  13.67f; **16**.26
  and Paul **8**.55; **9**.88f, 223;
  10.27f, **12**.177
Scruples **8**.180, 182, 194; **9**.73
Scythia **17**.159
Scythians **11**.155; **16**.97; **17**.194
Scythopolis **1**.81; **3**.124; **5**.147
Sea **2**.179; **9**.254; **17**.198
Seals **5**.145; **8**.87; **9**.78; **13**.14;
  14.244; **16**.166; **17**.1ff, 18,
  21–23, 66, 99
Sealing **10**.87; **12**.177; **17**.23
Seasons **10**.36
Secret See Mystery
Sectarianism **2**.291; **12**.265
Secularism **4**.81
Security **5**.86f; **6**.59; **14**.228–

| 1 Matt, v.1 | 3 Mark | 5 John, v.1 | 7 Acts | 9 Cor |
| 2 Matt, v.2 | 4 Luke | 6 John, v.2 | 8 Rom | 10 Gal, Eph |

230; **16.**61; **17.**103

Seed **15.**78

Seemism **15.**7

Seleucia **7.**97; **14.**39

Seleucids **14.**39; **16.**87

Self-centredness **1.**202, 219, 396;
3.335; **4.**164; **9.**22; **10.**48;
12.236; **14.**329

-control **1.**96f, 237; **2.**208;
10.52, 138; **11.**67, 75, 85f;
11.45; **12.**80, 144f, 239, 252;
14.302f; **15.**188f

-deception **1.**244; **4.**95; **15.**32–
34

-denial **2.**151, 173, 175, 182;
3.232; **4.**121; **11.**150; **12.**161

-esteem **1.**230; **2.**32, 325;
3.112; **4.**190; **5.**193; **12.**180

-examination **1.**244; 3.175,
261; **9.**249f; **10.**90, 135;
13.1

-pity **13.**178

Selfishness **1.**254, 323; **2.**103,
205, 210, 219, 326; 3.236;
6.114; **7.**125; **9.**121f, 232;
10.46; **11.**15, 23, 38; **12.**184,
259; **14.**118–120, 227, 329;
15.57, 190, 193f

in marriage **2.**205

in prayer **2.**190; **6.**180

in worship **9.**130

Sensationalism **4.**44

Senselessness **8.**38

Sensualism **9.**52

Sephoris **4.**121

Septuagint, The See Index VI

Seraphim **8.**117; **13.**17; **16.**157f

Seraphs **16.**158

Serenity **1.**256; **10.**75; **14.**75,

272

Sermon on the Mount **1.**5, 9,
33, *83–294*, 358, 372; **2.**206;
476; **5.**160; **8.**6; **12.**201;
14.22, 25, 126; **15.**83; **17.**153

Sermon on the Plain **4.**76

Serpent **8.**96; **16.**89f

The Ancient **17.**80, 82, 98

The Crooked **17.**58

Servant of the Lord **1.**310; **4.**38

Service **1.**97, 149, 169, 179, 225,
248f, 308f, 310, 361, 392,
400; **2.**25, 90, 186, 226, 230,
232, 279, 323f; 3.29, 38, 69,
123, 203, 257f, 301; **4.**52,
97, 118, 121f, 128, 132, 210,
264, 267f; **5.**87, 142; **6.**124,
136–140, 190, 217; **7.**78, 111;
8.157, 159, 161, 202f; **9.**114,
163; **10.**99, 124, 149; **11.**103,
187; **12.**52, 148, 173; **13.**61;
14.199, 255f, 293; **16.**25

Seven **1.**170; **5.**103; **7.**87; **8.**107;
13.36; **16.**11, 28f, 172;
17.117

Spirits **16.**31f, 116, 155

Seven, The **7.**19, 52, 64

Seventy, The **4.**133, 135

Shadow and reality **11.**79;
˙**13.**2f, 88

Shamelessness 3.175; **8.**179

Sharon, plain of 3.52

Sheba, Queen of **2.**50; **4.**151;
14.42

Shechem **5.**6, 150

Sheep **2.**184; **6.**56

Sheepfolds **6.**58

Sheol **6.**91; **9.**137; **16.**9, 181;
17.184

Shephalah 17.38
Shepherds 1.281f; 2.184f;
    4.22f, 200; 6.52–57; 14.215f
  false 6.61; 15.194
  Messianic 17.38
Shunem 4.48, 86
Sicarii, the 3.356
Sichem 5.150
Sicily 17.103
Sickness 1.44, 327; 3.49; 14.131
Sick-visiting 1.261; 6.90
Sidon 2.84; 3.177, 180
Signs 2.48f, 128–130; 3.185
Silk 17.160
Siloam 4.173; 5.6, 249; 6.42f
Silver 17.158f
Simony 7.67
Simoon, The 14.47f
Simplicity 1.41f, 243, 399f;
    2.14, 102, 212, 248–250, 325;
    3.8, 16, 38, 144, 247; 4.23,
    137; 8.161f; 9.23f, 130, 240;
    9.82, 114, 115, 134; 14.204,
    301
  of the Gospel 5.137; 11.96
  of the Law 2.117
Sin 1.14, 95, 141, 219–222, 287;
    3.26, 147; 4.44, 245f; 5.42;
    8.54f, 96; 10.29, 95f; 12.282;
    13.21, 45; 14.114, 230–233;
    16.116f; 17.17
  consequences of 6.38f; 7.29;
    8.186; 9.150f; 10.54; 13.77;
    17.9
  and death 8.80
  death of 6.94; 15.77f;
    17.198
  deliberate 1.142; 2.263f, 300;
    6.151; 8.194

  essence of 3.330; 8.28, 95;
    9.22, 181; 10.20; 12.37;
    14.107, 233f
  hardening of 4.153; 10.152f
  of ignorance 13.45
  influence of 2.178–181;
    4.215f; 9.219; 12.207;
    14.333; 17.142, 169f
  law of 8.90f, 110
  mortal 15.117–120
  original 3.187f; 8.55; 14.51–53
  personification of 14.28
  post-baptismal 13.56, 58;
    15.119
  pre-natal 6.37, 49
  of presumption 13.46
  satanic 3.23, 80
  sense of 1.219; 5.156; 6.192f;
    8.29f, 99, 146, 163f; 9.132;
    10.82, 162; 12.19f, 78;
    13.123f; 14.327
  and sickness 3.47–49; 4.62;
    5.183
  slavery of 8.89
  and suffering 1.327; 3.47f;
    4.62, 173; 6.37–39; 9.170,
    172; 11.110; 14.246f, 273
  total depravity 4.204
  types of 3.173, 230, 357;
    8.37; 12.36–40; 13.4, 125;
    15.33
  unforgivable 2.41–45; 3.79–
    81; 4.161f; 17.225
  universal 8.54; 14.82
Sinai, Mount 5.69; 16.94, 155;
    17.200
  covenant of 8.125
Sincerity 1.272, 289; 4.235;
    8.218; 12.34, 204

Sinope 14.145, 160
Sion, Mount 1.68; 2.305; 17.102
Sirius 1.26
Sirocco 17.19f
Six 5.103
Skull, place of 6.251
Slander 1.158, 325; 3.175; 4.148; 8.36; 9.259f, 264; 11.153; 12.116f, 189; 14.111
Slanderer, The 1.226; 3.22; 12.74, 189
Slavery 1.248f, 301f, 377; 2.223; 4.84f, 178, 209f; 8.89; 9.21f, 10.179f; 11.155; 12.39, 121f, 270; 14.208, 210; 17.162f
  and Church 1.377; 12.121–123; 14.210–213
  emancipation 12.271
  and Jews 2.80; 4.205; 14.38
  treatment of 9.40, 52; 12.39; 16.135; 17.99
Sling 6.55
Sloth 5.160
Smyrna 1.115; 14.162f; 16.17, 28, 73–76, 127
  Letter to 16.72–85
Snobbery 1.140; 8.38, 169; 9.118; 11.97; 12.28; 14.63f
Sobriety 12.79f, 247; 14.108, 183, 251f
Socnopaeus 14.263
Sodom and Gomorrah 1.371; 2.12; 9.221; 14.327f; 15.158, 184–186; 16.121; 17.71, 112
Solidarity, spiritual 8.79f, 103; 9.151
Solitude 3.214

'Son of' 1.109
Son of Man 1.312, 380–382; 2.26, 42, 49, 165, 234; 3.220f; 4.70, 222, 235; 5.185f, 192; 6.121f, 128; 7.14; 9.144; 13.23; 16.36, 45
Son of Perdition 11.212
Sons of God 1.109, 226; 3.22, 71; 4.103; 5.61f, 127; 8.133; 11.119; 14.322; 16.153; 17.80f, 89, 205
Sons of Thunder 5.16
Soothsayers 7.66
Sop, The 3.338
Sophists 9.19; 12.124, 207
Sorcery 1.34
Sorrow 1.93, 355; 3.116; 4.27, 87, 106, 124; 6.130, 269; 9.171, 213, 226f; 11.203; 14.174; 16.10; 17.105, 198
Spain 8.3f, 204; 12.10–12, 283; 14.9; 17.92, 158, 161
  Armada of 13.161
  Inquisition 6.190; 9.120
Sparrows 1.389
Sparta 1.333; 2.80; 3.223; 9.1; 12.196; 13.148; 14.195f
  elders of 12.70
Spartans 12.151; 14.261
Speech 4.83; 11.153f; 12.6, 112; 14.55f, 81–83; 17.129f
Sphinx 1.202
Spice 17.161
Spikenard 17.161
Spirit of God See Holy Spirit
Spirits, evil 1.320; 2.50–52, 112, 166, 359; 3.289; 4.250; 5.1; 6.258; 7.144; 8.101–103;

11 Phil, Col, Thes
12 Tim, Tit, Phlm
13 Heb
14 Jas, Pet
15 John, Jude
16 Rev, v.1
17 Rev, v.2

9.75; 10.182; 11.96, 134;
12.92
unclean 3.32; 4.148; 7.46;
17.129f
Spittle 3.181, 190; 6.41f, 45;
9.258
Stable 1.24–25
Stacte 17.161
Stars 1.26; 8.118; 11.96, 134f,
137; 16.153, 155; 17.14
of Bethlehem 1.31
Steadfastness 14.303; 17.97
Sterility 2.199
Stewardship
Christian 9.36; 14.255
eastern 4.168; 5.99; 14.255
Stoics 1.274; 2.313; 3.11, 279;
4.25, 79, 87, 103, 261, 285f;
5.197; 6.23; 7.104, 130, 132;
8.4, 28, 33, 45, 159, 189;
9.140, 235; 10.48, 108, 142;
11.84f; 12.75, 128, 146, ?75,
262, 265; 13.42, 87, 137,
157, 177; 14.27, 60, 75, 299,
341; 15.79; 16.159
Stones, precious 17.159, 212–215
Stoning 6.234; 7.61f
Strife 2.247; 8.35, 169; 9.30,
263; 10.47; 14.97, 225f
final 17.5f
Striking 9.251; 12.83, 237
Stripping 16.143
Stumbling 1.148; 2.180; 9.74,
94; 11.19
Sublime Porte 2.143
Submission 1.32, 209; 5.165;
10.51; 14.219
Suffering 1.111–116; 9.171, 214;
11.14, 17, 126; 13.165–171;

14.229f, 246f, 258–260;
16.62; 17.113
law of 14.273f
Suicide 6.17; 12.146
Sun 1.119; 12.100; 16.14
Sunday 3.64; 4.149, 291; 7.27;
8.184
Sunday Schools 12.73
Superstition 5.160f; 8.185;
9.47
Swiss Confession 12.55
Sychar 5.6, 14, 147, 167
Symbolism 1.25
Sympathy 1.104; 4.87; 13.192;
14.75f, 226f
Synagogues 1.80, 121, 188,
296; 2.290, 346; 3.30–32, 67,
300, 312; 4.45f, 48, 262;
8.60; 9.162; 12.70, 85;
14.129, 223, 263; 16.26;
17.119
Christian 14.21, 26
The Great 2.281f
and the Law 1.134; 3.295
prayers of 1.53f, 192f; 6.190f;
17.200
ruler of 1.80, 341–343; 2.92;
3.30f, 126f; 4.111
seats of honour 3.67; 4.156
teaching of 3.323; 4.262;
14.29f
Syria 1.72, 81, 363; 2.282, 359;
3.12, 124, 143; 4.20; 6.238;
7.73, 119; 9.5; 14.38
Syrians 1.73; 2.134; 4.5, 248;
17.103
Syro-Phoenician 1.363; 5.175;
6.63f
Syrtis Sands 7.183

Tabernacle   2.23, 161; 3.210;
    5.69; 13.94–97; 16.44; 17.10,
    121, 202
  brazen altar   13.95
  court   13.95
  golden lampstand   13.96
  heavenly   13.103
  holy place of   13.96
  laver   2.244; 13.95
  mercy seat   13.96
  sacrifices   13.113
  shewbread   13.96
  veil of   13.96
Tabernacles, feast of   3.323;
    4.9; 5.2, 4, 15, 177, 230, 247f;
    6.10f, 115–117; 7.21; 10.36
Tabor, Mount   2.157; 3.210
Talents   2.194, 321–324; 3.203;
    7.45; 13.11
Tallies   12.82
Tanners   2.197
Tarbert   9.1
Tares   2.72f
Tarichaea   1.77; 3.27, 159
Tarshish, stone of   17.214
Tarsus   7.76, 136, 159; 11.59
Tartarus   3.175; 14.321
Tavium   14.144
Taxation
  Palestinian   2.168, 272; 3.285;
    4.20, 64, 234, 247
  Roman   1.157, 329f; 8.175
  Temple   2.168, 244; 3.273;
    4.172, 241; 5.109; 14.172,
    241
Tax-collectors   1.5, 329f; 2.187,
    189; 3.53; 4.64, 224
Teachableness   14.56–58
Teaching   1.284; 2.55; 3.112f,

    244; 4.81; 9.25f, 84; 10.146;
    11.53; 12.31f, 82f, 96
  duty of   9.179; 12.204–206,
    207f; 13.49
  in Early Church   7.98; 9.115,
    208; 10.147f; 14.26, 79f;
    16.12
  false   8.218; 12.53, 92, 126–
    128, 173f, 240–242; 14.80,
    175, 318f; 15.5–7, 31f
  gift of   8.161; 9.130
  Jewish   See Rabbis
  teachers   12.144f, 180f, 252–
    254; 13.146f; 14.91–93
Telepathy   5.175
Tell Hum   1.74
Temper   1.139; 4.106; 9.122;
    10.48, 155; 11.153
Temple   celestial   1.52; 17.35
Temple, of Jerusalem   1.28, 32,
    68f, 80, 101, 189; 2.23, 244,
    304f, 353; 3.30, 143, 210, 258,
    272f, 307; 4.46, 223, 300;
    5.6; 6.11, 70; 7.32, 46;
    17.68, 213
  altar of incense   17.40, 211
  Beautiful Gate   2.244; 3.302;
    5.6
  captain of   4.273; 7.37
  courts of   1.143; 2.243f, 247,
    336f; 3.272f, 302; 4.10, 254;
    5.113, 243; 6.10, 120, 226;
    7.36; 10.111; 14.234f; 17.34f,
    67
  destruction of   1.383; 2.170,
    267, 273; 3.321
  of Ezra and Nehemiah   5.150
  gifts of   1.171; 3.302; 4.254
  Golden Vine   4.258; 6.172f

11 Phil, Col, Thes   13 Heb   15 John, Jude   16 Rev, v.1
12 Tim, Tit, Phlm   14 Jas, Pet   17 Rev, v.2

Hall of Hewn Stone 2.353;
　3.349; 4.276
Holy of holies 2.243, 371;
　3.63, 365; 4.288; 13.62, 96;
　16.94; 17.212, 221
Holy Place 2.23, 243; 11.10
inspectors of 5.110
Mount of 1.368
police 2.335, 351; 5.245;
　6.222
Royal Cloister 3.278
Royal Porch 1.68; 2.305;
　3.308; 4.44
profanation of 2.241; 3.267
sacrifices 1.142f; 2.26, 168;
　3.332f; 4.10, 22f, 242; 5.81
shewbread 2.23, 244; 3.63
of Solomon 5.69; 16.45;
　17.10, 203, 212
Solomon's Porch 1.68; 2.305;
　3.278; 4.44; 5.6
treasury 2.168, 245; 6.10, 70,
　239
Trumpets, The 3.302; 4.254;
　6.8
Water Gate 5.249
veil of 2.371; 3.365; 4.288
Temples, pagan 15.124
Temptation 1.199, 224–232,
　380; 2.80, 180; 3.130, 189;
　4.105f, 125, 144, 215, 270;
　8.221; 9.76, 90; 10.183;
　11.42, 71; 12.251; 14.42–44,
　50f; 15.54f, 76, 106; 16.119
avoidance of 9.59, 257
laws of 6.111
types of 9.89f
Tempter, The 1.64, 66; 2.148;
　3.199; 17.82

Ten 16.79
Ten Commandments 1.127, 130f,
　221; 2.115, 214, 281, 285;
　3.31, 163; 4.59f; 5.69; 8.52;
　9.190; 12.38, 187; 13.20;
　14.21, 60
Ten Tribes (lost) 5.149; 14.37;
　16.3
Tension 8.199f
Tent of witness 17.121
Testimony See Witness, Christian
Thanklessness 12.187
Thanksgiving 4.118; 10.167;
　11.77f, 132; 12.58
Theft 3.173; 8.39, 176; 9.52
Theocracy 2.272; 10.108
Theology 1.291, 342; 3.29;
　5.56f; 9.130, 161; 10.45;
　11.108f; 12.127; 14.140;
　15.88; 17.219
Theosophy 11.99
Thermai 11.180
Thessalonians, Letters to 11.179–
　183
Thessalonica 2.83; 4.182; 7.119,
　122, 127, 128; 11.73; 12.205
Thessaly 4.31
Thirst 1.99, 188
spiritual 5.153; 17.22
Thomist Church 6.277
Thought 1.136; 3.124; 4.150;
　11.210; 14.77
Thousand 17.192
Thrace 5.178
Thracians 16.97
Three 17.117
Three Taverns 7.190
Thrones 8.117; 16.148
Thyatira 16.28, 66, 101f

Letter to **16**.100–111
Thyine **17**.160
Tiber **2**.359; **17**.91
Tiberias **1**.77, 308, 317; **2**.105; **3**.146
Sea of **4**.56
Time **3**.368; **4**.171, 266; **6**.83; **8**.177; **9**.206; **14**.342; **17**.55, 198
Timothy, Letters to **12**.1–13
Tirabatha **2**.359
Titans **14**.321; **17**.101
Tithes **1**.286; **2**.293f; **4**.155, 224; **9**.80; **11**.10; **13**.75f
Tolerance **1**.338; **2**.41; **3**.110f, 226; **4**.130; **5**.252; **8**.170; **10**.89f; **12**.104, 259
Tombs **1**.320; **2**.296; **3**.324, 368; **4**.291; **6**.99, 266
Tongue, The **14**.82–88
Tongues, gift of **7**.21f, 66; **9**.96, 111f, 117, 127–130, 131; **15**.90
Topaz **17**.214f
Topheth **1**.141; **3**.231
Touchiness **12**.181
Trachonitis **2**.95; **3**.53, 115; **4**.3, 31
Tradition **1**.231; **3**.316; **6**.25; **9**.135, 142; **11**.81f; **15**.178
of the elders **2**.114; **3**.163–167
oral **15**.199
Tralles **16**.28
Transfiguration, Mount of **2**.157, 162f, 348; **4**.123; **5**.89; **6**.127; **11**.166; **14**.269, 310–312; **17**.54, 71
Transgression **8**.69
Travel **1**.44, 320; **4**.29, 145;

5.153, 203; **9**.167; **12**.231
Tray, The **7**.51; **12**.85
Treachery **12**.190
Treasure **1**.238–243
Tree, symbolism of **4**.179
Trent, Council of **14**.5f, 9
Trepanning **3**.33f
Trespasses **10**.95f
Tribulation **4**.259; **8**.166; **9**.213f; **16**.39f
The Great **17**.17f, 21, 23, 29
Tribunal, The **8**.188
Tribute-money **2**.272–274; **3**.284f; **4**.247–249; **8**.175
Trimitaria **16**.138
Trinity The **1**.199f; **3**.72; **6**.284; **7**.12, 18; **15**.110; **16**.30f
Tripoli **4**.282
Triumph, The (Roman) **9**.39, 183, 198; **11**.143; **16**.122; **17**.178
Troas **7**.19, 119, 122, 138; **16**.28
Trouble **8**.73; **9**.212; **12**.213
Trouble-makers **1**.110
Trumpets **17**.42, 125
Trust **1**.91, 218, 258; **5**.217; **6**.152; **8**.5, 21; **11**.56; **12**.138, 150–152; **13**.33f; **17**.169
of children **2**.176; **3**.242; **4**.226
Truth **1**.20–21, 49, 79, 82f, 158, 265–267, 337; **2**.16, 63, 69, 291; **3**.87, 99, 101f, 190, 315; **5**.46, 68, 213; **6**.29; **7**.45; **9**.123, 132; **10**.155, 164; **11**.82, 154; **12**.89; **14**.133; **15**.29f; **16**.23

belt of 10.183
criteria of 15.71
fundamental 11.52f
recognition of 2.43f; 4.99,
    244; 5.196
touchstone of 2.42; 6.21
triumph of 1.385; 2.377;
    9.146f; 12.168; 15.95
vastness of 3.226; 4.130, 179;
    5.72, 160
word of 10.87; 14.54; 15.25
Tubal 17.194
Tunic 1.167; 3.141f; 4.285;
    16.138
Turkey 2.143
Twelve, The 1.84, 86, 332, 359–
    362; 2.133; 3.8, 43, 144,
    158, 222, 269, 328f; 4.4, 75,
    115, 117, 119, 127, 133; 5.17,
    89; 10.7, 145; 14.17; 15.169f,
    171; 17.170
Twelve Tribes 14.21, 31, 40f,
    137; 17.24f, 210
Twins, sign of 17.214
Two ages, The 1.372f; 4.257;
    6.197; 7.25; 8.25, 118;
    9.196; 11.203; 12.92, 182;
    13.12, 57; 14.343; 15.60,
    80; 16.3, 22, 132
Two worlds, The 5.8; 13.87
Tyndale Version 2.294
Types 14.244
Tyre 3.176, 180; 7.138; 17.142,
    154, 158, 164, 166f
  King of 16.151
  and Sidon 2.12, 120f, 125,
    128; 3.70, 176; 5.2, 26;
    7.96
Tyrians 2.121

Tyropoeon Valley 3.308

Uganda, Church of 9.249f
Unbelief 6.131–133
Uncertainty 1.353; 3.116;
    13.128
Unchastity 1.151, 379; 3.238;
    4.211
Uncial scripts 6.290
Uncircumcized 11.55, 139
Uncleanness 1.303f; 2.110–117,
    295f; 3.129, 165f; 4.24f,
    156; 5.99; 6.106; 8.90;
    9.265f; 11.150f
United Church of South India
    3.62; 13.144
Universalism 1.17; 4.179;
    11.123f
Unleavened Bread, Feast of
    2.339; 3.323; 4.262
Urim and Thummim 13.99
Uselessness 1.48, 121; 2.183,
    254, 263, 322f; 3.272; 4.175,
    198; 6.174; 8.55; 12.245f;
    15.195

Valhalla 3.291
Valley of Hinnom 1.141
Veil, spiritual 9.192f
Vellum 11.142
Vendetta 1.164
Vengeance 1.163; 8.170; 17.41,
    148, 153
Venus 7.100
Vesta 14.147
Vesuvius 3.320; 17.45
Vice 3.173, 175; 9.56
Viciousness 8.35
Vienne 2.359

Vigilance 1.65; 9.89f; 14.272
Villainy 8.34
Vineyard 4.245; 6.173f
    of God 2.261f
Violence 2.351; 12.122, 237;
    17.97
Virgin, sign of 17.215
Virginity 9.66f; 17.106
    Jewish 1.19; 2.196; 4.12
Virgin's fountain 6.43
Virtue 1.96, 278; 8.164; 9.40;
    11.157; 12.39, 61f; 13.46;
    14.300–305
    healing 1.308
Visions 1.243–247; 11.145f
Votive shields 6.239f
Vows 2.208; 7.166
Vulgate, the 6.291; 15.111

Wady Hamam 2.72
Wages 1.99; 2.245
Wailing 1.344; 3.134; 6.96f
    women 4.111
Wallet 3.142f
Wantonness 10.47, 153
Warfare, Christian 1.393;
    10.181–184; 12.159–160
Washings 2.114, 362; 3.13f
Watchers, The 14.322f; 16.175
Watchfulness 2.317; 4.260f;
    16.118f, 120
Water 1.188, 322; 2.340; 3.331;
    5.98, 129, 153f, 178, 249;
    17.125, 221
    living 5.152, 250; 17.220
Water-carrier 17.215
Way of the Sea 1.73, 330
Way of the South 1.39
Weak, The 2.80

Weakness 1.365
Wealth 1.239f, 249, 252; 3.244;
    4.165, 228f; 12.132, 137;
    13.62; 14.115f
Weddings, Jewish 1.19, 335;
    2.266, 319; 3.59; 4.66; 5.96f,
    143f; 9.246
Wells 4.188
Westminster Confession 1.53;
    5.56
Wheat 2.73; 9.80
Whisperers 8.36
White 16.98
    day 16.97
    horses 5.178; 17.167, 179
    ones 16.31
    robes 16.121–123; 17.26, 29f,
    121
    stone 16.95–97
    throne 17.194
Wickedness 3.174f
Widows 9.62; 12.3, 105f, 109–
    115
    Jewish 1.19; 4.12, 254; 12.105
Wilderness 1.63; 3.16, 23;
    4.43; 17.143
Wind 17.19f
Wine 1.391; 2.340; 3.333;
    5.97; 10.49; 12.79f; 17.6,
    162
    -presses 2.261f; 17.116
    -skins 1.338; 3.61
Wisdom 1.273; 2.10; 5.33;
    7.56f; 9.109; 10.82f; 11.108f,
    129; 14.93–97, 295
    gift of 14.45
    and Greeks 9.19; 15.79
    O.T. 11.117
    personified 1.52; 5.31

11 Phil, Col, Thes   13 Heb   15 John, Jude   16 Rev, v.1
12 Tim, Tit, Phlm   14 Jas, Pet   17 Rev, v.2

Wisdom literature   **5**.31–34;
    14.25
Wise Men   **1**.9, 25–27, 30, 31–33;
    3.64
Witchcraft   **10**.47
Witness, Christian   **1**.391f;
    4.109, 251; **6**.49, 188, 235;
    7.12f; **9**.210f; **10**.14; **11**.26,
    167f; **16**.92; **17**.80, 176, 193
  law of   **1**.367; **2**.353; **12**.116;
    15.111f, 180; **16**.140; **17**.101,
    111f
  Tent of   **17**.121
Witnesses, The Two   **17**.66, 70f
Women   **1**.16f, 151, 153; **2**.80,
    197, 283, 329, 366; **3**.126,
    238f; **4**.4, 95, 110, 211; **5**.6,
    151, 162; **6**.89; **9**.98, 136;
    10.168f; **11**.161; **12**.66f;
    14.148, 218, 220–222
  and Church   **8**.208, 211f;
    9.96–100, 136; **10**.173; **11**.73;
    12.66–69, 86f; **13**.9; **14**.217–
    222
  emancipation of   **12**.192
  equality of   **14**.223
  and Greeks   **2**.80; **4**.4; **7**.133;
    9.136; **11**.161; **12**.67, 87, 250
  hair of   **4**.95; **6**.110; **14**.322f
  in Rome   **12**.67, 77f; **14**.218f
Wonder   **4**.226; **5**.71f; **9**.11
Wool   **9**.2; **11**.92
Word, The   **5**.25–40, 75; **8**.112f;
    10.184; **14**.191; **17**.181f
Word of God, The   **1**.215; **2**.59f,
    92; **4**.99, 134; **5**.28–30;
    12.167, 173; **13**.39f; **14**.57;
    15.24, 79
Words   **1**.391; **2**.46f; **12**.126,

    170f; **13**.38; **15**.24
Work   **1**.106f, 111, 118, 119, 184,
    218, 278–280; **2**.31f, 172, 225,
    263, 323; **4**.167, 237; **8**.214f;
    9.215; **10**.158, 181; **11**.164f,
    186, 200–202, 217f; **14**.196,
    213f; **16**.62, 160
  and Greeks   **9**.79, 249
  and Jews   **1**.128f, 310; **2**.22,
    223, 282; **3**.63, 293; **4**.60, 69f,
    156, 177; **6**.160f; **8**.64
Works   **1**.187, 191, 235; **5**.213f;
    8.102, 180; **10**.105; **12**.23;
    14.316; **15**.37; **17**.114
World, The   **1**.22, 236, 242, 391;
    2.154; **5**.42; **6**.167, 181, 214;
    7.109; **8**.157; **9**.44, 196;
    10.182; **13**.137; **14**.86f, 102f;
    15.16, 56f, 95; **17**.82
World to come   **1**.134; **3**.250;
    4.253; **13**.56f
Worldliness   **3**.247; **14**.103
Worms   **1**.141
Wormwood   **17**.44
Worry   **1**.254–261; **4**.165; **8**.200;
    11.77
Worship   **2**.66, 117, 271; **3**.103f;
    4.28, 180; **5**.112f; **7**.30f;
    8.126; **9**.95f, 130, 132; **11**.38,
    56; **13**.61, 102, 120f; **16**.160;
    17.109f, 222
  in Early Church   **7**.149;
    9.134f; **11**.159; **14**.127
  false   **5**.159–161; **12**.241
  Jewish   **2**.117, 295f; **3**.275,
    293
  and women   **9**.95–100
  true   **5**.158f; **8**.155–157; **14**.61f
Writing, ancient   **1**.279; **4**.115;

| **1** Matt, v.1 | **3** Mark | **5** John, v.1 | **7** Acts | **9** Cor |
| **2** Matt, v.2 | **4** Luke | **6** John, v.2 | **8** Rom | **10** Gal, Eph |

7.35f, 86; 8.ixf, 46, 165;
9.33; 11.142; 14.137; 15.147
pseudonymous 14.288; 15.172

Yemen 17.162
Yoke 2.17

Zanzibar 17.161
Zeal 8.165; 11.60; 14.91

Zealots, the 1.359; 3.74; 4.75;
6.59, 248; 8.173; 14.229;
17.68
Zebulun, tribe of 1.73
Zion, Mount 3.272; 10.143
Zodiac 16.158; 17.75, 214f
Zoroastrianism 4.263; 5.47;
9.196; 15.55; 17.59,
130

INDEX OF PERSONAL NAMES

Aaron 1.12; 2.276; 4.40; 12.194

Abbot, E. A. 3.287

Abbott, T. K. 11.155

Abednego 1.117

Abel 2.298; 8.213; 15.189

Abgar 1.81

Abiathar 16.133

Abijah 16.121

Abishai 1.225; 3.22

Abraham 1.12, 47, 55, 62, 224;
3.62, 87; 4.40, 54, 185; 5.14,
90; 6.24–26, 34–36; 7.55;
8.6, 12, 47, 62–71, 101, 116,
120; 9.221; 10.6, 24, 27f, 33,
41; 11.38f, 55, 57f, 138;
13.62, 142–145, 191; 14.29,
35, 42, 200, 327; 16.9, 25,
38, 52, 98, 121, 134; 17.11,
26, 151, 188, 200, 205f, 226
covenant of 8.125; 10.28;
17.205f
descendants of 9.252; 10.28;
14.41
faith of 13.144, 152; 14.78
friend of God 6.178
and Gentiles 8.41
and Gerizim 5.157
and Kingdom of God 1.210
legends of 13.142–144
and Melchizedek 13.69f
and Messiah 6.34f
promises to 10.41f; 13.146f
and rabbis 2.140
seed of 15.78
sons of 1.60; 4.33; 8.65f,.
120; 10.6

Abrahams, I. 2.246f

Abram See Abraham

Achaicus 9.6, 8, 166

Achan 1.239; 6.48; 8.79;
14.115

Acher 9.256

Achilles 3.335; 4.246; 7.39;
12.26; 13.110

Acilius Glabrio 8.210

Acland, Lady 7.18

Acton, Lord 3.286

Adam 4.40; 6.251; 8.79–81,
95f, 103, 110; 9.150f, 157;
16.69; 17.199
covenant of 16.161
and Eve 2.200; 9.246; 14.52;
17.17, 98
legends of 13.131; 14.50f,
53; 16.38
Life of Adam and Eve See
Index VI
rib of 9.98

Adonai 6.210f

Adonis 1.25

Adrian 12.124

Aelian 9.2

Aeneas 7.77; 12.61

Aesculapius 1.289; 9.110;
12.18; 14.89, 95

Aeschines 1.78; 12.106; 15.36

Aeschylus 8.202; 9.150; 10.82;
11.203; 13.48, 110; 14.143,
298; 16.113

Afranius Burrus 17.91

F

Agabus 7.19

Agamemnon 10.148

Agate, J. 1.348; 10.158; 11.210; 14.350

Agatharchides 2.29

Agesilaus 12.196

Aglaitidas 13.176

Agrippa 3.312; 7.4, 173–176, 178; 9.106; 14.40

Agrippina 8.32; 17.90–92

Ahab, King 12.102; 16.105

Ahasuerus 17.23

Ahaz 1.141; 3.231

Ahaziah 17.132

Ahijah 2.240; 3.339

Ahriman 3.23; 5.47; 9.196; 17.59, 130

Ahura-Mainyu 15.55

Ahura-Mazda 15.55

Aidan 8.16

Akiba, rabbi 1.152; 2.198; 3.239, 293; 4.212; 9.256; 10.169

Albert, King 4.161

Albinus 14.12

Alcibiades 5.140; 9.132; 12.205; 13.142; 14.114, 120; 15.85

Alcimus See Eliakim

Alexander, the apostate 12.53

Alexander, coppersmith 12.219

Alexander the Great 1.39, 98, 154f; 2.84; 3.124, 202; 7.122; 8.165f; 11.137, 179f, 186; 12.26; 14.39; 16.87, 115; 17.88

Alexander, of Herod 1.29, 36; 3.149

Alexander Philalethes 16.138

Alexander, rabbi 1.327; 3.187

Alexander Severus 1.274

Alexander, of Simon 2.366; 3.361; 4.283; 8.216

Alexandra 1.29, 36

Alexandrai, rabbi 14.131

Alford, Dean 11.175

Aliturus 6.183; 14.149

Allen, W. C. 2.40

Allenby, E. 1.39

Allshorn, F. 1.83, 124; 2.25; 4.53; 10.40; 12.103

Alypius 8.177f

Ambrose 4.209; 6.290; 11.31f; 12.35, 205f

Ami, rabbi 1.327

Amnon 12.79

Amos 1.193; 13.13

Amplias 8.9

Ampliatus 8.212

Amram 13.155

Anacreon 1.256

Ananias, high priest 7.164

Ananias, prophet 7.72, 75, 77, 161

Ananias and Saphira 12.44, 54, 82

Ananus 6.233; 14.12

Anaximenes 3.359

Andreas 17.225, 227

Andrew, apostle 1.77; 3.54; 5.5, 21, 23, 88, 91, 202, 204f; 6.120; 8.221; 14.162; 15.175

Andrew, Father 1.208

Andrews, C. F. 6.81

Andromache 12.26

Andronicus 8.212; 10.145; 14.17

Andronicus Rhodius 14.58

Anilaeus 14.38

Anna 4.4, 27f; 16.105

Annas 3.274; 4.3, 32; 6.225
  bazaars of 2.246; 6.226
  booths of 4.242
Anthony, saint 1.149
Antisthenes 8.199; 9.37
Antiochus Epiphanes 2.28, 241,
  282, 306; 3.172, 267, 310;
  6.69; 8.137; 13.30, 166f,
  183; 14.202; 15.62f; 16.137;
  17.26, 60f, 62, 69, 79
Antiochus the Great 11.93; 14.40
Antiochus of Sardis 16.115
Antipas 16.92
Antipater 1.29, 36; 3.149
Antiphanes 12.35
Antistius Vetus 14.219
Antoinette, Marie 1.42
Anton, P. 12.2
Antoninus 3.85; 6.37
Antonia 12.200
Antony 7.168; 11.3; 12.78
Apelles 8.213
Aphrodite 1.154; 7.134; 9.3,
  52; 10.162; 12.38, 67; 16.75;
  17.144
Apicius 17.156
Apion 14.202
Apollo 1.289; 7.89; 10.34;
  15.124; 16.75, 89
Apollonius 2.80, 16.75
Apollos 7.138f; 8.209; 9.14f,
  36, 38f, 165; 11.103; 12.68,
  266; 13.9; 16.60
Apphia 12.277f
Apuleius 5.73, 127
Aquila and Priscilla 7.136, 139;
  8.7–9, 208–211; 9.5, 167f;
  11.172; 12.68, 221f; 13.9;
  16.60

Aquinas 2.119; 8.35; 9.174;
  12.2, 80
Archelaus 1.39; 2.95; 3.150,
  284; 4.31, 35, 237; 6.237;
  7.93; 14.38
Archelaus of Macedonia 9.260
Archippus 11.174; 12.159, 273,
  277f; 16.139
Aristarchus 7.181, 192; 9.229;
  11.169
Aristeas 1.134
Aristides 6.185f; 13.142, 192;
  15.85; 16.73f; 17.155
Aristion 5.23; 14.162f
Aristippus 14.84
Aristobulus 1.29, 36, 74; 3.149f;
  4.35f; 5.123; 7.93; 8.213
  household of 8.9
Aristophanes 13.191; 16.88;
  17.130
Aristotle 1.96, 302, 375; 2.246;
  3.246; 8.ix, 28, 36, 37, 45;
  9.40, 79, 109; 10.52, 82, 113,
  137, 179; 11.34, 158, 179;
  12.35, 39, 45, 61, 80, 83, 104,
  107, 186, 235, 236, 238, 240,
  259, 271; 13.174; 14.40, 58,
  84, 95, 186, 211, 300, 302;
  17.211
Armitage, A.H.N.G. 5.22, 100
Arnobius 8.172
Arnold, M. 1.216; 3.132, 235,
  251; 5.212; 9.123f, 198;
  11.79; 13.120; 14.96, 128;
  17.198
Artemas 12.265
Artemis 1.196; 7.140f, 146;
  12.89; 16.89
  Temple of 16.59

Artemon 8.ix
Arthur, King 2.372; 10.125
Asclepios 16.75, 91
  A. Soter 16.89
Asher, *Testament of* See Index VI
Ashmedai 6.31
Asidaeus 14.38
Asquith, C. 13.122
Asquith, M. 3.140, 144
Assael 3.34
Astor J. J. 1.348
Athanasius 13.5; 14.5; 16.161
Athenagoras 8.172; 13.12; 14.280
Athene 10.174; 16.89, 91
Attalus II 16.125
Attalus III 14.145; 16.87
Augustine 1.133, 228f; 2.140; 3.161, 294; 4.63, 193; 5.13, 64, 86, 138, 155; 5.14; 6.81, 290f; 8.96, 168, 177f, 190; 9.18, 39, 192; 12.44, 263; 13.8; 14.4, 207, 279, 323; 15.6, 18, 41, 93; 16.119, 161; 17.37, 130, 190f
Augustus, emperor 1.27, 29; 3.71, 229; 4.31, 85, 237; 5.98; 6.238; 7.123; 9.249; 10.171, 180; 11.21, 137; 12.78; 13.177; 16.17f, 99; 17.89, 139, 146, 161
Aulus Fulvius 13.177
Aulus Plautius 12.223
Aurelius Archelaus 9.185
Aurora 1.271
Avery, M. 1.318; 5.209
Azai, rabbi ben 9.69, 256
Azariah 1.365
Azazel 14.322f

Bacchus 10.9
Bacon 6.242; 13.135
Bagehot, W. 12.204
Bailey, P. J. 12.171
Bain 1.348
Balaam 3.22; 14.332; 15.159, 164, 190; 16.66f, 92; 17.81
Balak 14.333
Baldwin, S. 1.324; 3.223; 13.200
Ball, R. 15.162
Balthasar 1.31; 3.65
Barabbas 3.173, 356–358
  Jesus B. 2.361; 6.248f
Barachios 2.298
Barak 4.47; 13.163; 17.132
Barclay, F. 4.153
Bar-Jesus See Elymas
Barnabas 1.109; 3.3, 361; 7.19, 75f, 90, 98f, 117f; 10.139, 145; 12.44
  apostle 14.17
  Letter of See Index VI
  and Hebrews Epistle 13.8f
  and Paul 7.96–101, 117, 118; 8.13; 10.19; 11.170; 12.21, 217, 232; 17.110
Barrett, C. K. 6.166
Barrie, J. M. 1.41, 149, 229; 2.250; 4.39, 168, 265; 8.64; 9.121, 171; 11.72; 12.210; 13.122, 138; 14.113, 273
Bartholemew 5.94f
Bartimaeus 3.260
Barton, B. 3.12f, 257; 4.267
Baruch
  Apocalypse of See Index VI
  Book of See Index VI
Basil 9.264, 265; 10.48, 135, 153
Basilides 12.8

Bathsheba 1.17; 3.85
Baxter, R. 15.161
Beare, F. W. 14.138, 142
Beatus 16.31
Becker 10.175
Beckwith 17.142
Bede 4.127
Beethoven 1.213; 7.189; 8.73, 166; 10.126; 13.117
Belden, A. D. 3.41
Belial 11.212; 17.59
Beliar See Belial
Belloc, H. 1.353
Benaiah 16.133
Bengel, J. 2.122f; 3.80, 174; 4.193; 6.126, 219; 8.59; 10.177; 11.13, 67, 163; 13.57; 14.220, 252, 300
Benjamin, *Testament of* See Index VI
Bennett, A. 4.137; 10.158
Bernanos, G. 5.233
Bernard, saint 16.147
Bernard, J. H. 5.74; 6.120; 10.135
Bernice 7.93, 174
Berokah of Chuza, rabbi 2.14
Beza 9.13; 12.173
Bias 14.55
Bigg, C. 14.143, 151, 176, 224, 230, 247, 300, 334, 348
Bilney, T. 4.91; 11.112; 13.56; 14.128
Binyon, L. 6.148
Birkett, N. 1.100; 3.153
Bishop, E. F. F. 1.121
Bithia 13.156
Black, J. 8.169
Blackie, J. S. 1.41

Blake, W. 2.373
Blastus 7.97
Boadicea, queen 17.5
Boanerges 5.16, 18
Boaz 6.146
Booth, W. 3.362; 4.68, 116; 9.208
Boreham F. W. 1.236; 4.8, 235; 8.124f; 10.89; 12.46
Borrow, G. H. 3.122
Boswell, J. 1.190; 3.152; 9.83, 160; 10.90
Botherich 12.205
Bottomley 15.161
Bradley, A. C. 1.244
Bridges, R. 1.223
Britannicus 17.91
Brooke A. E. 15.43, 47, 65, 77, 83, 97, 103, 115
Brooke, R. 1.115; 4.259f; 8.20
Brooks, C. 8.188
Brown, E. F. 11.103; 12.38, 40, 44, 55, 63, 80, 120, 129, 139, 193, 205, 248, 255
Brown, J. 1.285; 6.20; 7.18; 15.22
Brown, R. 1.227
Brown, R. McAfee 6.102
Brown, T. E. 3.186
Browne, T. 1.275; 14.92
Browning, E. B. 1.400; 3.186; 4.274; 5.142
Browning, R. 1.117, 214; 4.124; 5.155, 191; 6.32, 198f; 7.104; 8.20; 9.200, 202; 13.89, 178; 14.43, 247
Bruce, A. B. 3.5f; 4.195; 6.162; 9.179; 12.126; 13.70
Brugman 1.306

Brunner, E. **15**.143
Brutus **11**.3; **13**.125
Bryant, A. **1**.251
Buchan A. **3**.113; **10**.178
Buchan, J. **11**.197
Buchanan **10**.89
Bultmann, R. **2**.234; **9**.14, 22
Bunyan, J. **1**.51, 106, 395, 396,
      397; **3**.20, 77, 184, 314; **7**.12,
      24; **9**.173; **12**.132, 134;
      13.128, 129, 151; **14**.90, 128;
      15.163, 182
Burke, E. **1**.279
Burke, R. **1**.279
Burkitt, F. C. **2**.246; **11**.52
Burns, J. **3**.123, 277
Burns, R. **1**.227, 240; **2**.119;
      3.25, 139; **4**.66, 185; **8**.146,
      164, 194; **9**.68, 174; **10**.8,
      152; **13**.137; **14**.52; **16**.117
Burroughs, E. **2**.52
Burrus **17**.92
Burton **8**.2
Bushnell, H. **9**.132f
Butler, bishop **4**.71

Cadoux, C. J. **3**.89
Caedmon **5**.46; **9**.12
Caesar **8**.172; **12**.78; **16**.81
   godhead of **2**.134; **3**.192;
      9.107, 222
   image of **3**.287
Caiaphas, J. **2**.326, 373f; **4**.3,
      32; **6**.104f, 225
   house of **2**.373
Cain **13**.131–133; **15**.17, 84,
      159, 164, 189f
   daughters of **14**.323
Cairns, J. **3**.156; **4**.190; **6**.162;

      8.164
Caleb **9**.88; **13**.36; **14**.35; **16**.25
Caligula, emperor **2**.97; **3**.310;
      8.31; **14**.40, 221; **15**.63;
      16.18; **17**.89, 90, 93, 95, 139,
      146, 155f, 159
Callimachus **12**.243; **14**.346
Callistus **1**.377; **14**.211
Calvin, J. **9**.257; **10**.61; **12**.173;
      13.8; **14**.259, 277, 285, 348
Cambyses **1**.264
Cameron, R. **1**.213; '**4**.14
Campbell, T. **3**.140
Candace, queen **7**.68
Capitolinus **13**.87
Carabas **6**.247
Carey, W. **9**.121
Carleton, W. **5**.28
Carlyle, T. **1**.251, 284; **3**.16, 28;
      4.44, 63, 113f; **6**.112; **8**.97,
      164; **9**.44, 78, 235; **11**.194;
      12.196
   father of **6**.62; **8**.161
Carr **1**.37
Carrington, P. **16**.2
Carswell, C. **1**.189
Caspar **1**.31; **3**.64
Cassander **11**.180
Cassandra **4**.246
Cassian **5**.18
Cassiodorus **15**.18
Cassius **11**.3
Castor & Pollux **7**.189
Catullus **9**.155; **11**.203; **13**.136;
      14.187
Catiline **13**.177
Cato **1**.302; **2**.80; **10**.179;
      12.77; **14**.218, 220, 222
Cavour **3**.218; **13**.147

1 Matt, v.1	3 Mark	5 John, v.1	7 Acts	9 Cor
2 Matt, v.2	4 Luke	6 John, v.2	8 Rom	10 Gal, Eph

Cebes 1.278

Celsus 1.34, 289; 2.350; 5.73;
9.19, 21, 141; 10.122; 14.204
Against Celsus See Index VI

Cephas See Peter, apostle

Cerinthus 5.12, 18, 21; 15.7f,
108, 144; 17.190

Cervantes 3.226

Cestius 2.328; 3.324; 4.263

Chalmers, J. 3.227; 4.35; 9.261;
13.22

Chamberlain, N. 3.140

Chanina, rabbi 1.390

Chapman, J. 1.244, 247

Charlemagne, emperor 4.111

Charles, R. H. 16.29, 89, 98,
103, 173; 17.40, 120, 123,
149, 172, 180, 232

Charlie, prince 9.92f

Charrington, F. W. 9.222

Chase, bishop 14.286

Chesterton, G. K. 1.14, 348;
3.264, 316; 4.44, 75, 77, 92,
96; 6.18; 8.181; 10.130;
12.171; 13.24; 14.349

Chija ben Abba, rabbi 1.327

Chillingworth, W. 10.90

Chirgwin, A. M. 3.82f; 6.94;
12.146, 199f

Chiyya, rabbi 3.86

Chloe ix.6, 8, 13

Chopin, F. 4.272

Christ See *Jesus*

Christie, W. M. 1.317

Chrysippus 2.313; 14.341

Chrysologus, P. 1.302; 14.211

Chrysostom 2.349; 3.3; 5.211;
6.49; 8.42, 168; 9.19, 20,
119, 212, 213, 218; 10.50,

116, 138, 167, 173; 12.11,
102, 256; 13.60, 152; 14.303,
324; 15.73; 17.113

Churchill, W. 1.132, 374, 380;
3.201; 5.28; 8.199

Chuza 4.96

Cicero 1.14, 139, 153; 2.164;
3.125; 6.250; 7.163; 10.82,
83, 113, 161; 12.78, 104;
13.2; 14.38, 99, 207, 303;
16.74, 138

Clark, A. 9.124

Clark, G. N. 10.85

Clarkson, T. 2.76

Claudia 12.222

Claudia Procula 2.359

Claudias Lysias 7.4, 167; 14.23,
36

Claudius, emperor 1.114, 344;
3.134, 320; 7.136; 8.7, 32,
106, 208f, 213; 12.222;
16.18, 59; 17.89, 90f, 93, 139,
144, 146

Clement of Alexandria, 1.160,
307, 379; 2.207; 5.10, 17,
21; 6.154; 8.28, 32; 9.109;
10.160; 12.249; 13.5, 7, 149;
14.10, 64, 134, 277, 280, 285;
15.19, 28f, 97; 16.67

Clement (N.T.) 11.74

Clement of Rome 9.214; 12.10,
60, 158; 13.161; 14.137, 141

Clementine
Letters of See Index VI
Recognitions of See Index VI

Cleopatra of Egypt 5.98; 7.168;
17.156

Cleopatra of Jerusalem 3.150

Clogg, F. B. 14.286

Clough, A. H.　**2**.82; **4**.122;
　　12.154
Clovis　**9**.24
Cnaeus Domitius Ahenobarbus
　　17.90
Cockburn, Lord　**9**.188
Cogidubnus　**12**.222
Coleridge, S. T.　**1**.251, 280;
　　8.178; **9**.85; **10**.62, 123, 157
Colman, R.　**1**.262
Columella　**8**.4
Confucius　**1**.274; **4**.79
Conrad　**7**.63
Constantine　**1**.25, 120
Copernicus　**1**.339; **3**.101
Coponius　**6**.233
Cornelius Gallus　**17**.51
Cornelius (N.T.)　**1**.301; **2**.145;
　　7.4, 5, 19, 79f, 88, 114;
　　14.178; **15**.90
Cotton　**9**.244
Courvoisier, Prof.　**2**.31
Cousin, A. R.　**11**.193
Cowley　**3**.174
Cowper, W.　**8**.166; **16**.65
Cranfield, C. E. B.　**14**.169, 190,
　　195, 205f, 225, 227, 252
Cranmer, T.　**1**.255
Crassus　**5**.109
Crescens　**12**.218
Crispus　**9**.5, 16
Croesus　**16**.113f
Cromwell, O.　**1**.394; **3**.253;
　　4.130; **7**.45, 53; **8**.183; **9**.34,
　　88; **10**.184; **13**.52, 165;
　　14.340; **15**.145; **16**.91
Cromwell, T.　**3**.329
Cronin, A. J.　**4**.128
Crooks, W.　**3**.138f

Curzon, Lord　**3**.223
Cybele　**9**.117; **10**.44; **12**.17;
　　16.74f
Cynics　**3**.127; **9**.37, 65
Cyprian　**12**.59; **13**.5; **16**.84
Cyrenius　**3**.285
Cyril of Alexandria　**6**.283;
　　14.323
Cyril of Jerusalem　**6**.23; **9**.168;
　　14.280
Cyrus　**2**.33; **6**.5; **9**.89; **11**.92;
　　12.186; **13**.60; **15**.36; **16**.114f;
　　17.110, 128f

Dale, R. W.　**1**.184
Damaris　**7**.133
Damocles　**14**.158
Dan, *Testament of*　See Index VI
Daniel　**1**.234; **13**.164
Dante　**3**.156, 328
Daphne　**7**.89
Darius　**3**.202
Darwin, C.　**4**.162; **6**.114
David, King　**1**.9, 13, 47, 101,
　　225; **2**.23; **3**.22, 50, 63, 85,
　　193, 281; **4**.40, 70; **5**.82;
　　6.142; **11**.10, 54; **13**.90,
　　163f; **14**.293; **15**.69; **16**.25,
　　133; **17**.59, 81
　　city of　**1**.24
　　covenant of　**13**.90
　　house of　**2**.145
　　key of　**2**.144; **16**.127
　　kingdom of　**17**.206
　　line of　**4**.26; **7**.23, 105; **16**.2
　　servant of God　**6**.178
Davidson, A. B.　**10**.118
Davies, T. W.　**9**.97
Davies, W. H.　**7**.32; **12**.214

---

1 Matt, v.1	**3** Mark	**5** John, v.1	**7** Acts	**9** Cor
2 Matt, v.2	**4** Luke	**6** John, v.2	**8** Rom	**10** Gal, Eph

Deborah 4.47; 13.163; 16.105; 17.132

Deeping, W. 5.155

Deissmann, G. A. 4.76; 8.xif; 11.218; 17.100

Demas 4.286; 11.171; 12.212–215; 14.103; 15.153; 17.106

Demetrianus 12.59

Demetrius, prophet 15.132, 135, 153

Demetrius, silversmith 7.146; 12.214; 15.153

Demetrius, critic 8.ix

Democritus 12.131

Demonax 14.55

Demosthenes 1.153; 5.195; 10.170; 11.199; 12.106, 240; 13.11, 132; 15.36f

Denney, James 1.285; 2.8, 79f; 4.1; 7.67, 177; 8.87; 12.280; 13.22; 15.204

Diana 2.207; 7.140f; 12.67, 89; 15.124; 16.59

Dibelius 8.1

Dickinson, G. L. 13.111

Didymus 5.90; 6.87; 14.285
  called Thomas 7.100

Didymus of Alexandria 14.303; 15.168

Dill, S. 17.154f

Dio Cassius 10.79; 14.38

Dio Chrysostom 12.125, 207

Diocletian 13.57

Diogenes 1.44, 333, 386; 3.127; 9.23, 186; 14.315

Diogenes Laertius 12.75; 15.37

Diognetus, *Epistle to* See Index VI

Dion Cassius See Dio Cassius

Dionysius of Alexandria 16.13; 17.190

Dionysius the Areopagite 7.133; 9.21

Dionysius the Great 5.23

Dionysius of Halicarnassus 4.7

Dionysos 5.104

Dionysus 9.117

Diotima 1.155

Diotrephes 15.131f, 135f, 152f

Dismas 1.34f; 4.286

Dives 4.213f; 6.34, 102; 17.113

Dixon, McN. 8.185

Dodd, C. H. 2.82; 8.25, 92, 111, 112, 178; 14.140; 15.29, 39, 43, 56, 58, 65, 84, 98, 101, 115, 142, 144, 145, 153

Domatilla 8.212, 216

Domitian, emperor 5.17; 8.216; 9.21; 12.60; 15.173; 16.14, 19, 41, 164; 17.8, 89, 93, 101, 139–141, 147
  persecution of 13.6

Don Carlos 9.180

Dorcas 5.90; 6.87

Dore 6.268

Doris 3.149

Doryphorus 17.91

Drake, F. 7.10

Drinkwater, J. 10.131

Driver, G. R. 17.49

Drusilla 7.93f, 168, 171

Duguid, J. 1.135; 5.236; 7.175

Dumachus 4.286

Dundas 12.232

Dunsany, Lord 8.52

Easton 12.117; 14.30

Eby Kermit 13.40, 58, 73

Edersheim, A. 2.48, 114, 127,

161; **6**.225
Edward I **7**.44
Edward the Confessor **6**.95
Edwards, T. C. **9**.167
Egnatius **14**.218
Eleazar **4**.214; **6**.105; **8**.137;
    13.168
Elektra **15**.19
Elgar, E. **14**.273
Eli **2**.42; **12**.134; **17**.59
Eliakim **2**.145; **7**.100; **16**.128,
    133
Eliezer, rabbi **1**.56, 192, 194,
    274; **2**.48f, 116; **10**.111
Eliezer ben Hyrcanus, rabbi **1**.34
Eliezer ben Jacob, rabbi **1**.368
Elijah **1**.44f, 49, 64, 282; **2**.14,
    136f, 160, 287, 369; **3**.16, 22,
    147, 211, 213, 364; **4**.19, 48,
    90, 126; **5**.244; **6**.45; **8**.120,
    144; **13**.164, 166; **14**.29,
    132; **15**.69; **16**.6, 25; **17**.42,
    79, 143
  meaning of name **4**.17
  at Passover **3**.338
  return of **2**.6, 164f; **3**.195f;
    4.115; **5**.78f; **17**.70f
  at Transfiguration **2**.156–63;
    4.123
Eliot G. **1**.247; **9**.150
Eliot, T. S. **6**.242
Eliphaz **3**.47; **4**.173; **6**.126;
    10.158
Elisha **1**.239; **2**.159, 287; **3**.24,
    127; **4**.48, 86, 134; **13**.164,
    166; **15**.69; **17**.42
Elizabeth **2**.96; **4**.4, 10f, 17
Ellicott, C. J. **11**.13
Elliott, W. H. **1**.312

El Shaddai **9**.188
Elymas **1**.26; **7**.19, 100; **12**.54
Emerson, R. W. **6**.244; **12**.34
Enoch **8**.104; **13**.133–135;
    14.238–240; **15**.159; **16**.122;
    17.70
  Book of See Index VI
  Book of the Secrets of See
    Index VI
  legends of **13**.134
Epaenetus **8**.8
Epaphroditus **7**.192; **9**.230;
    11.6f, 48–50, 74; **12**.159
Epaphras **11**.94, 107, 171;
    12.269; **16**.25
Ephraim **5**.152
Epicharmus **1**.278f
Epictetus **1**.274, 283, 336, 396;
    3.114; **4**.65, 278; **8**.19, 113,
    197; **9**.55, 69, 140, 204, 254;
    10.13; **11**.85, 132; **12**.19,
    58, 125, 159, 204, 265; **13**.62,
    139; **14**.76, 207, 220, 304,
    326; **15**.115
Epicurus **1**.55; **8**.19; **9**.22;
    12.129; **13**.129, 139, 195
Epidaurus **9**.110
Epimenides **7**.132; **12**.243
Epiphanius **13**.17
Erasmus **1**.385; **11**.124; **12**.208;
    13.57; **14**.277; **15**.111
Erastus **9**.21; **12**.222
Esau **4**.17; **8**.120, 128; **11**.58;
    16.133
  legends of **13**.183f
Esdras, *Apocalypse of* See
    Index VI
Eudemus **12**.236
Eumenes **16**.88

Eunice **11.**47; **12.**68
Euodia **11.**71–74; **12.**68
Euripides **8.**202; **9.**140, 155;
   10.25, 48; **12.**80, 107f, 236,
   239; **13.**111, 132; **14.**95,
   298; **17.**4
Eusebius **1.**81; **2.**360; **4.**112;
   5.3, 17, 18, 23; **12.**11, 61,
   118; **13.**5; **14.**5, 12, 151,
   204, 285; **15.**7, 38, 127, 167;
   16.14; **17.**79, 141, 190, 231
Euthymius Zigabenus **6.**290
Eutychus **7.**149
Evans, C. **6.**124
Evans, E. **1.**312
Evans, M. **1.**247
Eve See *Adam & Eve*
Evelyn **1.**37
Ezekiel **14.**79
Ezra **1.**12, 74; **2.**281; **4.**40;
   5.150; **7.**65
Apocalypse of See Index VI

Faber **1.**341; **4.**6; **11.**83; **13.**162
Fabiola **2.**80
Falconer, R. **12.**144, 158, 164,
   235
Farmer, H. H. **5.**112
Farrar, F. W. **9.**2, 4; **14.**147
Farson, N. **1.**294
Faustus **6.**83
Felicitas **14.**211
Felix **3.**312; **7.**94, 166–168, 171;
   12.283
Festus **3.**312; **7.**4; 172–176,
   178; **11.**188; **14.**12
Findlay, J. A. **2.**319; **3.**62; **5.**192
Fisher, H. A. L. **10.**85
Fisher, Lord **14.**82

Flaccus **11.**93; **16.**139
Flavius Clemens **8.**216; **9.**21
Flavius Sabinus **8.**217
Fleming, A. L. **14.**128
Foch, Marshal **4.**53; **12.**160
Foligras, Andela di **3.**123
Forbes, R. **8.**72
Fortunatus **9.**6, 8, 166
Fosdick, H. E. **1.**288; **3.**42;
   4.68; **6.**129; **7.**101; **9.**120;
   12.218; **13.**130; **16.**65
Foster, J. **7.**10; **13.**43
Fowler, W. **12.**61; **14.**304
Fox, G. **1.**161, 396; **15.**145, 161,
   162
Foxe, J. **4.**151; **9.**214
Francis of Assissi **2.**326; **3.**24;
   4.95; **6.**138; **10.**56; **12.**254f
Francis of Sales **2.**107
Frankau, G. **1.**262; **6.**87
Frazer, J. G. **5.**178
Freeman, K. J. **2.**80
Freud, S. **9.**86
Friedlander, L. **14.**202; **17.**154
Frohman, C. **13.**138
Froude, J. A. **5.**58; **6.**112;
   8.26; **9.**147; **14.**340; **17.**86
Fry, E. **3.**107

Gabriel **10.**93f; **13.**18, 156;
   14.323, 325; **16.**31, 174;
   17.41, 175
Gaius **15.**131f, 135, 147f, 150
Gaius of Augustus **3.**229; **15.**37
   of Corinth **8.**220; **9.**16; **15.**148
   of Derbe **15.**147
   of Macedonia **15.**147
   of Rome **1.**302; **10.**180
Galba, emperor **3.**257; **8.**130;

16.19; **17**.89, 92f, 139

Galen 3.146; **12**.176; **13**.82, 193; **14**.129; **16**.89

Galerius **12**.59

Galileo 3.101f; **4**.68

Gallio 7.3f, 137; **9**.5; **16**.15

Galloway **6**.93

Galsworthy, J. 3.28

Gamaliel 7.49f, 160; **11**.59

Gamaliel II, rabbi **6**.89

Gandhi 2.254

Garfield, president 1.231

Garibaldi, G. 1.375; 3.201; **6**.191

Gee, H. L. 1.399; 2.62f; **6**.206; **9**.172, 261; **10**.129

Gehazi 1.239

George V **6**.275; **9**.172

Gibbon, E. 3.205; **4**.85; **8**.173

Gibbs, P. 3.108; **6**.242; **10**.91, 113

Gideon 4.47; **13**.163; **17**.180

Gilbert, H. 7.184

Gilbert, W. S. **13**.136

Gladstone, W. E. **4**.148

Glaucus **12**.151

Glover, R. 2.143, 145, 175

Glover, T. R. 1.323, 394, 397; **4**.130; **5**.73; **6**.138; **7**.128; **8**.15, 185; **11**.85; **15**.41

Godet, F. L. **5**.91; **6**.100

Goethe, W. 1.75; **5**.48; **8**.181

Gog **17**.60, 194

Goldsmith **10**.90

Goodspeed, E. J. 3.287; **5**.7, 26; **10**.68; **11**.126; **12**.269, 274; **14**.30, 138; **15**.7; **16**.16

Goodwin, T. **12**.46

Gore, C. **9**.145

Gorgias **12**.156

Gorion **5**.123

Gosse, E. 3.122

Gossip, A. J. **4**.8; **6**.162; **10**.13; **12**.160; **13**.45, 72

Gough, J. B. **10**.54

Graham, Billy 3.13

Gray, T. 1.279

Green, B. 7.72

Gregory the Great 2.235; 3.258

Gregory of Nazianzen **13**.82

Gregory of Nyssa 2.234; 3.258; **8**.16; **12**.127

Grenfell, W. 1.135; **5**.105, 191, 236f; **7**.175

Grenville, G. 2.76

Grice, S. Le 1.220

Gunkel, H. **17**.133

Gunther, J. **10**.11

Haarhoff, T. J. **10**.123

Hadrian 1.25; **9**.54; **13**.87

Hagar 8.128; **10**.41; **11**.58

Hamilton, W. **6**.162

Hananiah 2.240; 3.339

Handel **6**.195; **9**.195; **16**.151

Hankey, D. **6**.140; **8**.15; **14**.337

Hannah 4.15; **14**.112; **17**.59

Hannibal **13**.126f

Hanum **16**.143

Hanway, J. 1.339; **6**.185

Hardy, H. E. 1.208

Hardy, T. 1.215; 3.344; **4**.189; **5**.219; **8**.15; **10**.91

Harnack, A. 3.33; **10**.69; **13**.9, 193

Harris, R. **14**.238; **15**.130

Harrison, P. N. **12**.155

Hastings, J. **9**.97

| 1 Matt, v.1 | 3 Mark | 5 John, v.1 | 7 Acts | 9 Cor |
| 2 Matt, v.2 | 4 Luke | 6 John, v.2 | 8 Rom | 10 Gal, Eph |

Hawkins 1.190
Hazael 15.69
Healy, G. 1.16
Heawood, G. 1.353
Hegesippus 14.10, 12, 14
Heine 1.204; 8.43
Heli 4.41
Heliodorus 12.149
Helofernes 13.164
Helvidius 14.20
Henley 8.74
Henry V 1.126; 7.111; 9.216
Henry VI 12.176
Henry VIII 1.386; 3.206; 4.186
Henry, O. 3.230; 4.15; 6.109;
    16.64
Heracles 17.103
Heraclitus 3.57; 5.34f; 15.124;
    16.60
Herbert, G. 1.41, 183; 9.65;
    12.123, 128
Hercules 12.26
Hermas, *Shepherd of* See Index VI
Hermes 5.222; 7.109
Hermogenes 12.156; 17.140
Herod Agrippa I 2.97, 135;
    3.256; 7.93, 96f; 14.9
Herod Agrippa II 7.93
Herod Antipas 1.39, 71, 331;
    2.1, 93–98, 133, 136; 3.53,
    146, 150, 160, 187f, 213, 237,
    284; 4.3, 31, 35f, 115, 186,
    222, 237, 278–280; 6.237;
    7.93
Herod the Great 1.12, 28–30,
    36–39, 43; 2.95, 134; 3.53,
    149–153, 284; 4.31, 35f, 237;
    5.116, 237; 7.93, 167; 12.78
Herod Philip 2.94, 97; 3.150,

191; 4.3, 31, 35, 173, 237;
    6.237; 7.93
Herodias 2.94–96; 3.149f, 152f;
    4.35f; 7.93
Herodion 8.213
Herodotus 1.365; 4.7; 6.119;
    9.154; 11.92, 180; 12.17,
    151; 13.48; 14.261; 17.103,
    128
Histories of See Index VI
Hervey, H. 12.216
Hesiod 1.278; 5.178; 10.82
Heywood, T. 16.75
Hezekiah 5.134; 6.43; 12.150;
    13.164, 166; 16.128; 17.22
Hieronymus See Jerome
Hilarion 2.81
Hilary of Poitiers 14.3
Hillel, rabbi 1.170, 263, 273,
    284, 367, 390; 2.198, 200;
    3.113, 164, 239, 293; 4.79;
    6.70; 10.169
  school of 1.152; 4.212
Hind, L. 3.51
Hippocrates 12.280; 16.89
Hippolytus 14.312; 15.70;
    16.67; 17.25, 85
Canons of See Index VI
Hitler, A. 5.234; 15.63; 17.100
Hogan 9.244
Holland 3.181
Holmes, O. Wendell 1.120
Homer 3.138, 335; 5.98; 9.167;
    10.109; 12.234; 13.110, 117;
    14.216; 16.73, 75
Honorius 3.204
Hood, T. 9.203
Horace 1.279; 9.155; 12.78,
    245; 17.156

Horder, Lord 3.140
Hort, F. J. 12.24, 25, 207;
     14.42, 45, 46, 55
Housman, A. E. 1.180
Huldah 16.105
Huna, rabbi 2.14f
Hunt, H. 1.32; 16.148
Hunt, L. 9.30
Hutton, J. 5.132; 9.25
Huxley, T. 5.92; 9.240
Hymenaeus 12.53, 174f, 178

Iamblichus 12.80
Iberina 1.157
Ibsen 1.120; 13.58
Ignatius 2.175; 6.283; 12.19,
     106, 275; 14.137, 139; 15.8,
     142; 16.28, 42, 58, 60; 17.11
Inchfawn, F. 4.295f, 298
Inge, R. 12.214
Irenaeus 5.18, 20, 115; 6.154;
     8.125; 12.94, 192; 14.129,
     141, 278, 309; 15.29, 108,
     137, 166; 16.67, 160; 17.101,
     189, 231
Irwin, M. 6.242
Isaac 1.62, 210; 4.54; 8.120,
     128; 10.41; 12.76; 13.151–
     154; 14.35, 42, 78
  covenant of 8.125
Isaiah 2.136; 4.157; 8.145;
     13.13, 166; 16.25
  Ascension of See Index VI
Iscariot See Judas Iscariot
Ishii, T. 3.60, 80; 6.94
Ishmael (O.T.) 8.120, 127f;
     10.41
Ishmael, rabbi 1.171
Ishtar 17.80

Isis 2.65
  Mysteries of 3.91; 5.222;
     12.51
Isocrates 1.274; 4.79; 12.97,
     207
Israel See Jacob
Issacher, *Testament of* See
     Index VI

Jacob (O.T.) 1.23–24, 93, 210;
     3.62; 4.17, 54; 5.90, 147,
     152; 6.79; 8.120, 128; 11.39;
     13.3, 183; 14.35; 16.25,
     98, 133; 17.180
  blessing of 13.153f
  covenant of 8.125
  called Israel 5.90
Jacob (N.T.) 14.31
Jah 17.169
Jahweh 3.298; 6.210; 13.99;
     14.101; 15.53
Jair 6.118
Jairus 1.342; 3.8; 4.110–112;
     5.9, 89; 6.86, 100
Jambres 12.194
James, apostle 1.77; 2.228,
     230f; 3.54, 253; 4.127, 129;
     5.16, 23; 8.221; 10.93;
     14.8f, 162; 17.148
James of Jerusalem 6.164, 178;
     7.96, 115; 9.144; 10.145;
     14.9–12, 14–23, 292; 16.134
  Book of See Index VI
  'the just' 7.115; 9.144
  legends of 9.144; 14.11
  martyrdom of 14.12–14
  and Paul 10.17; 14.22f, 73f
  religion of 13.1
James, father of Judas 14.8

James, son of Alphaeus **14**.8, 15
James the Younger **2**.229;
   14.8, 15
James of Compostella **14**.9
James VI **1**.385
James, M. E. C. **11**.163
James, W. **9**.85
Janet **1**.306f
Jannes **12**.194
Jason (N.T.) **7**.128; **8**.219f
Jason (Gk) **9**.3
Jay, W. **8**.55
Jeans, J. **1**.207
Jeffrey, G. J. **3**.18, 314; **15**.182
Jeffrey, Lord **1**.262
Jehoida **2**.298
Jehovah **3**.298; **4**.143; **5**.60;
   6.210; **9**.107; **11**.39; **17**.179f
Jehu **2**.239; **3**.266; **4**.47; **15**.69;
   17.132
Jehudah, rabbi **17**.175
Jephthah **13**.163
Jeremael **16**.31
Jeremiah **2**.136f, 240, 337;
   5.215; **14**.79
   covenant of **13**.92–94
   legends of **13**.166; **16**.94
Jeremias, J. **2**.349
Jeroboam **2**.240; **16**.3
Jerome **2**.361; **4**.139; **5**.18,
   96, 111; **6**.65, 284, 290;
   9.120, 144, 258; **10**.132, 171;
   11.173; **12**.11; **13**.8, 178;
   14.3f, 10, 11, 15–17, 32, 187,
   286; **15**.110, 167, 168, 196;
   16.14, 41; **17**.190
Jerome, J. **7**.18
Jesse, root of **16**.170
Jesus

acceptance of **5**.190f
   accursed **10**.26
advocate **15**.14, 35–38
alpha and omega **16**.37f;
   17.204, 225f
the Amen **16**.140
anger of **2**.247, 281, 288; **3**.7,
   272–275; **5**.14, 105, 108–
   114; **10**.156
anointing of **2**.329f; **5**.5f
apostle **13**.30f
appearances of **12**.149f, 203;
   15.75f
arrest of **2**.350–352; **3**.345f;
   4.273f; **6**.223f
ascension of **4**.299; **5**.1, 227;
   6.127, 149, 270; **7**.13f;
   10.144f; **12**.91; **14**.286;
   15.171; **17**.78
authority of **1**.133–135; **3**.35,
   37, 279; **4**.51; **6**.14, 223;
   13.75
awe of **3**.6
baptism of **1**.58–60, 83, 358;
   2.3; **3**.18–20; **4**.37f; **5**.1, 80,
   83–85; **6**.127; **13**.47; **15**.70,
   107, 108, 109
birth of **1**.20, 23–27, 30; **3**.11;
   4.12f, 21–25; **5**.1; **6**.28, 36;
   17.21, 78
blood of **5**.221, 223–226;
   9.103–105; **11**.122; **14**.141,
   170; **15**.15, 30; **16**.34; **17**.30–
   34, 83f
body of **9**.103–105; **13**.103,
   119, 197, **15**.7
the Branch **1**.40
the Bread of Life **5**.9, 216–
   220; **9**.103–105

the Bridegroom 1.336; 5.143
burial of 2.371f; 3.365f;
    4.289f; 6.262–4
carpenter 1.41f, 59; 2.17;
    3.6, 76, 138, 193, 254; 4.37,
    237; 5.123, 174, 219, 236,
    239; 6.20, 107, 160, 222;
    11.218
centrality of 1.79; 5.82; 9.130;
    14.337; 15.22, 93, 178;
    17.180
and children 2.174–181, 211f;
    3.7, 224, 241; 4.127, 225–227
Christ, The 2.137f; 3.196;
    5.88; 8.86; 10.32, 132;
    11.11, 15, 32, 67, 104, 131f,
    148f, 152f; 15.13f
commission of 2.378
compassion of 1.297f, 354f;
    2.15–18, 99; 3.6f, 182f;
    4.86, 117; 5.9; 6.39; 11.18
courage of 2.19f, 242, 350;
    3.252, 268, 283, 335, 351;
    4.107, 230, 239f; 5.187, 236,
    243; 6.108, 119, 126, 223,
    244
courtesy of 4.295
and creation 5.40f; 6.18;
    11.95, 114, 119f; 13.15, 31;
    14.185; 16.140f
cross of 1.32f, 60f, 65, 70, 104,
    337; 2.18, 33, 99, 120, 136,
    147–149, 156f, 161f, 211, 227f,
    230, 326, 343; 3.60, 192, 210–
    212, 215f, 220, 241, 251, 282,
    327, 340, 343f, 350f; 4.67,
    119f, 127, 196, 230f; 282–
    289, 297f; 5.135; 6.19f, 101,
    171, 204; 7.26; 9.33; 10.25,

26f, 114; 12.9; 13.58f;
    14.185f; 15.107
crucifixion of 2.363–370; 3.8,
    360–365; 4.153, 288, 297f;
    5.2, 5, 13, 134f; 6.234, 245,
    292; 7.33f; 9.15; 15.8
day of 9.12; 15.118
death of 3.362f; 4.287f; 5.135,
    251; 6.67, 261; 8.93; 9.17,
    202, 209; 11.122f, 142;
    14.185, 242; 15.109; 16.177f;
    17.30–34
deity of 2.135, 206; 3.6; 4.51,
    138; 5.14f, 39, 52, 74, 148,
    183, 188; 6.68f, 74f, 161,
    215, 217f; 7.25; 9.151;
    11.34–37, 39, 70, 95, 115;
    13.4, 14, 19, 31, 44, 119;
    14.154, 294; 16.110, 127,
    180; 17.138
deliverer 9.23
and Hades 14.232, 236–243;
    16.52
disciples of 2.77f, 120f, 125f,
    133, 212, 224, 229, 249, 304,
    333, 377; 3.27–29, 38, 74,
    83, 155, 218, 252f; 4.267f,
    274, 292; 5.5, 16, 85–95;
    6.190, 213f; 7.15
the Door 6.58f
emotions of 3.6f
eternal 6.36; 16.49; 17.226
exaltation of 13.15, 84, 86f,
    117f; 14.141, 185
example of 4.293; 11.34f;
    13.173; 14.214
exodus of 2.160, 162
expiation of 15.14f, 39f; 17.31
faithful 17.178

family of   2.229; 4.102; 5.231
  233; 6.83, 257; 7.15, 95;
  14.9f, 14–20; 15.171
fasting of   1.234, 325
feeding of five thousand   2.98–
  103, 125f; 3.1f, 7; 5.4, 10,
  10, 200–208
finality of   2.130; 11.95, 116–
  118; 16.23
the Firstborn   11.119, 121;
  16.32
the First-fruits   9.149–151
the Forerunner   6.155; 13.63
forgiveness of   2.345; 3.49–
  52; 6.203, 231
the Foundation   2.140; 9.32
friendship of   1.369; 2.10;
  3.26; 6.177
fullness of   5.71; 11.118f
and the future   2.300
in Galilee   2.126f; 3.41, 70,
  73, 237, 262f; 4.45; 5.2, 4,
  91, 106, 141
genealogies of   1.8–9, 11–13,
  14–15; 3.298; 4.3, 12, 40f;
  7.23; 13.74, 161
generosity   14.297
and Gentiles   3.177–179
gentleness of   9.238
in Gethsemane   1.65; 2.148,
  191, 256, 343, 348, 350f; 3.8,
  343, 347f; 4.271f; 5.1, 89,
  126, 221; 9.199; 13.47, 74;
  14.272; 17.97
glorification of   6.81, 123, 204
glory of   2.162; 3.211; 5.9,
  14, 68–70; 6.81, 148f, 219f;
  11.210; 13.14f, 86f; 16.150,
  180

'Lord of glory'   1.25; 8.197
goodness of   8.81
gospel of   8.221; 12.149
grace of   7.142; 8.199; 9.144,
  169; 10.143; 12.44, 48;
  17.232
greatness of   3.190; 5.226;
  6.152, 195; 14.296–298
healings of   1.80, 83, 354;
  3.39, 119, 131f; 4.177f, 187
the Herald   1.352f, 362
the High Priest   6.254; 13.4,
  31, 41–48, 70f, 79, 80–82,
  119f; 15.93; 16.45f
and history   4.137f; 8.222;
  12.230; 15.93
holiness of   13.83; 16.127
honesty of   1.111, 374, 393f;
  2.231, 310; 3.201, 250; 4.131,
  259; 6.154
honour of   16.180
our hope   12.19–21
hour of   3.70; 4.37, 45; 5.102,
  231; 6.78, 81
humanity of   2.314; 3.6f; 4.41,
  50, 138; 5.14, 65, 147f, 223;
  6.50, 258, 261f; 8.103;
  11.34–37, 95, 98, 115, 118;
  12.90, 164; 13.4, 31, 44, 84;
  15.9, 14, 23f, 93f, 143, 180
humility of   6.137; 11.6, 38
image of God   11.116–119
incarnation of   1.104; 3.80,
  139; 4.23, 40, 274; 5.13, 14,
  63–70; 6.148; 8.14, 157, 222;
  9.18f, 141, 157; 10.144f;
  11.36f; 12.90, 127, 256f;
  13.103f, 15.6–9, 14, 23f, 61,
  93, 105, 142f; 16.22, 63, 160;

17.58, 62

influence of 2.6; 6.164

and Jerusalem 2.158f, 160, 299; 3.262f; 4.124, 186; 5.2f, 106f; 6.101

of Judah 13.70, 79; 16.169, 172

the Judge 2.316; 3.51; 5.9, 189f; 6.15, 20, 246; 7.14, 132; 9.206f; 12.202; 13.111; 14.22, 141, 195; 15.176; 16.146; 17.194f

justice of 14.294

and the keys 2.144; 16.48

kindness of 2.127, 231

kingship of 1.9, 32f, 40, 115, 371; 2.104, 137, 239, 242f, 361; 3.15, 27, 144, 160, 256f, 265; 4.26, 169, 238–240, 247, 278; 5.43, 50, 80; 6.116, 130, 241f, 243, 246f, 252; 9.107; 10.141; 11.39, 111; 12.136, 203; 13.15, 110, 118; 14.122, 347; 15.93; 16.32, 46, 146; 17.183

knowledge of 11.63–65; 14.178f

'Lamb of God' 4.23, 5.80–82, 153; 14.185; 15.77

the Lamb 16.27, 157, 168– 172; 17.30, 83, 96, 98, 102, 107f, 112, 118, 141f, 147, 172f, 208

language of 1.88, 314; 6.271

and the Law 1.9, 126–133, 298; 2.118; 4.72; 10.114f

law of 10.78; 14.21

legends of 4.286

liberator 1.13; 2.341

life of 1.40–43; 2.11; 3.1f, 5f, 139f; 4.1, 134, 185f; 5.75, 106f; 6.279; 7.9, 10; 9.24, 130

life-giver 5.43, 189; 6.60, 158; 15.15, 100

the Light 1.122–125; 5.9, 10, 45; 6.10f, 13, 64; 6.85; 10.164f; 13.56; 16.53

limitlessness of 5.72

loneliness of 3.7, 251; 6.202

lordship of 1.114; 2.123, 234, 312, 342; 4.261; 6.183; 7.14, 26; 8.11, 139; 9.11, 107; 10.141; 11.9, 39, 70–72, 122, 132; 12.91, 136f; 13.118; 14.21, 184f; 15.24, 68; 16.16, 33, 169; 17.89, 183

love of 1.293f; 6.149f; 9.125, 144; 10.9, 132f; 11.18, 56; 16.33

loveliness of 2.211f; 3.80, 191

made sin 2.369; 3.19f, 364

majesty of 6.243; 9.184; 16.172

master 2.239; 4.3; 5.76

mediator 12.29, 62f; 13.15, 89; 17.176

meekness of 16.172

mercy of 15.54

merits of 9.13

messiahship of 2.353; 3.264f, 350; 4.239; 5.154, 161f, 185f, 192; 6.72, 118; 14.24; 15.6, 68, 93, 107, 110; 16.170

miracles of 1.308f; 2.101f; 3.37f; 5.9, 52, 119, 232

mission of 1.72, 80; 4.14

the Morning Star 16.110f;
17.228
names of 1.19; 2.177, 361f;
3.225; 5.63; 6.200; 7.144;
9.9, 15, 16; 11.38f, 160;
15.53
nature of 15.13–15
obedience of 4.30, 120; 5.136,
165f, 188; 6.20, 33, 66, 148,
206, 219f, 224, 273; 11.38;
13.105, 114f
omnipotence of 16.171
omniscience of 5.15
only begotten 5.74
opposition to 1.324f, 358;
4.147
parables of 1.8; 2.53–56, 78f,
88, 320; 3.93; 4.99, 236;
5.2; 6.200
and passover 2.338–340; 5.2,
4; 9.45
patience of 10.139
our peace 8.72; 10.114
'Prince of peace' 3.357f;
6.118
perfection of 13.26
personality of 1.312
pioneer 13.25f
pity of 6.8
power of 2.83, 378; 3.23, 270;
4.87f; 14.297; 16.179, 180
praise of 16.173
and prayer 1.197f; 3.41; 4.4,
261, 288; 6.165, 213–220
preaching of 1.75f, 82, 210;
3.84; 4.211; 7.11
pre-existence of 5.14, 37;
6.36; 12.90; 16.49
presence of 1.233; 8.186;

9.42; 11.11, 164; 12.245;
13.173; 17.216
priesthood of 1.32f; 16.160
promises of 14.297
and prophecy 1.16; 9.176f;
17.37
prophet 2.305, 328; 3.303–
322; 4.173, 247; 5.206, 235,
252; 6.45, 51; 16.46
the Propitiation 15.38–40
rabbi 3.138; 4.3, 94, 96; 5.87
the Ransom 2.234f; 14.317;
16.177
redeemer 1.58, 200; 14.184–
186; 16.177
resurrection of 2.50, 143f, 156,
206, 218, 228, 256, 343, 375f;
3.212, 283, 368–371; 4.231,
291–293, 297; 5.23, 48, 55,
117, 227; 6.149, 168f, 207,
266–272, 282, 288; 7.4, 24,
27f, 34, 132, 177; 8.14, 139;
9.17, 78, 115, 137, 142–151,
202; 10.92, 146; 11.39, 64,
69, 121f; 12.90, 164; 14.24,
140, 185f, 245, 286, 310;
16.12, 32, 45–51, 81f, 103;
17.224
resurrection and life 5.10;
6.93, 103; 13.118
revealer of God 2.130, 280;
3.25, 51; 4.19, 137; 5.38, 40,
74f, 133; 6.33, 98, 161, 186f;
7.132; 9.146, 197; 11.115,
116–119; 12.33; 13.12, 14,
28, 117, 188; 14.197; 15.54,
88; 16.23, 32
riches of 11.100; 13.51;
16.179

---

11 Phil, Col, Thes 13 Heb 15 John, Jude 16 Rev, v.1
12 Tim, Tit, Phlm 14 Jas, Pet 17 Rev, v.2

our righteousness **9**.22

robe of **2**.367; **6**.254

the Rock **2**.140

sacrifice of **2**.264; **8**.58; **9**.45,
   229; **10**.161; **11**.124; **13**.4,
   15, 79, 81, 85, 102–105, 106,
   109f, 113–115, 116f, 187,
   197; **14**.170, 185, 233;
   15.14f, 54, 81, 100, 109f;
   16.161, 171f, 177; **14**.234;
   17.33f, 84, 96, 227

Saviour **1**.19, 22f, 33, 41f,
   200, 334, 341; **3**.58; **4**.2,
   39, 71, 237, 283; **5**.43, 51,
   170–172; **8**.55, 135; **11**.9;
   12.91, 230; **13**.48, 82; **14**.195;
   15.15, 88, 94, 100, 110;
   16.89, 108; **17**.138

sayings of **1**.148; **2**.118;
   3.233f, **5**.228; **6**.14, 98f;
   9.103; **12**.177; **16**.94

'orphan sayings' **2**.84, 289,
   349; **3**.98; **13**.149; **14**.168

second coming of **1**.7, 381f;
   2.304, 308f, 312–317; **3**.208,
   303, 306f, 315, 320–322; **4**.167,
   220, 258, 261; **6**.155f, 184;
   7.14, 24, 36; **8**.177; **9**.17, 58,
   61, 70, 160, 169; **10**.172;
   11.16, 69, 76, 148, 182f, 197,
   201, 202–205, 212; **12**.182,
   257; **13**.123; **14**.21, 26, 121–
   124, 139, 141, 148, 248, 249f,
   284, 287, 310–312, 337–339,
   343–347; **15**.46, 71, 75f, 142;
   16.4, 26, 36f, 119, 132f, 146;
   17.224, 232

self-determination of **5**.15

self-renunciation of **11**.38

serenity of **4**.188, 274

the Servant **5**.1; **13**.82, 110

the Suffering Servant **1**.60,
   311; **4**.54; **5**.236; **14**.185,
   214

the Shepherd **6**.52–63; **7**.152;
   10.148; **13**.201; **14**.215, 270;
   17.38f

the Chief Shepherd **14**.269

sin-bearer **12**.282; **14**.244;
   15.14

sinlessness of **2**.158; **3**.18;
   6.158, 193; **8**.103; **9**.151;
   12.90; **13**.41, 48, 71, 83–85;
   14.214, 228; **15**.14; **16**.49

Son of David **1**.8, 9, 11, 13,
   15, 341, 349, 393; **2**.35, 48,
   123, 237, 279; **3**.261f, 265,
   297; **4**.252; **5**.7; **7**.23;
   8.101; **16**.170, 172; **17**.228

Son of God **1**.35f, 60, 70, 200;
   2.15, 135, 137, 140, 143, 147,
   158, 161, 169, 257, 264, 266,
   280, 353, 367; **3**.6, 20, 71f,
   148, 192, 365; **4**.14, 23, 29,
   87, 203, 247, 272, 276f;
   5.43–45, 51, 82f, 135f, 151,
   187, 189, 245; **6**.15, 26, 50,
   51, 72, 77, 99, 169, 201, 243;
   8.127; **13**.14, 20f, 85; **15**.13,
   67, 68, 88, 101, 105, 110;
   16.160

Spirit of **3**.236; **9**.193f;
   17.229

the Stone **2**.264f; **4**.247;
   8.135; **14**.193–195

the Corner Stone **2**.141

submission of **3**.256; **4**.272;
   9.151

sufferings of 2.147, 227, 348f,
363f; 3.342; 4.271f, 275f;
5.14; 6.244, 246f; 11.64;
12.168f; 13.26f, 47; 14.258,
286, 311; 15.14; 16.131f

sufficiency of 10.65f; 11.134f;
12.241

supremacy of 5.12, 92, 142,
144; 13.14, 16, 31, 33

our surety 13.61

sword of 16.93f

sympathy of 2.344; 4.87;
5.149; 6.96–99, 203; 13.27f,
42f

and the synagogue 2.53f;
3.29–32

the Teacher 1.311, 353;
2.339; 3.31, 84, 138; 5.152

teaching of 1.4, 8, 83–87;
2.1, 54, 273; 3.32f, 144; ~
5.2, 20–23; 14.25, 60

and the Temple 2.20, 243–
248; 5.2, 4, 107, 114–117;
6.101; 10.51

temptations of 1.61–70, 83,
224f, 358; 2.36, 148, 171,
252; 3.6, 21–24, 160, 199;
4.41–44; 5.1, 80, 204;
6.161; 13.42; 16.33; 17.82,
143

transfiguration of 2.156–163;
3.209–211; 4.123f; 5.4;
16.51

trial of 2.343, 352–362, 373;
3.354f; 4.275f, 277–281;
5.53; 6.233–249; 12.136

the Truth 5.66f; 13.13;
14.316; 17.178

touchstone of truth 2.42, 129;
15.143

unifier 10.66

uniqueness of 5.165; 6.66;
8.139; 11.95, 115, 134;
12.31, 153; 13.33, 87, 101;
14.233; 15.13, 68, 163, 165,
180; 16.23, 32

victory of 2.220, 228, 312,
369f; 4.288; 6.258; 8.21;
9.183; 11.87, 142f; 13.118;
14.242f; 15.77f, 106; 16.178;
17.3f, 66, 167f, 177–183

the Vine 5.9; 6.172–176; 9.80

voice of 17.229

the Way 5.46; 9.17; 13.82

wisdom of 2.308; 5.242;
9.22; 16.179

the witness 16.32

woes of 2.288–299

work of 2.3; 3.23; 5.52, 104;
6.205f, 209–211; 7.82f; 8.23,
103; 10.101–104, 122–125;
11.143; 14.231–243; 15.35–
40, 112; 16.33–35; 17.17,
31f

worship of 1.30, 297f; 2.123

yoke of 2.17f

Jesus Barabbas 2.361f

Jesus ben Sirach 14.45, 63, 82,
113

  Book of See Index VI
  Wisdom of See Index VI

Jesus called Joshua 7.100

Jesus called Justus 11.170

Jezebel (O.T.) 1.64, 152; 2.198;
3.175, 239; 4.48; 9.266;
10.47; 16.105

Jezebel of Thyatira 16.66, 102–
110

11 Phil, Col, Thes
12 Tim, Tit, Phlm
13 Heb
14 Jas, Pet
15 John, Jude
16 Rev, v.1
17 Rev, v.2

Joab **16**.133

Joachim **13**.18

Joad, C. M. **4**.175; **11**.151

Joan of Arc **4**.14; **6**.124, 133, 204f; **9**.199; **12**.221

Joanna **4**.96

Joash **2**.298

Job **14**.29, 35, 125; **16**.25

Jochanan, rabbi **1**.368, 387f; **2**.182; **5**.150; **13**.103, 199

Jochebed **13**.155

John, apostle **1**.77; **2**.228, 230f; **3**.54, 253; **4**.127, 129, 265; **5**.15–18; **6**.266f; **7**.1, 32, 38; **8**.221; **14**.162; **16**.134; **17**.148

  Acts of See Index VI

  beloved disciple **3**.329; **5**.19; **6**.145

  legends of **5**.96; **10**.94

  name of **4**.17

  religion of **13**.1

  the un-named disciple **6**.228

John, Augustus **1**.348, 371

John the Baptist **1**.7, 43–60, 71; **2**.1–7, 10, 92–98, 99, 136, 258; **3**.11–20, 30, 146, 150f, 154, 213, 279; **4**.31–36, 89f, 115, 244; **5**.141–146, 245; **6**.25, 163; **9**.261; **14**.72; **15**.23, 109; **17**.143

  baptism of **4**.37; **5**.79f, 84; **6**.79; **7**.139, 141

  birth of **4**.8–11, 14, 16–19

  death of **7**.93

  disciples of **1**.78; **2**.2; **4**.5; **7**.141f

  emergence of **4**.3; **5**.2f

  in John's Gospel **5**.49f, 70f, 141

  prayers of **4**.143

  preaching of **3**.20f; **4**.6; **5**.45; **7**.141f

  sect of **5**.11f, 50

  witness of **5**.75–82, 85, 195f; **15**.112

John of Damascus **14**.4

John the Divine **16**.11–13

John the Elder **5**.23f; **14**.162; **15**.128

Johnson, L. **1**.350

Johnson, S. **1**.190, 242, 268; **2**.218; **3**.39, 247, 361; **4**.134, 156, 191; **5**.206; **9**.83f, 160; **10**.155; **11**.154; **12**.171, 216; **13**.73; **14**.336; **17**.198

Johohanan **4**.17

Jonadab **12**.119

Jonah **2**.49; **4**.151

  and Jesus **2**.20

  sign of **2**.129

Jonathan **16**.46

Jones, S. **4**.15

Jose ben Chalafta, rabbi **13**.29

Jose ben Jehuda, rabbi **2**.193

Joseph of Arimathea **2**.219, 372–374; **3**.263, 366f; **4**.289f; **6**.263

Joseph, husband of Mary **1**.8, 18f, 33f, 39, 41; **3**.65, 139; **4**.12f, 21, 29f, 41; **5**.96; **14**.17–19

Joseph (O.T.) **1**.15f, 39, 93; **4**.40; **5**.147; **7**.56f; **13**.153f; **14**.31; **15**.37; **16**.143; **17**.23

  Life of See Index VI

Josephus **1**.12, 27, 37, 45, 72, 77, 161, 295f, 359; **2**.28f,

37f, 84, 93, 96f, 98, 121,
134f, 179f, 182, 196, 197f,
307f, 328, 329; 3.27, 68, 134,
177, 229, 300, 308, 311, 324,
333; 4.35, 45, 147, 234, 258f,
263, 281; 5.178, 248; 6.23,
59, 104, 233, 237; 7.58, 97;
9.266; 10.47, 112; 11.155,
157; 12.76, 77; 13.164, 168,
191; 14.11, 37, 40, 277, 291,
322, 326; 16.45; 17.95, 213

Joses 2.229

Joshua 1.19; 2.281; 3.102, 178;
6.178; 8.12; 9.88; 11.10;
12.227; 13.37; 14.35, 79,
293; 16.25; 17.134

called Jesus 2.362; 7.100

Joshua, High Priest 17.81

Joshua ben Levi, rabbi 3.178

Joshua ben Nehemiah, rabbi
1.176

Josiah 1.141; 2.183; 3.231;
4.47; 9.221; 17.132

Jotham 3.89

Judah 1.234; 8.47; 16.133
Testament of See Index VI

Judah the Patriarch, rabbi 6.37

Judah the Prince, rabbi 3.85

Judah, rabbi 3.129

Judas Barsabas 14.275; 15.169

Judas of Damascus 15.169

Judas the Gaulonite 3.285

Judas of Galilea 1.395; 4.121;
6.23; 7.50; 15.169f

Judas Iscariot 2.328; 331–338,
350f; 3.8, 23, 173, 221, 328–
330, 335, 345f, 348; 4.153,
172, 263, 273f; 5.5, 15, 48,
229; 6.109, 111–113, 142–

148, 151, 222, 292; 7.15–17;
10.3, 146; 14.267, 279;
15.169; 16.133; 17.82
meaning of 'Iscariot' 7.16

Judas of Jerusalem 7.116;
15.170, 173

Judas Maccabaeus 2.136, 241,
306; 3.267; 5.82; 6.70;
13.160, 170; 17.69

Judith, *Book of* See Index VI

Julian the Apostate 1.120;
2.264f; 4.112f, 195; 7.90;
13.58; 16.81

Jülicher, A. 16.6

Julius Caesar 6.60; 9.3f; 11.137;
13.125; 14.38, 221; 16.17;
17.159

Julius, centurion 7.181

Julius Vindex 17.92

Junias 8.212; 10.145; 14.17

Juno 17.140

Jupiter 1.379; 10.129; 17.40
crown of 9.184
J. Stator 14.147

Justin Martyr 1.24; 2.360; 5.244;
6.25, 246; 8.41, 172; 12.59,
76, 100; 13.12; 14.129, 242,
279; 15.150; 16.26; 17.189

Justus 9.5

Juvenal 1.157; 3.12, 236; 5.203;
8.31f, 48, 49, 50; 10.171,
180; 11.199; 12.78, 151,
270; 14.187, 202; 16.166;
17.141, 144, 154f, 161

Kagawa, T. 2.233; 12.56, 102

Kant 1.208; 5.58

Keats 1.262; 4.87, 167; 8.177;
13.137

Keble, J. 12.250
Kennedy, A. R. S. 2.194
Kennedy, S. 6.253; 10.46
Kepler, T. S. 16.1; 17.100, 169
Khayyam, O. 1.212, 259; 8.75
Kingsley, C. 3.217; 6.175;
    12.171
Kingsley, H. 6.265
Kipling, R. 1.221; 3.28, 257,
    357; 4.68; 5.58; 6.128;
    8.43; 9.122, 205, 208, 244,
    265; 10.14; 14.77
Kirkpatrick, A. K. 14.194
Klausner, J. 2.364
Klopstock 3.328
Knox, C. 1.262f; 4.65; 9.68
Knox, J. 1.386; 2.94; 4.161;
    5.27f, 165; 7.41; 9.179f;
    10.61; 11.32; 12.49f, 52, 55;
    17.100
Kollybos 5.110
Korah 2.16; 9.89; 12.177;
    15.159, 164, 191; 17.152
Kuria 15.130, 138

Laban 4.17
Lacordaire 12.129
Lactantius 1.377
Lagrange 3.274
Lamb, C. 1.220; 3.270
Lamb, M. 9.182; 11.163
Lang, A. 1.223
Lang, C. 6.123f
Langton, S. 9.223
Laodice 16.137
Latimer 1.386; 4.186
Laubach, F. 6.40
Laurentius 1.242
Law, W. 14.96

Lawrence, Brother 2.84
Lawrence, J. 14.208
Lawrence, T. E. 5.219; 6.146;
    8.76
Lazarus of Bethany 2.329;
    3.263; 5.5, 9f, 15, 69; 6.80f,
    96, 101, 109–111, 114
    as Beloved Disciple 5.19;
    6.145
Lazarus, rich man 4.213f; 6.34,
    102; 11.54; 17.113
Lecky 1.157; 5.26
Legion 3.118; 4.108
Leighton 4.73; 8.169
Leontinium 1.155
Lessing 1.201; 5.136
Levi (N.T.) See *Matthew, apostle*
Levi (O.T.) 13.70
    Testament of See Index VI
Levi, rabbi 1.195
Levison 2.73, 79
Lewis, C. D. 6.242
Lewis, S. 5.155
Licinius 13.193
Lightfoot, J. B. 9.90, 121, 211;
    10.138; 11.18, 26, 28, 49, 53,
    60, 67, 81, 91, 92, 116, 132,
    155; 12.271; 14.19
Lilley, P. 14.92
Lincoln, A. 1.109; 3.28; 4.130,
    175, 205; 6.204; 9.120, 173,
    263; 14.66; 15.145; 17.165
Lind, J. 3.219
Lindsay, D. 12.49
Linklater, E. 1.383
Linus 12.222
Lipman, W. 11.126
de Lisle, R. 5.28
Lister 1.339; 4.68; 13.51

1 Matt, v.1   3 Mark   5 John, v.1   7 Acts   9 Cor
2 Matt, v.2   4 Luke   6 John, v.2   8 Rom   10 Gal, Eph

Liszt 4.272
Livingstone, D. 4.292f; 7.12, 129; 8.203
Livy 8.31; 10.113
Lock, W. 12.55, 129, 236
Locke, W. J. 4.195
Lois 11.47; 12.68
Loisy 3.292
Lollia Paulina 14.221
Lombard, P. 2.235
Longfellow 13.138
Longinus 9.33; 13.172
Lord, W. 1.348
Lot 9.221; 12.79; 14.327; 17.151
Lovelace 1.394
Lowell, J. R. 3.19; 11.106
Lucan 8.4, 204; 13.178
Lucian 3.53; 9.186; 12.125; 14.99; 15.133; 16.73
Lucifer 3.81; 12.73; 15.183; 16.111; 17.59, 133
Lucius 7.98; 8.219
Lucius Antoninus 8.49
Lucius Valerius 14.220
Lucretius 8.31; 9.254
Lucullus 5.178
Luke 1.76; 4.2, 82; 7.6, 121f, 148, 192; 9.229, 231; 12.215f, 233
    author of *Acts* 7.1–3; 12.11
    doctor 4.1f, 52, 86; 7.3, 189; 11.171
    historian 7.6
    and *Letter to Hebrews* 13.7
Lull, R. 9.82
Lunn, A. 11.151, 163
Lunn, H. 11.103
Luther, M. 1.65, 209, 357; 3.61,

99, 102; 5.205; 6.107, 214; 7.42; 8.25; 9.182, 257; 10.22, 157, 178; 11.163; 12.127, 169; 13.5, 8f; 14.3, 5–8, 24, 59, 77f, 169; 15.143; 16.1; 17.100
Lydia 7.123; 11.5, 73f; 16.102, 105
Lysanias 4.3, 31
Lysimachus 16.74
Lyte, H. F. 6.195; 10.132

Maartens, M. 9.86
Macaulay, Lord 1.37; 6.224
Macauley, R. 3.41
Maccabaeus, J. 2.28; 12.149, 156f
Macdonald, chief 4.89
Macdonald, A. B. 4.58
Macdonald, C. M. 1.244, 246f
Macdonald, G. 1.253; 2.212, 250; 3.206, 241f; 6.160
Macdonald, R. G. 1.v
Macdonald Maclean, C. 1.244, 246f
Macgregor, W. M. 3.145; 4.195; 5.22; 6.162; 9.244; 11.193; 12.126; 13.46, 73; 15.41
Mackail, D. 4.168; 14.113
Mackay, J. 1.287
Maclaren, A. 1.44
Maclaren, I. 5.238
MacLean, A. 1.259f; 9.202; 10.75
Magog 17.60, 194
Mahafty, J. P. 1.391
Mahomet 3.229
Maimonides 1.53, 57; 2.22;

11 Phil, Col, Thes
12 Tim, Tit, Phlm
13 Heb
14 Jas, Pet
15 John, Jude
16 Rev, v.1
17 Rev, v.2

6.90, 227
Malchus 2.351
Maltby, F. R. 4.77; 10.124
Malthake 3.150; 4.35
Manaen 7.98
Manasseh 1.58; 3.231; 5.150,
    152; 9.221; 13.166
Manasses 13.164
Manoah 10.129; 13.3, 192
Marcion 10.68; 12.3, 139;
    15.144; 17.106
Marcus 12.192
Marcus Antonius 12.39
Marcus Aurelius 1.154; 3.11,
    25; 4.285; 5.58, 64; 10.170;
    13.87, 111, 139
Marduk 11.212; 15.61; 17.58,
    77, 133, 198
Mariamne the Boethusian 3.150;
    4.35
Mariamne the Hasmonaean
    1.29, 36; 3.149; 4.35; 7.93f
Mark, John 3.3f, 72, 347f; 7.97,
    101f, 192; 10.39; 11.169f;
    12.217f; 14.278
Marlow, N. 1.339
Marlowe, C. 6.83
Martha 1.104; 2.329; 3.263;
    4.4, 141f; 6.80, 91, 96f, 109–
    111; 15.138
Martial 1.157; 8.4, 204; 10.171;
    12.222; 14.187
Martin, H. 2.77, 225
Martin, J. 1.v
Martin, K. 11.200
Martin of Tours 11.326
Martineau 12.204
Marvell, A. 4.171; 8.177
Matthias 16.133

Mary, queen 2.194; 9.180
Mary of Orange 2.320; 11.205
Mary Tudor 12.52
Mary of Bethany 1.104; 2.329;
    3.263; 4.4, 141f; 6.80, 91,
    96f, 109–111
Mary, wife of Clopas 2.229;
    6.255; 14.16
Mary, mother of James & Joses
    2.374; 5.96–98; 14.16
Mary, mother of Jesus 1.18–20,
    33, 41; 2.79, 96, 373; 3.139;
    4.4, 5, 12–16, 21, 29f, 39, 41,
    181; 5.19, 101f; 6.28, 82f,
    255–257; 11.136; 12.68;
    13.11f; 14.17, 19f; 15.138
Mary Magdalene 2.229, 376;
    4.4, 96; 5.19, 48; 6.256,
    264–267; 12.68; 14.16
Mary, mother of Mark 3.3,
    347; 7.95; 12.217
Mary, the other 2.376
Mary (Rome) 8.214
Masterman, E. W. G. 1.295;
    3.43
Mathathias 13.170
Matheson, G. 9.124; 10.103
Matthew, apostle 1.4–5, 329–
    332, 359; 2.189; 3.53–57,
    74, 83; 4.64, 75, 82; 5.3, 23,
    94; 11.136; 14.8, 162
Maugham, S. 2.205; 14.223
Maurice, F. D. 6.175
du Maurier 10.97
Maurois, A. 1.380; 10.85, 155
Maximus of Egypt 4.21
Maximus of Tyre 12.51
Maxwell, W. D. 1.195
Mayor, J. B. 14.46, 47, 134,

286; **15.**157
McCaig **4.**197
McCosh, A. **1.**v
McFadyen, J. E. **6.**92, 93;
 9.138; **14.**117
McNeile, A. H. **1.**335; **2.**163,
 200; **10.**64; **14.**21
Meander **1.**173
Meir, rabbi **3.**85
Melanchthon **12.**127
Melba, N. **1.**262
Melbourne, Lord **12.**191
Melchior **1.**31; **3.**65
Melchizadek **5.**157; **13.**63–72,
 80f
Meleager **3.**125
Melito **16.**42
Melville, A. **1.**385; **3.**102; **4.**36;
 9.147; **12.**167f
Men **16.**138
Menander **2.**46
Menippus **3.**125
Menuhin, Y. **8.**160
Meredith, G. **13.**138
Merrick, L. **3.**277
Meshach **1.**117
Mesori **1.**26
Messalina **17.**144
Metallus **12.**77
Metillus **1.**157
Meyer **14.**30
Micah **4.**157
Michael, archangel **13.**18;
 14.324f; **15.**158, 166; **16.**31,
 54, 174; **17.**11, 40, 41, 80f,
 96, 175
Michelangelo **5.**91; **8.**201
Milligan, G. **8.**x; **10.**24
Milton **1.**355; **8.**43, 53; **14.**266,

334
Mimnermus **13.**110
Minerva **17.**140
Minucius **14.**114
Miriam **13.**155; **16.**105
Mithra **5.**222; **17.**33
Mnason **14.**254
Modestinus **1.**156
Moffatt, J. **6.**19, 97, 108; **9.**139,
 143; **10.**64; **11.**73; **13.**117,
 121, 122, 129, 133, 158, 174,
 182, 191, 202; **14.**32, 138,
 142, 150, 191, 238, 276, 286,
 294, 299, 305, 327, 336, 345;
 15.19, 62, 92, 151, 157, 160,
 192, 203f; **16.**104, 118, 142
Moiseiwitsch **9.**244
Mommsen **14.**39; **16.**75
Monobaz **1.**241; **12.**137
Montaigne **1.**264; **3.**26; **9.**110
Montanus **15.**90
Montefiore, C. G. **1.**52f, 172;
 2.6, 223
Montgomery, Lord **11.**163f
Montrose, Earl of **6.**205
Moody, D. L. **1.**125f; **8.**56, 203
Moore, G. F. **1.**52f
Mordaunt, E. **10.**178
Mordecai **11.**58; **17.**228
More, H. **10.**156
More, T. **12.**235
Morley, J. **3.**226
Morris, W. **7.**30; **13.**135
Morrison, G. **12.**204
Morton, Earl of **4.**36; **9.**147;
 12.50, 167
Morton, H. V. **1.**25, 77; **4.**139;
 5.167; **6.**56f, 222, 229, 281
Moses **1.**47, 98, 234, 375; **2.**281;

3.21f, 132, 211, 281; **4.**133;
5.52, 134, 215, 237–239, 241;
6.27, 45, 54f; **9.**88, 189–192;
10.27; **11.**10, 187; **12.**70,
134, 177, 194, 227; **13.**3, 31,
33, 89, 154–159; **14.**35, 181,
262, 292; **16.**25, 123; **17.**70f,
98, 143, 152, 196, 200
Ascension of See Index VI
Assumption of See Index VI
body of **15.**158, 166
and the Law **1.**366; **2.**160f;
3.293; **5.**72; **8.**118, 123;
10.6, 29f; **16.**24, 161
law of **2.**16, 281; **4.**250; **5.**5;
7.21; **8.**81; **10.**6; **13.**17,
185f
legends of **7.**58; **9.**125; **13.**18,
155, 156, 201f
pre-existence of **17.**96
and Samaria **2.**359; **5.**157
seat of **1.**7
servant of God **6.**177; **8.**12
Song of **17.**117–120
at Transfiguration **2.**159f,
163; **4.**123
uniqueness of **13.**28f
veneration of **1.**187
Moule, C. F. D. **11.**106, 108,
110, 150, 152, 165, 168
Muir, E. **1.**220
Muirhead, L. **6.**162
Muller, M. **11.**155
Muratori **5.**21; **14.**152
Muratorian Canon See Index VI
Muretus **4.**16; **14.**47
Murray, A. V. **3.**215
Murray, G. **12.**20, 80; **16.**159
Mussolini **15.**63

Myers, F. W. H. **3.**132, 191;
8.124; **9.**254; **15.**121, 122;
16.52

Naaman **1.**239; **3.**127; **4.**5;
5.187; **14.**112, 116
Nabal **17.**59
Naboth **4.**47
Nain, widow of **4.**4; **5.**9; **6.**100;
16.168
Nannacus **7.**107
Naphtali, *Testament of* See
Index VI
Napoleon **1.**39; **2.**138; **5.**211,
235; **6.**5f; **7.**109; **9.**121;
13.159; **15.**28, 63; **17.**100,
132
Narcissus **8.**9, 213
Nathan **3.**50, 85, 89
Nathanael **2.**252; **5.**91–95;
16.150
Nebuchadnezzar **8.**166; **13.**129,
164; **14.**39; **17.**77
Necho **17.**132
Nehemiah **1.**74, 230; **2.**168,
281; **4.**40; **5.**150; **6.**117;
7.65
Nelson, Lord **1.**32; **4.**265; **7.**30;
8.169; **10.**48; **12.**88
Nelson, J. **11.**52
Nemeseis **16.**75
Nepos **17.**190
Nereus **8.**9, 216f
Nero **1.**27, 112; **2.**135, 328;
3.324; **4.**263; **6.**183; **7.**167;
8.4, 106f, 172f, 204, 213;
9.21, 53f; **10.**121f; **11.**128;
12.11, 18, 59, 78, 166f, 211;
13.6, 58, 130; **14.**10, 138,

146f, 156–159, 209, 221;
  15.63; 16.14, 18f, 59; 17.7,
  63f, 89, 93, 129, 139, 145,
  146f, 155f, 160
  life of See Index VI
  N. redivivus 15.63; 17 64, 90,
    93, 101f, 129, 138, 141f, 184
  'saviour of the world' 17.89
Nerva 16.14, 20
Newbigin, L. 3.62; 7.55; 13.144
Newman, B. 11.186
Newman, J. H. 13.3; 14.327
Newton, F. E. 1.121
Newton, I. 4.57
Newton, J. 11.163; 12.46
Nicanor 12.149
Nicholls, B. 1.353
Nicias 17.103
Nicklaus 9.244
Nicodemus 2.219; 5.5, 120–125,
    131f, 152, 163, 237, 254;
    6.86, 263; 16.32
  Gospel of See Index VI
Nicolaos 7.53
Nicolaus 16.66f
Nicoll, W. R. 1.253
Nicolson 1.324
Nicomedes 5.123
Niger (N.T.) 3.361
Niger, sophist 12.124f
Nightingale, F. 9.79; 10.150;
  13.121
Nimrod 13.143
Noah 2.315; 12.79; 13.140–142;
    14.238, 240, 325f
  covenant of 8.125; 16.161
  legends of 13.140
North, B. 3.353; 7.176
Northcott, C. 1.269; 2.76, 233

Nympha 11.171

Octavia 8.107; 17.91
Octavius See Augustus
Oerstereley, W. O. E. 3.92
Onesimus 11.164, 169; 12.269f,
    271, 274; 14.213
Onesiphorus 12.155, 222
Onias 2.136f; 12.149
Onosander 12.75
Origen 1.34, 217, 289, 320;
    2.96, 149, 207, 234, 361;
    3.232, 258; 6.153; 8.176;
    9.33f, 120; 10.54, 98; 11.124;
    13.5, 7–9, 192, 193; 14.4, 9,
    134, 280, 285; 15.167; 16.54,
    70; 17.106, 190
Ormuzd 2.364; 3.23; 5.47;
    9.196; 17.59, 130
Orpheus 3.336
Osiris 2.65; 3.91; 5.222
Otho 9.54; 16.19; 17.89, 91,
    93, 139
Ovid 8.98; 12.35, 78; 14.55
Oxenham, J. 1.278; 3.19;
    4.104; 6.249

Paedaretos 3.223
Paley 1.207
Pallas 7.167, 171
Palmer 5.100; 9.244
Palmerston, Lord 9.188
Panthera 6.28
Papias 1.4f; 2.345; 3.4; 5.23;
    6.291; 14.161, 278, 309;
    15.127, 137; 17.189
Paris 17.140
Parry 12.25, 241
Pascal, B. 14.92

Passfield, Lord See Webb, Sidney

Pater, Walter **2**.55

Paterson, J. **5**.27; **17**.81

Patmore, C. **1**.326

Paul **1**.15, 79; 161, 301, 363; **2**.128, 256; **3**.77, 89, 202, 248f, 312, 315; **4**.2, 77, 95, 120, 285; **5**.16, 94; **6**.164, 190, 193, 287; **7**.1, 3, 6, 19, 97, 101, 117f; **8**.94, 98; **10**.17, 18–20, 39; **11**.57–61; **12**.41–43, 45–48; **13**.130, 201; **14**.146, 347f; **17**.93

Acts of See Index VI

ambassador **9**.209–212

Apocalypse of See Index VI

apostleship **8**.12; **9**.78f; **10**.3f, 74; **11**.9, 27, 103; **12**.17f, 63f, 142f, 148, 227f; **14**.17

apostle to Gentiles **7**.100, 151; **8**.45f, 148; **9**.14; **14**.22

appearance of **9**.242f, 257; **12**.279f

in Arabia **10**.14

in Athens **9**.23; **10**.6

authority **9**.267; **12**.228

baggage of **7**.154

bonds of **11**.174f

businessman **9**.231

chronology of **7**.73; **12**.9–12

in Cilicia **10**.15

conversion of **7**.5, 70–72; **10**.12f

in Corinth **8**.19; **9**.4–8, 14, 23f, 31, 41; **11**.45; **17**.93

courage **7**.73f, 110, 129, 147, 152–154; **10**.14f; **12**.50

courtesy of **11**.48–50, 169

in Crete **12**.9

'crisis legislation' **9**.70

in Damascus **7**.73; **10**.14

death of **12**.208f

at Ephesus **9**.4, 5, 13, 31, 154, 166f, 172; **11**.45, 93; **16**.60; **17**.93

epilepsy of **9**.258

eyesight of **9**.258

in Galatia **10**.38f

greatness of **8**.17; **9**.40, 181

and healing **7**.189

humility of **9**.38–40, 145, 188f, 217; **11**.216

humour of **12**.283

imprisonments of **8**.206; **10**.61, 121, 182f; **11**.20, 21f, 27, 47, 168, 174; **12**.10f, 145, 155, 165–167

independence **9**.80f, 248; **10**.4; **14**.266

industrious **7**.143

influence of **2**.6

and Jerusalem **10**.4, 14f; **17**.93

and Jesus **4**.13; **9**.42, 193f; **11**.27, 34–40, 46; **12**.244

and Jewish feasts **7**.150

and Jews **3**.148, 168f; **7**.191

journeys of **7**.97, 119, 138; **9**.254f

letters of **8**.ix–xiii, 45; **10**.68f, 172; **11**.47, 52, 104, 172, 174; **12**.8f, 275; **14**.288, 348

prison-letters **7**.192; **10**.61; **12**.165

love of **9**.169, 178f, 218;

| 1 Matt, v.1 | 3 Mark | 5 John, v.1 | 7 Acts | 9 Cor |
| 2 Matt, v.2 | 4 Luke | 6 John, v.2 | 8 Rom | 10 Gal, Eph |

10.39
in Macedonia 11.179
marriage of 9.60f; 10.73;
  11.75
ministry of 9.82–84
mother of 3.361
at Neopolis 11.5
obedience of 11.9
opposition to 9.176, 242, 251,
  259; 10.3f; 11.182, 188;
  14.26
parchments of 12.219
pastor 9.255; 10.44f; 11.194–
  196; 14.192
persecutor 7.64; 11.11, 60;
  12.45; 17.85
Pharisee 7.70; 8.13; 11.59f
at Philippi 8.19; 10.7, 8, 248;
  11.3, 5, 13, 86, 188; 17.93
prayers of 10.28; 11.128,
  196f
preaching of 7.103–105; 9.23f,
  195; 10.24f; 14.28
rabbi 7.98, 135, 160, 180;
  8.118; 9.60, 79, 131, 243;
  10.27, 29, 41; 11.218
in Rome 7.5; 8.2f; 12.10
and Sanhedrin 10.172
servant of God 6.178
sickness of 7.102f, 121
slave of Christ 8.11f, 202;
  9.40; 10.9f, 124; 11.9;
  12.227
in Spain 8.3f, 204; 12.10–12,
  283
strategy of 8.4
style of 10.64; 14.142
sufferings of 9.253, 257–260;
  10.38f, 56f, 124; 11.30, 126,

128; 12.197
in Syria 10.15
tact of 8.201
of Tarsus 7.62, 70f; 9.252;
  10.15; 11.58f
tent-maker 7.136, 175; 11.167
at Thessalonica 8.19; 11.47,
  86, 181f
thorn of 9.257; 10.38
trial of 7.161f, 169–173;
  11.20; 12.220
in Troas 9.183, 224; 11.5
visions of 9.256f
vocabulary of 10.64; 12.8f
vows of 7.138
Paul of Nisibis 14.4
Paula 8.216
Pausanias 5.104; 6.153
Peake, A. S. 1.v; 13.158
Pekah 1.75
Pelagius 12.237
Penn, W. 3.226
Pericles 1.155, 231; 10.108f;
  12.87; 16.97
Perpetua, saint 14.211; 17.118
Perrot, A. 2.31
Perseus 12.26
Persius 6.42; 12.20; 14.335;
  15.121
Peter 1.8, 15f, 65, 77; 2.156–
  163, 169, 171, 175, 193, 220,
  226, 343–347; 3.54, 80, 214,
  248, 250, 346, 351–353, 369;
  4.4, 57, 119, 121, 126f, 153,
  265, 269–271, 285, 292, 296;
  5.19, 23, 88ff, 163; 6.87,
  151f, 224f, 266f, 282f, 285–
  288; 7.1, 4, 19, 32, 38–42,
  44f, 76f, 80–88, 95, 100, 114;

8.100, 221; **9**.14f, 36, 143f; **10**.17, 18–20, 102; **14**.145, 162, 292, 347f; **16**.134; **17**.108

Acts of See Index VI
character of **2**.106f
Chief Apostle **14**.262
confession of **2**.137–139; **3**.180, 192f; **5**.230; **14**.195
courage of **2**.351; **14**.154f; **17**.97
denial of Jesus **3**.351–353; **6**.227–231; **14**.90, 268; **15**.119
faith of **2**.140f
and Gnosticism **11**.136
Gospel of See Index VI
house of **3**.39
and James **4**.16; **14**.10
and John **4**.16
in John's Gospel **6**.101, 141
and the keys **2**.139–146
legends of **3**.145; **10**.93; **13**.58
and Mark **3**.72
and Paul **10**.17, 18–20; **14**.347f
preaching of **2**.345; **3**.4f, 7–8, 157; **7**.5, 24–29, 33f
rebuked **1**.65, 225; **2**.51, 148–150; **3**.174, 199; **5**.4
religion of **13**.1
wife of **14**.277
wife's mother **1**.307f; **3**.36–38
Peter Lombard **3**.258
Peter Pan **1**.149f; **9**.160; **13**.51, 138
Petronius **17**.157
Phaniel **13**.18
Pharaoh **8**.120, 131; **12**.194

Philemon **1**.173; **11**.164, 169; . **12**.270, 273, 274, 278, 283
Philemon the Greek **14**.46
Philetus **12**.174, 178
Philip, apostle **1**.39; **5**.5, 15, 16, 23, 52, 91, 94, 202, 204f; **6**.120, 159, 163; **7**.62; **14**.162; **17**.107
Philip, evangelist **7**.4, 19, 62, 64f, 69, 88; **12**.68; **15**.89; **16**.105
Philip II **9**.120
Philip of Macedon **2**.84; **7**.122f; **11**.3, 180
Philip of Neri **13**.173
Philip, Tetrarch **2**.95, 133, 135; **3**.53, 150
Phillips, J. B. **16**.118
Philo **1**.134; **2**.358, 364; **3**.196; **4**.79; **5**.36, 64, 83, 183; **6**.237, 247; **8**.96; **10**.99; **11**.117, 159; **12**.39, 80, 107, 131; **13**.2, 12, 52, 80, 91, 134; **14**.55, 60, 84, 98, 126, 323; **15**.37, 190; **16**.70
Philodemus **3**.125; **12**.236
Philostratus **9**.19; **12**.124, 125
Phineas **11**.60
Phocylides **12**.131
Phoebe **8**.7, 207; **9**.186
Phygelus **12**.156
Pilate **1**.8; **2**.353, 357–363, 377; **3**.354; **4**.3, 31, 153, 172f, 277–281; **6**.231–249; **13**.130
Acts of See Index VI
bodyguard **2**.363
character of **6**.237–240
shade of **2**.362
wife of **2**.359

Pindar 8.46
Pitt, W. 2.76; 12.98
Pius 1.377
Pizarro 1.374f; 6.191
Plato 1.27, 136, 173, 279; 2.203, 313; 3.17, 113, 174; 4.36, 124; 5.8, 73, 140; 6.38, 168; 7.63; 8.167; 9.35, 51, 53, 79, 140, 186; 10.52, 83, 90, 113, 153, 183; 12.80, 81, 98, 107, 109, 207; 13.1, 2, 39, 88, 191; 14.99, 114, 186, 203, 217, 288, 316, 337, 341; 15.41, 42, 123, 149; 16.151; 17.199, 211
Definitions of See Index VI
Plautius 9.21
Plautus 1.385
Pliny 1.378, 398; 5.212; 6.42, 189; 8.36, 49; 9.21, 107; 10.179; 11.159; 12.67, 78, 99, 270; 13.193; 14.128, 155f, 161, 221; 16.97, 137; 17.155, 158f, 160, 213, 214
Letters of See Index VI
Plotinus 9.204
Plummer 1.73, 311, 359, 374; 2.14, 46, 288; 15.107, 118, 121
Plutarch 1.119; 3.202; 5.64, 8.45; 9.18, 19, 40, 71; 10.51, 83, 99, 156; 12.62, 124, 182, 185, 237; 13.43, 46, 207; 14.295, 302; 16.21; 17.103
Pluto 14.346
Pole 9.120
Polybius 1.301; 4.84; 12.237, 242, 258

Polycarp 1.115; 5.20; 9.107, 171; 11.7, 15; 12.19, 169; 14.137, 141f, 162; 15.9, 144; 16.76
Polycrates 6.228
Pompey 2.28; 3.68, 125; 5.123; 12.78; 14.38
Pomponia 12.223
Pomponia Graecina 9.21
Pomponius Mela 8.4
Pope 3.129
Popilius Laena 13.30, 167
Poppaea Sabina 6.183; 12.78, 14.149; 17.91
Potter, G. 2.24
Pouyanne 2.31
Praxiteles 7.141
Premanand 2.99, 101, 111, 211, 291; 11.103
Prescott 1.375
Primasius 17.142
Prisca See Aquila and Prisca
Priscilla See Aquila and Prisca
Priscillian 15.110
Prometheus 1.200
Propertius 8.31; 12.78
Prudentius 17.33
Psammetichus 14.39
Ptolemy 1.155; 16.88; 17.179
Ptolemy Lagos 2.29
Publius 7.188f
Publius Sempronius Sophus 14.219
Pudens & Claudia 12.222
Pusey 1.294; 4.106
Pythagoras 2.47; 8.112; 9.26; 10.99, 156; 12.80; 13.52, 62, 196; 16.21
Pytho 7.124

Quartus **8**.220; **11**.103
Quintilius **1**.279
Quintillian **1**.97; **8**.4, 204; **9**.35;
      13.195; **14**.220
Quintus Fabius Cunctator **3**.202f
Quintus Lucretius Vespillo **12**.78
Quirinius **4**.20; **7**.50
Quiroga, V. **12**.201

Rab, rabbi **2**.14
Rabbula **14**.4
Rachab See Rahab
Rachel **1**.24, 38; **11**.58
Rafael See Raphael
Raguel **16**.31; **17**.41
Rahab **1**.17; **13**.161, 191; **14**.29;
      15.62
   legends of **14**.78f; **17**.58, 77
Rainy **11**.201
Ramsey, W. **9**.98; **16**.41, 68,
      87, 113, 125, 137
Raphael **13**.8; **14**.323, 325;
      16.31, 174; **17**.41, 175
Rawlinson, A. J. **3**.80, 286
Rebecca **8**.128; **12**.76
Redwood, H. **3**.54
Rehoboam **1**.24; **2**.240; **12**.134;
      13.92; **16**.3
Reith, Lord **6**.87; **8**.74
Remiel **17**.41
Renan, E. **6**.101f; **14**.138; **17**.83
Resh, rabbi **3**.276
Reuben **1**.233; **16**.133; **17**.25
   Testament of See Index VI
Rhine, J. B. **1**.306
Rhoda **16**.54
Richard of Chichester **1**.v
Richards, L. **1**.231
Rieu **6**.97

Robert of Burgundy **2**.180
Robertson, E. H. **14**.234
Robertson, F. W. **10**.156
Robertson, J. A. **4**.283; **6**.175
Robinson, A. T. **2**.288
Roby, W. **8**.56
Rockefeller, J. D. **4**.268
Rogers, E. **14**.185
Roland **4**.111; **6**.190; **16**.80
Roma **1**.113; **6**.182; **16**.17, 75
Ropes **14**.33, 45, 64, 80
Rossetti, C. **11**.215; **13**.41;
      16.173
Rough, J. **11**.32; **12**.49
Rowe, N. **13**.137
Rufinas **12**.205; **17**.231
Rufus **2**.366; **3**.249, 361; **4**.283;
      8.7, 214–216
Ruinhart **17**.106
Ruskin, J. **4**.195
Russell, G. **13**.1
Ruth **1**.17, 24; **6**.146
Rutherford, M. **1**.202, 244, 246f,
      264; **4**.58; **11**.209
Rutherford **9**.170; **11**.193
Ryle **15**.185

Sadd, A. **6**.224
Saiguael **16**.31
Salisbury, F. **5**.239
Sallust **10**.80; **13**.177
Sallustius Lucullus **17**.140
Salome, of Herodias **2**.95f;
      3.150, 152f, 7.93
Salome **2**.229; **3**.353; **5**.16, 96;
      6.256; **14**.16
Sambathe **16**.101, 105
Sammael **6**.31
Sammlai, rabbi **3**.293

Samson **10.**129; **13.**163; **14.**115f

Samuel **1.**234; **2.**276, 296; **4.**17; **5.**82; **6.**126; **12.**134; **15.**69

Samuel, Viscount **1.**340

Sanballat **5.**150

Sanday, W. **1.**65; **8.**1

Saphira See Ananias & S.

Sarah **8.**128; **10.**41; **14.**222

Sariel **17.**41

Satan **1.**65; **2.**36f, 40, 51, 148–150, 317; **3.**22f, 78f, 174, 330; **4.**150, 263, 270, 273f; **6.**31, 126; **8.**34, 219; **9.**181f, 195f, 246; **10.**182; **11.**193; **12.**91, 93; **14.**50; **17.**47, 59, 80–84, 86, 88, 130, 168, 184, 190, 191f

  and death **16.**141

  delivery to **9.**44; **12.**53f; **15.**118

  depths of **16.**108f

  power of **11.**112, 212

  prosecuting angel **13.**18

  seat of **16.**88–90

  synagogue of **16.**80

Saturninus **12.**94

Saul, king **2.**276; **4.**17, 47; **11.**54, 58; **15.**69; **16.**46, 133

Saul of Tarsus See Paul

Schopenhauer **3.**25; **5.**231

Schürer **2.**303; **3.**194

Schweitzer, A. **9.**83

Scipio **12.**18

Scott, E. F. **5.**160; **10.**66, 67, 68; **12.**217; **13.**5; **14.**283

Scott, R. **4.**126; **11.**72

Scott, W. **4.**19; **8.**74; **9.**219; **13.**83

Scythinus **3.**57

Seago, E. **5.**112

Seeley, J. **6.**3; **14.**229; **15.**204

Selwyn, E. G. **14.**143, 178, 190, 257

Semjaza **14.**322

Seneca **1.**27, 32, 139, 157, 283, 344; **3.**12, 25; **4.**26, 181; **5.**55, 58; **6.**23; **7.**137; **8.**4, 19, 31f, 39, 98, 204; **9.**54, 140, 204, 235, 254; **10.**81, 171, 176; **11.**199; **12.**19, 34, 51, 78, 130, 131, 159, 231, 245; **13.**139, 157; **14.**60, 64, 82, 113, 207, 221, 335; **15.**100, 121; **16.**117, 159; **17.**91f, 145, 161

  Epistles of See Index VI

Serapis **1.**111; **3.**181; **9.**72

Sergius Paulus **7.**3, 100; **9.**21

Seth (Greek) **2.**65; **3.**91

Seth (O.T.) **14.**323

Sennacherib **6.**43; **17.**22

Severus, A. **14.**129

Shackleton **1.**375

Shadrach **1.**117; **8.**166; **9.**119; **13.**129, 164

Shaftesbury, Lord **1.**94, 166; **10.**155

Shakespeare, W. **1.**117, 244; **2.**225, 297; **3.**19, 206, 329; **5.**224; **6.**51; **8.**33; **10.**64, 82; **12.**128, 189; **13.**117, 135, 136, 137; **14.**92, 266, 329; **17.**28

Shammai, rabbi **1.**273; **2.**198, 200; **3.**164; **6.**70; **10.**168

  school of **1.**152, 158; **3.**239; **4.**212

Shaw, G. B. **3.**28; **4.**11; **5.**58; **6.**129; **7.**75; **8.**40

Shearjashub **8**.145
Shebna **16**.133
Shelley **4**.87; **6**.128
Shemaiah **12**.134
Shemachsai **3**.34
Sheppard, D. **1**.218; **9**.187;
    13.124
Shibta **3**.165
Shimei **17**.59
Short, A. R. **2**.80, 112; **3**.33,
    36, 119f
Shylock **5**.110
Sidney, P. **3**.85
Silas **7**.117, 125, 136; **9**.5, 74;
    11.181; **12**.22; **14**.17, 143,
    274; **15**.169
Silesius **13**.128
Silvanus **10**.145; **14**.143f, 145,
    274–276
Sim, A. F. **9**.121
Simeon ben Jocai, rabbi **4**.224
Simeon **4**.26
Simeon, called Niger **3**.361;
    7.98f
Simeon (O.T.) *Testaments of*
    See Index VI
    tribe of **14**.31
Simeon (Peter) **2**.145, 4.26, 228
Simeon, rabbi **1**.257; **14**.55
Simeon ben Yohai, rabbi **1**.55
Simon the Canaenaen **1**.359;
    3.74; **4**.3
Simon of Cyrene **1**.168; **2**.366;
    3.360f; **4**.282f; **7**.98f; **8**.215f
Simon ben Eleazar, rabbi **1**.139f
Simon ben Gamaliel, rabbi
    2.246; **3**.274
Simon the Leper **2**.329; **3**.325
Simon Maccabaeus **1**.74, 233f;

2.239; **3**.266; **6**.117
Simon Magus **1**.26, 69; **15**.89
Simon Peter See Peter
Simon the Pharisee **2**.329; **4**.4,
    5, 94; **11**.157
Simon the Righteous, rabbi **3**.293
Simon ben Shetah **12**.77
Simon the Sorcerer **7**.66f
Simon the Tanner **7**.80; **14**.254
Simon the Zealot **1**.359; **3**.83;
    4.3, 75
Simpson, E. K. **12**.106, 122, 130,
    158
Simpson, J. Y. **1**.41f, 119, 224,
    338; **3**.127; **4**.68, 136
Sirach See Jesus ben S.
Slessor, M. **8**.184
Small, A. H. **8**.71
Smart, W. J. **12**.56
Smith, Adam **10**.86
Smith, Alexander **3**.13
Smith, D. **10**.177
Smith, G. A. **1**.63; **2**.247; **4**.47,
    201; **5**.28; **6**.53; **9**.118;
    14.216; **15**.184–186; **17**.38
Smith, R. **17**.103
Smith, W. H. **1**.276
Smith, W. T. **3**.134
Snowdon, R. **8**.76; **10**.113, 115
Socrates **1**.78, 154, 155, 278,
    396; **2**.313; **5**.140; **6**.23,
    168, 187; **8**.112; **9**.53, 79,
    132; **10**.170; **11**.45, 85;
    12.61, 186, 205, 239; **13**.130,
    142; **14**.114, 120f, 304, 341;
    15.41, 42, 85, 122f
Solomon, King **1**.17, 45, 225;
    2.37, 50; **3**.22, 210; **4**.147,
    151; **5**.82; **11**.187; **13**.19;

| 1 Matt, v.1 | 3 Mark | 5 John, v.1 | 7 Acts | 9 Cor |
| 2 Matt, v.2 | 4 Luke | 6 John, v.2 | 8 Rom | 10 Gal, Eph |

14.42; 15.87; 16.3; 17.81, 206
and Jesus 2.20
Odes of See Index VI
Psalms of See Index VI
temple of 2.161
Solomon, pianist 9.244
Solon 1.154; 10.162; 12.38, 106; 16.114
ben Soma 9.256
Sopater 8.220
Sophocles 1.173; 8.202; 9.136, 158; 10.25, 110; 14.172, 298
Sosipater 8.220
Sosthenes 11.103
Spence 5.142f
Spenser 12.209; 17.114
Sporus 17.91
Spurgeon, C. H. 5.100, 163; 12.204
Spurius Carvilius Ruga 1.156; 8.32; 10.171
Stalin, J. 4.114
Stalker 9.7
Stanley 7.12
Stanton 6.204; 9.120
Starbuck, E. D. 6.40f
Statius Quadratus 9.107
Statilla Messalina 12.78
Stephanas 9.15f, 166
Stephanatus 9.6, 8
Stephanus 3.299; 9.223; 15.111
Stephen 4.285; 6.86, 233; 7.4, 5, 19, 53f; 14.259
   defence of 7.54–61
   and Paul 7.74f
   prayer of 7.62, 72; 8.168
Stevenson, R. L. 1.100, 121, 222f; 3.153, 245; 4.66, 106, 167; 5.55; 8.22, 64, 91, 177; 9.196, 203, 235f; 10.182; 13.120, 150; 14.92; 15.55; 16.82
Stewart, H. F. 14.92
Stewart, J. 9.24
Stilicho 3.204
Stoddart, J. 1.276
Stowe, H. B. 9.188
Strabo 11.91; 14.40; 16.58, 74, 87, 126; 17.45, 166
Strachan, R. H. 6.87
Stradivari, A. 7.45
Strahan 16.41
Streeter, B. H. 14.151, 163
Struma Nonius 14.221
Struthers, J. P. 1.285; 3.327; 7.31; 13.151
Studd, C. T. 3.58; 12.56
Sulla 12.78
Suetonius 1.27; 3.181, 229, 313; 6.182; 8.31; 10.171; 14.157; 17.139f, 154, 156
Suidas 14.107
Sullivan, A. 10.123
Sulpicius Gallus 14.218
Sulpicius Severus 14.149
Sunday, B. 3.12
Sutherland, H. 12.213
Swedenborg, E. 1.305
Swete, H. B. 3.80; 16.33, 38, 50, 51, 121, 151, 154, 156, 159, 169, 172; 17.17, 26, 41, 77, 79, 83, 93f, 110, 117, 120, 130, 131, 132, 133, 151, 171, 172, 176, 177, 180, 190, 192, 197, 209, 219, 221, 224, 225, 227, 229

11 Phil, Col, Thes
12 Tim, Tit, Phlm
13 Heb
14 Jas, Pet
15 John, Jude
16 Rev, v.1
17 Rev, v.2

Swinburne 1.120, 213; 4.195;
 8.72; 13.135
Symeon (Peter) 14.291f
Syntyche 11.71–74; 12.68

Tabitha 5.90; 6.87; 7.77
Tacitus 1.27; 2.218, 364; 3.313,
 320; 6.41f, 182, 250; 7.168;
 8.31, 49, 50; 12.20, 36, 78,
 167, 190; 13.111, 178; 14.147,
 149, 202; 15.124; 16.138;
 17.83, 145, 146, 154, 160
 Histories of See Index VI
Tagore 10.8
Tamar 1.17
Tarphon 1.367
Tatian 12.59; 14.152; 17.106
Tatlock, R. 11.33
Tauler 1.260f
Taylor, Fr. 10.113
Taylor, J. 3.122, 174; 8.36;
 12.80; 13.27
Taylor, V. 10.45; 15.143
Telemachus 2.77; 3.203–205
Temple W. 2.117; 3.89
Tennyson, A. 1.227; 2.321;
 3.200, 226; 4.226, 276; 13.1,
 20, 27; 14.132
Terah 13.143
Tertius 8.xii, 45, 220; 11.174
Tertullian 1.111, 267; 2.349,
 360; 3.13, 317; 8.27, 172;
 9.63, 222, 258; 12.1, 59, 64,
 170; 13.5, 8, 149, 192;
 14.20, 129, 279, 280; 15.70,
 169; 16.26, 70, 92; 17.12, 70,
 141, 189
 and Scripture 14.3, 151
Tertullus 7.168f

Thackeray 9.219
Thaddeus 1.82
Thalasius 2.80
Thecla, *Acts of Paul* See
 Index VI
Theocritus 11.203
Theodore of Mopseuestia
 2.349; 12.116f, 204
Theodoret 1.266; 2.349; 8.34f;
 11.124
Theodorus 3.125
Theodosius 12.159, 205
Theodota 1.155
Theognis 10.110
Theophilus (N.T.) 4.1, 3; 7.2, 9;
 12.11
Theophilus of Antioch 12.59
Theophorus 2.175
Theophrastus 8.37, 38; 12.186;
 13.191; 14.105, 265; 15.58,
 197
Theophylact 8.37; 12.186;
 13.182; 14.105
Theresa, saint 8.71
Thermouthis 13.156
Theudas 1.69; 7.50; 9.18
Thomas, apostle 5.5, 23, 90;
 6.87f, 101, 156f, 270, 275–
 279; 14.161, 162, 179, 294
 Acts of See Index VI
 called Didymus 7.100
Thomas à Kempis 15.87
Thompson, F. 6.160; 8.153;
 9.199
Thomson, W. M. 1.77, 316, 322,
 344; 2.21, 72f, 76, 84, 134,
 253; 6.57, 61, 281
Thorwaldson 2.249; 9.92
Thurio 12.127

| 1 Matt, v.1 | 3 Mark | 5 John, v.1 | 7 Acts | 9 Cor |
| 2 Matt, v.2 | 4 Luke | 6 John, v.2 | 8 Rom | 10 Gal, Eph |

Thucydides 9.3, 155; 14.82, 108, 143

Tiamat 11.212; 15.61; 17.58, 133, 198

Tiberius 2.359; 3.125, 286; 4.3, 31; 6.239; 8.31; 10.171; 11.21, 137; 16.18, 75, 115, 126, 135; 17.89, 93, 139, 146, 160

Tiberius Claudius Cogidubnus 12.222

Timothy 3.4, 71; 7.120, 136; 8.219; 9.5, 6, 8, 41, 165; 11.47f, 74, 103f, 181, 195; 12.21–23, 49, 50, 51f, 96, 98, 133f, 138, 164f, 197; 15.171

Tiridates 1.27

Titus (Emperor) 2.302, 306; 9.183; 16.19; 17.89, 93, 101, 139, 146

Titus (N.T.) 9.7, 8, 183, 224–226; 10.16; 12.71, 218f, 232

Tobias 1.273

Tobit, *Book of* See Index VI

Tolstoi 4.40; 9.188

Toplady 6.262

Torpacion 14.129

Toscanini 1.135; 3.17; 4.51; 10.126

Tournier, P. 1.327; 2.31; 3.35, 37f, 47; 6.5; 13.60

Trajan 1.391; 6.189; 9.21, 107; 11.159; 12.99; 13.193; 14.128, 155f, 159

Trench, R. C. 8.42; 9.170; 10.51, 136; 11.157; 12.37, 61, 80, 83, 236, 239, 240; 14.330; 16.60, 63, 133, 140, 141, 144, 145, 148

Tristram, C. 1.345; 2.157, 251; 5.153, 212f

Trophimus 7.157; 10.112; 12.222

Tryphaena and Tryphosa 8.214

Trypho, *Dialogue with* See Index VI

Tsze-Kung 1.274

Tullia 12.78

Tulloch, Mrs 1.105

Turgeniev 9.262

Turner, C. H. 7.4

Twitchell, J. 9.132f

Tychicus 7.192; 10.61f, 185; 11.169; 12.219, 265

Tyndale, W. 1.255; 3.180; 4.152; 6.189; 8.167; 12.220

Tyrimnus 16.101

Tyrranus 7.142f

Tyrrell 5.51

Ulysses 3.336; 8.186; 9.52

Unamuno 4.182; 10.124; 17.118

Urban VIII 3.101f

Uriah 1.17; 3.85

Uriel 13.18; 14.325; 16.31; 17.41

Valentine 12.127

Valentinus 12.8

Valerius Maximus 17.156

Varro 1.302; 10.179; 14.211

Varus 1.395

Vaughan, C. J. 8.55, 96; 13.14

Vedius, P. 10.180; 12.270

Verrall, A. W. 1.153

Verrius Flaccus 9.249

Verus 1.154; 10.170

Vespasian **2**.170; **3**.181; **6**.41f;
  8.216; **11**.137; **14**.14; **16**.19,
  126, 135; **17**.89, 93, 101,
  139, 146
Vettius Epagathos **15**.38
Victor of Capua **11**.173
Victoria, Queen **1**.105
Victorinus **16**.14, 161
Vidyasagar **2**.100
Vincent of Lerins **12**.139
Vincent, M. R. **11**.11, 77
Vinicius **3**.145
Virgil **1**.27, 279; **4**.87; **8**.30;
  9.129; **14**.76; **16**.11, 16
Vitellius **2**.359; **11**.21; **16**.19;
  17.89, 93, 139, 157
Voltaire **3**.227

Wagner **9**.191
Waldmeier, M. **1**.314
Walker, A. **6**.270
Walpole, H. **2**.218; **3**.341
Walton, I. **14**.138
Warren, M. **9**.240
Washington, B. **7**.188; **8**.170
Watkinson **4**.132
Watson, W. **4**.91, 132; **6**.80;
  13.15
Watt, J. **4**.57
Watts **8**.196
Way, A. S. **9**.155; **12**.107
Weatherhead, L. **10**.7, 126;
  13.194
Webb, S. **4**.177; **6**.5
Welch, A. C. **4**.149; **10**.166
Wellington, Duke of **11**.186
Wells, H. G. **1**.100, 315; **2**.78;
  3.77, 108; **4**.63, 177, 269;
  6.22; **7**.41; **8**.72, 110, 200;

  10.91; **15**.31
Wendt **1**.314
Wesley, C. **4**.130; **13**.119;
  14.234; **16**.71; **17**.84
Wesley, J. **3**.61, 84, 110; **4**.56,
  73, 130, 164, 195; **7**.110, 111;
  9.46, 214, 259; **10**.133, 156;
  11.51f; **12**.171, 181; **14**.109,
  131; **15**.161, 162, 182; **16**.80
Wesley, Samuel **4**.130
Wesley, Susannah **2**.163
West, B. **10**.178
Westcott, B. F. **3**.5; **5**.71; **6**.111,
  273; **13**.104, 182, 183;
  14.151, 176; **15**.35, 44, 47,
  56, 64, 82, 116, 122, 123
Wetstein, J. J. **1**.188
Weymouth **15**.92
Whale, J. S. **12**.127
Wharton, Lord **1**.394
Whitefield, G. **3**.84; **6**.5; **8**.163;
  12.260
Whitley, Bishop **2**.101
Whittier **1**.215; **2**.25; **3**.252;
  8.157; **15**.26
Whyte, A. **1**.361; **8**.196; **9**.115;
  10.13; **15**.22
Wilberforce, W. **1**.166; **2**.76;
  5.165; **9**.243; **10**.155; **14**.134
Wilde, O. **1**.309; **10**.84f, 100
William, Conqueror **2**.181
Williams, K. **3**.226; **15**.92
Williamson, K. **4**.216
Wilson, Bishop **12**.205
Winn, G. **1**.183
Wishart, G. **7**.62; **12**.55
Withers, J. H. **1**.16
Wolsey **3**.206, 329
Wood, H. G. **6**.114

| **1** Matt, v.1 | **3** Mark | **5** John, v.1 | **7** Acts | **9** Cor |
| **2** Matt, v.2 | **4** Luke | **6** John, v.2 | **8** Rom | **10** Gal, Eph |

Wordsworth **1**.208, 262; **5**.22, 155; **9**.191, 202; **10**.98; **15**.3
Wren, C. **3**.89; **10**.121
Wyclif **1**.255; **3**.53; **4**.151; **6**.167; **7**.10
Wyon, O. **2**.107

Xenophanes **5**.73
Xenophon **1**.78, 155; **8**.38, 112; **10**.170; **12**.61, 87, 186, 239; **13**.176; **14**.114, 304; **15**.36, 41, 122; **16**.69f
Xerxes **5**.178; **11**.92, 180

Yeats, W. B. **1**.305, 309, 326, 347, 348, 350; **2**.16
Young, E. **3**.249; **6**.64

Zachaeus **2**.189, 219; **3**.53; **4**.5, 234f
Zacharias (N.T.) **2**.298; **4**.9–11, 17–19; **5**.76; **16**.160

Zacharias (O.T.) **4**.159
Zadok **16**.133
Zadok, rabbi **1**.284, 367
Zarephath, widow of **4**.5
Zebedee **2**.229; **5**.15; **6**.229
Zechariah **13**.166
Zedekiah **16**.171
Zenas **12**.266; **17**.176
Zeno **3**.279; **14**.55
Zera, rabbi **3**.86
Zeus **1**.201, 271; **3**.267; **10**.129; **13**.25, 167; **14**.321; **16**.29f, 89, 91; **17**.226
  of Olympias **2**.241, 306; **3**.310; **6**.70; **17**.60
  and Paul & Barnabas **7**.109
  temple of **16**.74f
  tomb of **12**.243
Zeus Xenios **12**.81f; **13**.191; **15**.149
Zeuxis **16**.138
Zophar **14**.295
Zwingli **16**.1

11 Phil, Col, Thes
12 Tim, Tit, Phlm
13 Heb
14 Jas, Pet
15 John, Jude
16 Rev, v.1
17 Rev, v.2

INDEX OF FOREIGN WORDS, TERMS AND PHRASES

A 17.159
Abaddon 17.51
Abba 2.349f; 3.8, 344; 10.35
Acharistos 12.187
Acharista mathemata 13.48
Achreioo 8.55
Adiaphora 8.189
Adelphos 14.16f
Adiakritos 14.97
Adikia 8.34
Adokimastos 12.173
Adokimos 12.246
Adolos 14.192
Adonai 17.180
Adoxos 10.135
Ad salutem 12.231
Ab umbris et imaginibus ad veritatem 13.3
Adunaton 13.57
Aeons 12.6; 15.164
Aergos 2.46
Agallian 17.172
Agalliasthai 1.116
Agapan 1.173; 4.78; 16.144
Agape 1.113, 173–175, 224, 376; 6.184; 9.95, 99f, 216; 10.18, 49f, 139f; 12.98, 134f; 14.148, 203; 15.139
Agape, he 15.192; 16.80
Agapetos 15.148
Agathos 1.125; 3.326; 6.62; 7.31; 8.42; 14.202
Agathosune 10.51, 164
Agenealogetos 13.74

Agennes 10.135
Aggareuein 1.168
Aggareus 1.168
Aggelos 7.47f; 13.17; 16.54
Agon 12.210
Agorazein 16.177
Aionios 2.182, 216; 5.44, 129; 6.207; 12.228; 15.113
Aischrokerdes 12.237; 14.265
Aischrokerdeia 14.265
Aischrologia 11.153
Akakos 13.83
Akatastasiai 9.265
Akatharsia 9.265; 10.47; 11.188
Akeraios 8.218; 11.43
Akeratos 1.106
Akolasia 14.303
Akolouthein 6.12
Akrasia 14.303
Akrates 12.189
Akratisma 8.178; 9.53; 16.147
Akropolis kakon 12.186
Alazon 8.38; 12.185f; 15.58
Alazoneia 8.38; 12.186; 14.114; 15.58
Ale 12.185
Aleph 5.213; 16.38; 17.226
Aletheia 5.9; 10.164
Alethes 5.9, 54; 16.127
Alethinos 5.9, 54; 6.173; 16.127; 17.178
Allotriepiskopos 14.259
Allotrios 14.259f
Alpha 16.37

Amachos **12.**84, 259
Amarantos **14.**174
Amemptos **11.**43, 60
Amen **9.**177; **16.**37, 140
Ameth **5.**213
Ametor **13.**74f
Amiantos **13.**84; **14.**173
Amixia **8.**50
Amnos **16.**171
Amomos **10.**78; **11.**44; **15.**207;
  17.108, 161
Amphiblestron **1.**77; **2.**88f;
  3.27
Anagke **9.**213
Anakainosis **8.**158
Analuein **11.**28
Analusis **12.**209
Anamartetos **6.**4
Anapempein **12.**274, 281
Anastrephesthai **12.**88
Anastrophe **14.**201
Anathema **8.**124
Andrapododes **10.**135
Androphonoi **12.**38
Andropodistai **12.**39
Aneleemon **8.**39
Anemeros **12.**190
Anepileptos **12.**75
Anhupotaktoi **12.**37
'Ani **1.**91
Anoche **8.**42
Anomia **1.**221; **3.**357
Anomoi **12.**37
Anosios **12.**37, 188
Anothen **5.**125
Antallagma **2.**154
Anthropos **6.**244
Anti **15.**61
Antilutron **16.**177

Antistrategos **15.**61
Antitheseis **12.**139
Antitupos **14.**244
Anupokritos **14.**97
Aorgesia **1.**96
Apagoge **1.**144
Aparabatos **13.**82
Aparche **17.**108
Apatheia **6.**98; **9.**18; **13.**42;
  14.75f
Apator **13.**74f
Apatouria **10.**34
Apaugasma **13.**14
Apechein **1.**186
Apecho **1.**186
Apeitheia **8.**38
Aphanismos **13.**92
Aphilagathos **12.**190
Aphorozein **8.**12
Aphrosune **3.**175
Aphthartos **14.**173
Apo **11.**26; **16.**21
Apokalupsis **3.**305; **14.**122;
  16.2, 21
Apokaradokia **8.**110f; **11.**26
Apokatallassein **10.**117
Apokruphos **11.**130, 148
Apokruptein **11.**148
Apollyon **17.**51f
Apologia **11.**17
Apolutrosis **8.**59; **10.**81
Apostellein **5.**165; **10.**74; **12.**17;
  15.176
Aposthesthai **14.**189
Apostolos **4.**74; **7.**177; **10.**74f;
  11.49f, 103; **12.**17, 148; **13.**30;
  15.176
Aproskopos **11.**19
Aptaistos **15.**206

Arbel **17.**50
Arbiter bibendi **5.**99
Arbitri **13.**89
Arche **11.**121; **16.**141; **17.**204f
Archegos **13.**25f
Archetheoria **8.**202
Architriklinos **5.**99
Archomenoi **13.**52
Archon **5.**123
Areskeia **12.**62
Areskos **12.**236
Arete **11.**81; **14.**301f
Argurion **2.**332
Ariston **16.**147
Arles **9.**177
Arnion **16.**171
Arnoumai **17.**101
Arnoume **17.**101
Arrabon **9.**177, 205; **10.**87
Arsenokoitai **12.**38
Artemisia **17.**44
Asebeis **12.**37
Asebes **12.**37
Aselgeia **3.**174f; **8.**179; **9.**265f;
   10.47, 153; **14.**319; **15.**180
Aselgese **15.**180
Asher **4.**56
Ashere **1.**88
-Asmos **8.**91
Asotia **12.**234
Asotos **12.**235
Aspondos **12.**188
Assarion **1.**389; **4.**171
Asthenein **1.**365
Asthenes **1.**365
Astorgos **8.**39; **12.**188
Astrateia **8.**49
Asunetos **8.**38
Asunthetos **8.**38f

Ataktein **11.**217
Ataktos **11.**217
Ataraxia **8.**199
Atheotes **8.**49
Athetesis **13.**79
Athlein nominos **12.**161
Atimia **9.**217
Augustus **17.**138
Autarkeia **9.**235; **11.**84; **12.**128
Autarkes **11.**84
Authadeia **12.**62, 236
Authades **12.**236; **14.**329f
Autodiakonos **1.**90
Autos **14.**329
Ayont **9.**203; **13.**150
Azazel **13.**100

Baptizein **3.**255; **4.**169; **5.**84
Barbaroi **7.**187; **13.**148
Basileia **16.**40
Basilikos **5.**174
Bastazein **6.**112; **8.**197
Bath **5.**98
Bath qol **3.**20; **6.**127
Bdelugma **12.**246
Bdeluktos **12.**246
Be **16.**34
Bebaiosis **11.**17
Bebaptismenos **3.**255
Bebelos **12.**37f; **13.**182
Bela **16.**66
Bema **9.**206
Beneficiarius **9.**185
Biblia **12.**219
Biblos **1.**12
Blasphemia **1.**324; **3.**175;
   11.153; **12.**187
Brekekekex coax coax **17.**130
Brosis **1.**239

Burnous 1.99

Capax dei 12.55
Carob 3.16
Cavaletta 17.50
Centuries 7.79
Chaburah 5.120
Chairein 14.23, 36; 17.172
Chairete 2.376
Chalepos 12.182
Chalkolibanos 16.49
Challah 9.80
Chamaizelos 10.135
Chara 10.50
Character 13.14
Charagma 17.99
Charaz 4.81, 160; 8.55; 14.30
Charis 9.163; 10.9, 75f; 11.12
Charisma 8.91, 160; 9.12
Charismata 8.160; 9.108
Charosheth 2.340; 3.333, 338
Chazzan 3.31; 4.48
Cheirographon 11.141; 12.283
Cherem 6.47; 7.166
Chesedh 1.103; 12.24f
Chilios 17.186
Chiton 1.167; 3.141f
Chliaros 16.141
Chloros 17.9
Choinix 17.7
Choregein 14.299
Choregia 8.202; 10.25
Choregos 14.298
Chortazesthai 5.203
Chremata 3.246
Chrematizein 13.188
Chrestologos 8.218
Chrestos 2.17; 8.42; 10.51, 159f

Chrestotes 8.42; 9.216; 10.51; 11.157; 12.261
Christemporos 15.135
Christos 3.297; 10.107; 15.70; 17.60
Cilicium 7.136
Cognomen 8.212
Conversari 11.29
Cor 16.10
Corban See Korban
Cubit 3.308

Damnatio memoriae 10.69f
Dayyaneh gezeloth 4.222
Dayyaneh gezeroth 4.222
Deesis 12.57
Deilos 17.206
Deipnein 16.147
Deipnon 9.103; 16.147f
Delator 3.313; 17.83
Delatores 12.190
Deleazein 14.332
Denarius 1.389; 2.194, 222, 329; 3.159, 285, 326; 4.171, 247; 5.202; 17.7
Derush 10.41; 13.67
Desmios 11.21
Deus pater 10.129
Diabolos 1.227; 3.22; 10.157; 12.74, 189; 17.82
Diadema 11.70, 193; 16.83; 17.3, 179
Diakonia 8.161; 9.163; 10.149
Diakonos 9.163
Dialogismos 3.173; 11.43; 12.65
Diaspora See Subject Index
Diatheke 13.90, 107
Didache 7.22; 9.25f

Didaktikos **12**.82

Didaskalos **1**.311; **5**.87

Didrachma **2**.168; **4**.172

Diekrithete **14**.65

Dikaios **8**.23; **9**.79f; **12**.239; **13**.142

Dikaiosune **8**.23, 34; **10**.164; **11**.62; **12**.134

Dikaioun **8**.22, 57

Dilogos **12**.85

Diolkos **9**.1

Diorussein **1**.239

Dipsuchos **14**.46

Dispensator **14**.255

Dives **4**.213

Divus **17**.89, 138

Dokein **5**.13, 65; **11**.26; **15**.7, 180

Dokimazein **11**.18

Dokime **8**.74

Dokimion **14**.43

Dokimos **12**.173; **14**.48

Dolos **3**.174; **8**.35f; **14**.190

Doloun **8**.36

Domina **15**.138

Dominus **17**.89, 138

Dorcas **7**.77

Douleuein **1**.248

Doulikos **10**.135

Douloprepes **10**.135

Doulos **1**.248; **6**.177f; **8**.11f; **11**.9; **12**.227; **14**.35f, 210, 292, 293; **15**.175; **16**.24f

Doxai **14**.323

Drachma **2**.168, 222; **4**.172, 202

Dunamis **5**.119; **7**.180

Dusnoetos **14**.349

DWD **1**.9

Ebedh **16**.25

Ebion **1**.91

Ecclesia haeres crucis est **12**.169

Echein **14**.318

Echthroi **8**.152

Egguos **13**.81

Egkomboma **14**.270

Egkombousthai **14**.270

Egkoptein **11**.193

Egkrateia **10**.52; **14**.302f

Egkrates **12**.239

Eikon **11**.116–118; **13**.112f

Eikonion **11**.118

Eile **11**.19

Eilein **11**.19

Eilikrineia **9**.174, 185

Eilikrenes **11**.19; **14**.337

Eilikrines dianoia **14**.337

Eimi **16**.30

Eirein **11**.12

Eirene **10**.9, 50, 76; **11**.12; **14**.95, 97

Eirenikos **14**.95

Ek **15**.92

Ekbasis **9**.90

Ekklesia **2**.142; **12**.88f; **14**.21, 26

Eklektos **14**.167

Ektenes **14**.252

Ekzetesis **12**.5

Electrum **16**.49

Eleemon **1**.103

Eleemosune **9**.164

Elegchein **6**.192; **12**.239; **16**.144

Elegchos **16**.145

Elekte **15**.19, 129f, 138

Elekte kuria **15**.129f, 138

Eleos **12**.24; **14**.96

Eleutheria **12**.9

Elohim **6.77; 13.24**
Eloi, eloi, lama sabachthani **3.8**
Emathen aph hon epathen **13.48**
Emblepein **5.90**
Embrimasthai **6.97**
Emphutos **14.57**
En **9.104**
Enarchesthai **10.25; 11.17**
Endeiknumai **12.219**
Energein **11.41**
En kairo eschato **14.176**
Ennoia **13.40**
Enteuxis **12.57f**
Enthumesis **13.40**
Entugchanein **12.58**
Eophema **11.80**
Epaggelia **8.68**
Epagonizesthai **15.179**
Epainos **8.47**
Epekteinomenos **11.66**
Eperotema **14.244**
Ephebos **10.34**
Ephphatha **3.8**
Epichoregein **14.298f**
Epieikeia **9.238; 11.75f; 12.83**
Epieikes **12.83, 259; 14.95, 124**
Epignosis **14.294f**
Epikaleisthai **14.67**
Epiorkoi **12.39**
Epiousios **1.216f**
Epiphaneia **12.149f, 203; 14.122**
Epiphanes **16.87**
Epipothein **14.192**
Episkopein **12.71**
Episkopos **12.70f, 81; 14.139, 216; 14.259**
Epistomizein **12.242**
Epitage **12.17**
Epitelein **11.16**

Epiteleisthai **10.25**
Epi ten gen **2.126**
Epi ten thalassan **2.105**
Epi thumia **8.28f, 176; 10.100**
Epitropos **4.97**
Epoptes **14.310**
Eran **1.173; 4.78**
Eranos **9.99, 162**
Ergon **2.46**
Eris **8.35, 179; 9.263**
Eritheia **9.264; 10.48; 11.23; 14.91**
Erithos **10.48**
Eros **1.173; 10.49, 139**
Errimenoi **1.356**
Eschato **14.176**
Eskulmenoi **1.355**
Eta **9.15**
Euaggelion **3.24**
Euanthas **17.101**
Eucharistia **12.58**
Euergetes **4.267**
Eulogetos **14.90**
Eulogia **9.164**
Eupeithes **14.96**
Euphemia **11.16**
Eusebia **12.61, 134; 14.297, 303f**
Eusebes **14.304**
Euseistos **11.91**
Exagorazein **16.34, 177**
Exaleiphein **11.142**
Exedoke **5.20**
Exia **14.318**
Exodos **2.160; 14.308**
Exousia **1.134; 3.37**

Familia **13.17**
Fortis **6.167; 7.10; 9.171**

Frail 3.184
Fugitivus 10.180; 12.122, 270

Galil 1.72; 4.45
Gallicinium 2.347; 3.352; 6.230
Gan 4.56
Gazam 17.50
Geneseos 1.12
Genomenos 16.30, 81
Genus Boswellia 17.162
Geraskon 13.92
Geron 12.280
Gerousia 12.70
Gignesthai 11.37
Gignomai 16.30
Ginoskein 11.63
Gnesios 12.22f
Gnosis 9.109, 130; 12.139; 14.294, 302; 15.10
Goggusmos 5.237; 11.43
Goggustes 15.197
Graphein 6.3
Gumnasiarcha 8.202
Gumnos 13.40
Gunai 5.98
Gunaika 16.104
Gune 16.104

Ha'am 16.66
Hadon 14.329
Hadrotes 9.163f
Haggadah 3.338
Hagiasmos 8.91; 13.181f
Hagios 15.4, 176; 16.93, 127; 17.152
Hagiazo 9.10
Hagiazein 6.77, 216
Hagiazesthai 1.205
Hagios 1.205; 6.77, 216; 7.78;

8.94; 9.10; 10.77, 108; 11.10; 13.181; 14.188, 199
Hagnos 11.80; 14.95
Hagnotes 9.215
Hairein 12.265
Haireisthai 14.316
Hairesis 10.48; 14.316
Hairetikos 12.265
Halal 17.169
Hallel 2.342; 3.338; 5.249; 6.116; 17.169
Hallelujah 17.168f
Halusis 11.21f
Hamartia 1.220; 6.17; 10.95f; 14.233; 15.33
Hamartolos 3.56f; 12.37; 14.107
Hanukkah 6.69
Haplos 1.245
Haplotes 1.245; 8.161f
Haplous 1.245; 8.162
Hargol 17.50
Harpagmos 11.36
Harparchein 11.35
Harpax 9.53
Hasil 17.50
Hathos 8.118
Hedraioma 12.89
Helkuein 5.220
Heupferd 17.50
Herrenvolk 1.304; 2.224
Hestiasis 8.202
Heteira 1.154f
Heteros 8.118
Hieron 2.244, 336; 3.272f
Hilaskesthai 15.39
Hilasmos 15.38–40
Hilasterion 8.58
Himation 3.142

Holokleros **14.44**
Homilia **7.23**
Honestus **14.202**
Hora **5.231**
Horan **15.23**
Hosanna **2.239; 3.267f; 6.116;**
  17.169
Hosios **12.37, 239; 13.83**
Hubris **8.37; 9.266; 12.45;**
  17.154
Hubristes **8.37; 12.45**
Hugiainein **12.40**
Huios **1.29, 109; 12.9**
Huiothesia **12.9**
Hupage satana **2.150**
Huparchein **11.35**
Huper **9.152f**
Huperephanos **8.37; 12.186;**
  14.105
Huperetes **1.145; 9.36**
Huper hamartion **14.233**
Hupo **8.54**
Hupodeigskia **13.88**
Hupogrammos **14.214**
Hupo hamartion **8.54f**
Hupokrinesthai **14.190**
Hupokrisis **14.190**
Hupokrites **1.188; 2.288;**
  3.168; 14.190
Hupomenein **9.124**
Hupomone **8.73f, 196; 9.170,**
  212f; 11.83, 109f, 210; 12.135,
  197; 13.173; 14.43, 125,
  303; 16.40, 62; 17.97
Huposchesis **8.68**
Hupotithesthai **12.96**
Hupotuposis **12.48**
Hupselokardia **1.97**
Hupsoma **8.118**

Hupsoun **5.134**
Hus **1.29**
Hyperephania **3.175**

'Iakobos **14.31**
-Iani **7.90**
Ibis ad crucem **6.250**
Idiotes **9.247**
IHWH **6.210f; 13.99; 17.179f**
Illi servire est regnare **11.10**
-Im **13.17**
Imsh' Allah **14.114**
-Inos **9.29**
Intermundia **13.43**
Iodh **1.127**
IOGD **14.257**
Iota **9.15**
Io triumphe! **9.184**
Isos **14.291**
Isotimos **14.291**
Ius gladii **6.233; 16.90**

Jaba **2.349**
Jeshuah **3.213**
Jot **1.85, 127**

Kaboth **8.125**
Kadasha **1.267f**
Kadosh **1.267; 11.10**
Kainos **8.158; 9.189; 10.116;**
  13.92; 16.98, 176
Kairos **5.231; 8.165**
Kakia **8.35; 11.153; 13.83;**
  14.189f
Kakoetheia **8.36**
Kakos **3.174; 8.35, 38**
Kakos krites **8.35**
Kalein **1.333; 15.175**
Kalos **1.125; 3.326; 6.62; 7.31;**

12.52; 14.202
Kalupsis **16.**21
Kaluptesthai **1.**317
Kamelos **2.**217; **4.**229
Kamilos **2.**217; **4.**229
Kara **11.**26
Kartarizein **14.**273
Kartartismon **10.**149
Kartartizein **10.**149
Kata **6.**3; **8.**159
Katagraphein **6.**3
Katalalein **14.**111
Katalalia **9.**264; **14.**111, 190
Katalalos **8.**36
Katalambein **5.**49
Katanoein **13.**29
Katapausis **13.**35
Kataphilein **2.**335; **3.**345
Katastrophe **12.**172
Katatemnein **11.**55
Katergazesthai **11.**41
Katharizein **15.**30
Katharos **1.**105f; **10.**47; **12.**33f
Kathekonta **8.**33
Katheudein **1.**345
Katiasthai **14.**116
Katoikein **10.**132; **16.**91
Kauson **14.**47
Kenoun **11.**36
Kephas **2.**139
Kerugma **7.**22; **9.**25; **14.**140
Kerussein **1.**75, 362
Kerux **1.**75, 362; **12.**148; **14.**326
Khan **4.**21
Kethubah **12.**77
Kiddush **2.**202; **3.**337
Kinnor **4.**56
Kiomasthai **1.**345

Kleptes **3.**173
Kleronomia **14.**173
Kleros **14.**267f
Klopai **3.**173
Koimeterion **1.**345
Koinonia **9.**163
Koinonia pisteos **12.**278
Koinos **3.**164
Koite **8.**178
Kolakeia **11.**189
Kolaphizesthai **9.**40
Kollubistai **5.**110
Kollubos **5.**110
Kollurion **16.**138
Kolumban **5.**178
Kolumbethron **5.**178
Kombos **14.**270
Komos **8.**178; **10.**49
Kophinos **2.**126; **3.**158, 184; **5.**203
Kopian **8.**214; **11.**44f; **16.**62
Kopos **9.**215; **16.**62
Korban **2.**115f, 214f; **3.**8, 169–171; **6.**239
Korinthiazesthai **9.**2
Kosher **2.**112
Kosmios **12.**80f
Kosmos **6.**18; **14.**86f, 103; **15.**56, 105
Krabbatos **5.**180
Krasis **14.**58
Kraspedon **1.**346; **2.**286
Kratein **12.**189; **16.**61
Krauge **13.**47
Kretizein **12.**243
Krinein **11.**19
Krites **8.**35
Krustallon **16.**156
Kubeia **10.**151

11 Phil, Col, Thes
12 Tim, Tit, Phlm
13 Heb
14 Jas, Pet
15 John, Jude
16 Rev, v.1
17 Rev, v.2

Kuberneseis 9.116
Kunaria 2.122
Kuppah 7.51; **12.**85
Kuria **15.**130, 138
Kurios **1.**248; **3.**298; **8.**11, 139,
    165; **9.**107; **10.**141; **11.**39;
    15.130; **17.**89, 138, 179
Kurios kai theos **16.**164
Kuriotes **14.**323
Kusi ballomena **11.**62

Lalein **13.**188
Lambanein **14.**62
Laos **9.**10; **16.**66
Lapis lazuli **17.**213
Lateinos **17.**101
Latreia **6.**190; **8.**156
Latreuein **8.**156
Latreuein kallei **8.**156f
Legatus **9.**209f
Legion **3.**118; **4.**108; **7.**79
Leipesthai **14.**44
Leitourgia **8.**202; **9.**164
Leitourgos **8.**202f; **11.**49f
Lepton **3.**302; **4.**171, 255
Lestes **3.**173; **4.**248
Lex talionis **1.**163
Libellus **1.**114
Liberalia **10.**34
Lictors **9.**184, 253
Lilin **3.**35
Lilith **1.**320; **3.**35
Limne **1.**76
Log **4.**155
Logia **8.**52; **9.**163; **14.**256
Logikos **14.**190
Logizesthai **9.**122
Logos **5.**7f, 35f, 56; **8.**113;
    11.117; **14.**191, 230

Logos akoes **15.**24
Logs **5.**249
Loidoresthai **9.**40
Lolium temulentum **2.**72
Loudaioi **5.**76
Louein **16.**34
Luein **16.**34
Lulabs **6.**116
Lumen Asiae **16.**58
Lutron **16.**177
Lutroun **10.**81
Lutrousthai **16.**177

Ma'ah **4.**241; **5.**109
Machai **14.**98
Magna est veritas et praevalebit
    2.377
Major domo **9.**36
Makarios **1.**89
Makrothumein **9.**119
Makrothumia **8.**42; **9.**216;
    10.50, 138; **11.**110, 158; **12.**196
Mal'akim **13.**17
Malakos **9.**52
Mamon **1.**249
Mancipatio **8.**106
Mandata dei **12.**127
Manthanontes **13.**52
Maran atha **9.**169; **14.**124
Marin **6.**247
Martha **15.**138
Martus **7.**13; **16.**92
Massah **13.**33
Mataiologoi **12.**241
Mataios **12.**241
Mathein **13.**48
Mathetes **6.**20
Mazzikin **3.**34
Mechitsah **1.**296

Megabyzi **15**.124
Megalopsuchia **9**.40
Melissae **12**.67
Mellon aion **13**.57
Memphesthai **11**.60; **16**.197
Mempsimoiros **15**.197f
Memra **5**.30
Menein **11**.28
Mens sana in corpore sano
  12.119
Meribah **13**.33
Merimna **1**.255
Merimnan **1**.255
Merismos **16**.32
Mesites **13**.89
Mesos **13**.89
Messiah **10**.107; **15**.69; **17**.60
Metamorphousthai **8**.157
Metanoia **3**.26; **13**.53, 184
Methe **8**.178
Methistemi **11**.111
Methos **9**.53
Methuskein **17**.159
Metraloai **12**.38
Metriopatheia **13**.47
Metriopathein **13**.46
Mezuzah **3**.295
Miainein **14**.173
Millenium **17**.186
Mimesis **10**.160
Min **5**.213
Minah **4**.172
Misanthropia **8**.50
Miseria **6**.4
Misericordia **6**.4
Mnemonic **1**.13
Moicheiai **3**.173
Moira **15**.197
Monai **6**.153

Monogenes **5**.74
Moriturus **8**.85
Moros **1**.140
Morphe **8**.157f; **11**.35–37
Mulos onikos **2**.179
Mumcheh **5**.110
Muopazon **14**.306
Murex **17**.160
Muscipula **2**.235
Musterion **2**.64; **3**.92; **9**.26;
  16.153; **17**.143

Nai **16**.37
Naos **2**.243, 305, 336; **3**.273
Neos **8**.158; **9**.189; **10**.116;
  13.92; **16**.98, 176
Neotes **12**.98
Nephalios **12**.79f, 247
Nephein **12**.207; **14**.252
Nephilum **14**.322
Ne plus ultra **15**.90
Neron **17**.102
Nezer **1**.40
Nikan **16**.66
Nimbus **16**.84
Nomen **8**.212
Nomenclatores **17**.163
Nomikos **12**.266
Nominos **12**.161
Nothros **13**.49
Nouthetein **9**.41
Nun aion **13**.57

Odinai **16**.7
Odium theologicum **2**.34;
  12.162; **14**.92
Ofanim **13**.17
Oiketai **14**.210
Oikiakoi **1**.383

---

11 Phil, Col, Thes   **13** Heb   **15** John, Jude   **16** Rev, v.1
12 Tim, Tit, Phlm   **14** Jas, Pet   **17** Rev, v.2

Oikonomia 10.84
Oikonomos 9.36; 10.84
Oikos 12.88; 13.31
Ololuzein 14.115
Omega 16.37
Onos 2.179
Opheilema 1.221
Opisthograph 16.166
Opsonia 8.91
Orge 1.139; 10.159; 11.153;
  12.236
Orgilos 12.236
Orgilotes 1.96
Orgizesthai 1.138
Orphanos 6.168
Orthotomein 12.173
Ouai 2.12, 288
-Oun 8.57

Paggim 2.252
Paidagogos 9.41; 10.31
Paidia 15.51
Paliggenesia 12.262
Palkos 11.151
Paneguris 13.186
Panta 11.123
Pantokrator 16.38f; 17.173f
Para 11.28
Parabasis 1.220f; 13.22
Parabolani 11.50
Paraboleuesthai 11.50
Parachrema 2.251
Paragellein 1.362
Parakalein 11.129; 15.36
Paraklesis 7.22; 11.83; 13.9
Parakletos 4.162; 6.166f;
  15.14, 36–38
Parakoe 13.22
Parakolouthein 12.195

Paralambanein 11.81
Parallage 14.54
Paramenein 11.28; 13.82
Paraptoma 1.221; 10.53, 96
Pararrein 13.21
Parastesai 12.173
Paratheke 12.4, 138f, 150–153
Paratithesthai 12.50; 14.261
Pareisduein 15.179
Parepidemos 13.148, 200
Paroikein 13.148
Paroikos 10.118; 13.148;
  14.167, 200
Paroimia 6.200
Paroinos 12.79f, 237
Parousia 2.312; 14.122
Parresia 15.114
Parthenos 15.19
Paschein 1.103
Pastor 6.54; 10.148
Panthei mathos 13.48
Pathein 13.48
Patientia 14.303
Patraloai 12.38
Patria potestas 1.156; 8.38,
  106; 10.79f, 175; 11.161;
  13.176; 14.218
Paupatheia 12.135
Pax romana 3.287; 6.182;
  8.174; 10.67; 12.231; 14.95;
  16.16, 137
Peah 5.203
Peirasmos 14.42
Peirazein 1.62, 224; 14.42
Pempein 5.165
Penes 1.90
Penia 16.78
Penthein 9.44
Pera 1.367; 3.143

Pergamene charta 16.88
Peri hamartias 14.233
Periousios 12.257
Peripatein 2.105; 11.29f
Perisseia 14.57
Peritemnein 11.55
Peshat 10.41; 13.67
Petalos 6.228
Petra 2.139
Phainole 12.219
Philadelphia 14.304
Philadelphos 16.125
Philagathos 12.238
Philanthropia 12.261
Philautos 12.184
Philein 1.173; 2.335; 3.345; 4.78; 7.2; 16.144
Philia 1.173; 10.49f, 139
Philostorgos 8.164
Philoxenos 12.81, 238
Phobeisthai 13.38
Phoinos 17.160
Phonos 3.173; 8.35
Phos 17.209
Phosphora 9.165
Phoster 17.209
Phosteres 11.44
Photismos 13.56
Photizesthai 13.56
Phratmai 10.34
Phronesis 10.82f; 14.251
Phrourein 11.78; 14.174
Phthonos 8.35; 10.48; 14.90
Phusioseis 9.264f
Phusis 8.45
Pietas 12.61; 14.304
Pikria 10.159
Pinein 6.109
Pisteuein 5.44

Pistikos 6.109
Pistis 10.51; 12.134; 14.301; 17.97
Pistos 6.109; 12.158, 179
Pithanologia 11.131
Planos 9.217
Plektes 12.83, 237
Pleon 14.318
Pleonektes 9.53
Pleonexia 3.173f; 8.34f; 10.153; 11.151f; 14.318, 332
Pleroma 5.71; 11.118f
Pneuma 1.22, 49; 5.131f; 8.101–103; 9.28; 13.39; 14.93; 15.11, 165f, 201f; 17.129
Pneumatikos, oi 9.28f; 15.11, 165f, 201f
Poderes 16.45f
Poiein 1.361
Poikilos 10.36; 14.177
Poimen 14.215
Polemoi 14.98
Polis 4.47
Politeuesthai 11.30
Polu- 13.11
Polumeros 13.11, 13
Polupoikilos 10.127
Polutropos 13.11, 13
Poneria 3.174; 8.34
Poneros 1.245; 3.174; 8.34
Pontifex 1.32; 6.254; 12.1; 13.31, 66; 14.196; 17.193
Porneia 3.173; 9.265
Pornoi 12.38
Poros 10.152
Porosis 8.146; 10.152
Poroun 8.146
Porte 2.143
Praenomen 8.212

Praetor 8.106; 10.80
Praitorion 11.20
Praktor 1.145
Praotes 1.96; 10.51f, 137;
   11.158
Prasiai 3.158
Praus 1.96; 10.52, 137f; 12.259
Prautes 9.238; 14.58
PRDS 10.41
Presbeutes 9.209f; 12.280
Presbuteros 12.70f; 15.127
Presbutes 12.280
Proagon 15.143
Prodotes 12.190
Prodromos 6.155; 13.63
Prographein 10.24f
Proi 5.88; 6.265f
Proistasthai 12.264
Prokope 11.20; 14.299
Prokoptein 11.20; 12.174
Prokoptontes 13.52
Propetes 12.191
Prosagein 14.235
Prosagoge 8.73; 14.235
Prosagogeus 10.117; 14.235
Prosechein 13.21
Proselutos 2.290
Proseuche 12.57
Proskunein 1.297
Prosopolempsia 14.62
Prosopon 14.62
Prosopon lambanein 14.62
Prosphiles 11.80
Prostasia 13.18
Pros thanaton 15.120
Proton 5.88
Prototokos 11.119; 16.32
Pseustai 12.39
Psithurismoi 9.264

Psithuristes 8.36
Psuche 9.28; 13.39; 14.93;
   15.11, 166, 201
Psuchikos, oi 9.28; 14.93;
   15.11f, 165f, 201f
Psuchros 16.141
Ptocheia 16.78
Ptochos 1.90
Ptoein 6.271
Ptossein 1.90
Publicanus 3.53
Pule 17.210
Pulon 17.210

Qolbon 2.245
Quadrans 4.171
Quahal 2.142
Quaternion 6.250; 7.95
Quelle 1.4
Qui cessat esse melior cessat esse
   bonus 13.52
Quo vadis? 13.58

Rabban 7.49
Rabbi 1.311; 6.269
Rabbounai 6.269
Raca 1.139
Raphis 7.2
Ratio marmorum 17.161
Recto 16.165
Rede 17.162
Religio licita 14.146, 156
Religiones (licitae et illicitae)
   14.156
Remaz 10.41; 13.67
Renatus in aeternum 5.127;
   17.33
Roizedon 14.344

Ruach **1**.22, 49; **5**.83, 131;
  8.102
Ruparia **14**.57
Rupos **14**.57

Sacramentum **12**.160; **14**.245
Sagan **7**.37
Sagene **1**.78; **2**.89; **3**.27
Salaam **1**.108
Salem **13**.69
Sar **4**.56
Sarkikos **9**.29f
Sarkinoi **9**.29f
Sarx, sarka **5**.65; **8**.101–103,
  158; **9**.29f, 239f
Satana **2**.149f
Satraps **17**.141, 147
Schema **8**.157f; **11**.35–37
Schismata **9**.14
Scintilla **12**.175; **15**.79; **16**.159
Scribo **15**.50
Scrip **6**.55
Seah **10**.32
Sebaste **16**.43
Sebastos **17**.89, 138
Seiros **14**.321
Seismos **1**.317
Seleniazesthai **2**.166
Semeion **5**.9, 119
Semnos **11**.79; **12**.61, 236, 247
Semnotes **12**.61f
Senate **12**.70
Senechomai **11**.27
Senex **12**.70
Sepein **14**.115
Serif **1**.127; **4**.211
Sesterces **9**.249
Setobrotos **14**.116
Shalom **1**.108; **6**.171; **10**.9, 50, 76

Shechinah **2**.161f; **5**.69; **8**.125;
  14.259; **17**.35f, 94, 202f
Shedim **1**.320; **3**.35; **9**.92
Shekel **2**.168; **4**.172, 241; **5**.109
Shekinah See Shechinah
Shema **1**.192, 196; **2**.278;
  3.295; **17**.119
Shomeron **6**.31
Shomeroni **6**.31
Shemoneh 'esreh **1**.192f; **14**.89f
Shoshben **5**.143
Shub **1**.52
Sicarii **2**.332
Siloam **6**.43
Sindon **3**.141f
Siros **14**.321
Skandalethron **1**.148; **3**.342
Skandalizein **2**.170; **3**.342
Skandalon **1**.148; **2**.170; **3**.342;
  4.215
Skene **17**.35, 94, 202
Skenoun **17**.35
Skia **13**.112
Skleros **5**.226
Skolops **9**.257
Skotia **5**.47
Skotos **5**.47
Skubala **11**.62
Sod **10**.41; **13**.67
Solam **17**.50
Soluitur ambulando **12**.171
Soma **14**.93; **15**.11, 201
Soma sema **12**.175
Somatikos **11**.95
Sophia **5**.31; **9**.109; **10**.82f, 90;
  11.108, 130; **14**.295, 302
Sophron **12**.80f, 239, 247, 251
Sophronein **14**.251
Sophronismos **12**.144f

Sophrosune 12.80; 14.251, 302
Soter 12.18; 16.89; 17.138
Soteria 8.19; 9.24f; 14.176
Sou 16.104
Sozein 14.175, 251
Spatalan 14.119
Spectatus 16.96
Speira 2.363; 6.222
Spendesthai 12.209
Spernere mundum, spernere te
 ipsum, spernere te sperni
 13.173
Sphragis 12.176
Sphurides 2.127
Sphuris 2.126; 3.184
Spilas 15.193
Spilos 15.193
Splagchnistheis 1.354
Splagchna 1.354; 9.218f;
 11.17f
Sponde 12.188
Stade 17.212
Stater 2.171
Stauros 12.9
Stauroun 12.9
Stekete 11.71
Stenochuria 9.213
Stephanos 11.70, 193; 14.48;
 16.83, 154; 17.3
Stereoma 11.131
Stergein 1.173
Sterixein 14.273
Sthenoun 14.273
Stigmata 10.56
Stilbein 3.211
Stipulatio 14.244
Stoa 3.279
Stoicheia 10.35; 11.95f, 136f;
 13.50

Storge 1.173; 8.39, 164;
 10.50, 139; 12.188
Strategos 15.61
Stulos 12.89
Sulagogein 11.136
Sumbolon 15.149
Sumposium 10.166
Sunagoge 14.21, 26; 16.80
Sunedrion 1.140
Suneidesis 12.34
Sunesis 11.130
Suntheke 13.91
Sunzugos 11.74
Sur 2.140
Susschematizesthai 8.157
Sustatikai epistolai 8.207
Syn 1.103

Tabitha 7.77
Taborion 3.210
Talaiporein 14.108
Talent 2.194; 4.172
Talith 4.113
Talithi cumi 3.8, 136
Tamhui 7.51; 12.85
Tapeinophrosune 10.135;
 11.158
Tapeinos 10.135
Tartaroun 14.321
Tau 5.213; 16.38; 17.226
Taurobolium 5.127; 17.33
Taxis 11.131
Te Deum 17.168
Teitan 17.101
Teknia 15.51
Tekton 3.138
Teleioi 13.52
Teleiomenoi 13.52
Teleios 1.777; 9.26; 11.65–67;

13.26, 48, 52; **14.**14, 61
Teleiotes **13.**52
Teleioun **13.**26, 48
Telos **1.**177; **17.**205
Tephillin **2.**286
Tephra phrygia **16.**139
Teras **5.**119
Terma **12.**11
Terumah **4.**155; **9.**80
Teshubah **1.**52
Tesserae **16.**96
Tetelestai **2.**369; **6.**258
Tetrachelismenos **13.**40
Tetragrammaton **6.**210; **17.**180
Tetrarch **2.**95; **4.**31
Tetuphomenos **12.**191
Thalassa **1.**76; **5.**208; **16.**41
Thanatos **17.**9
Theasthai **5.**64; **15.**23
Theion, s **1.**119; **17.**138
Themelioun **14.**274
Theologos **16.**13
Theos **5.**39; **7.**2; **12.**50, 138
Theostugeis **8.**36f
Thlipsis **8.**73; **9.**170, 213; **16.**40, 78
Threskia **14.**61
Thuia articulata **17.**160
Thumos **1.**138; **9.**264; **10.**159; **11.**153; **12.**236
Timan **12.**138
Time **12.**50; **14.**291
Tittle **1.**85, 127
Toga **10.**34
Tolman **14.**329
Tolmetes **14.**329
Torah **3.**31f
Trierarchia **8.**202

Trimita **16.**138
Triremes **9.**3, 36
Trochos geneseos **14.**87
Trope **14.**54
Truphein **14.**119
Tsaraath **3.**44
Tupos **14.**244
Tzedakah **1.**187
Tzelatzel **17.**51

Urbs candida **16.**122

Vehemens **14.**252
Verso **16.**165f
Vilicus **14.**255
Vilis **11.**69
Vindicatio **8.**106

Xenos **10.**118; **13.**148; **15.**149

Yada **11.**63
Yashmak **9.**97
Yetzer hara **8.**98; **14.**50
Yetzer hatob **8.**98; **14.**50

Zadik **1.**57
Zanah **2.**73
Zelos **8.**179; **9.**263f; **10.**47; **14.**91, 104
Zelotes **1.**359; **14.**229
Zen **5.**43
Zestos **16.**141
Ziz **6.**228f
Zizanium **2.**73
Zizith **1.**346; **2.**286
Zoe **5.**43
Zugon **8.**55
Zunim **2.**73

INDEX OF ANCIENT WRITINGS

Acts of John   15.7

Acts of Paul and Thecla   9.242;
    17.106

Acts of Peter and Paul   2.360

Acts of Pilate   6.35

Acts of Thomas   6.277

Ad Uxorem   14.280

Against Apion   2.29

Against Celsus   See Contra
    Celsum

Antiquities of the Jews   1.359;
    2.29, 37, 93, 96f, 179f, 196;
    4.147, 281; 5.248; 6.23,
    233; 10.112; 12.76, 77;
    13.168; 14.12, 322, 326;
    16.45; 17.95

Antitheseis, The   12.139f

Apocalypse of Baruch   1.373;
    3.194, 290, 313; 5.187;
    8.63, 109; 13.145; 14.246

Apocalypse of Paul   16.175

Apology, The   8.172

Apostolic Canons   12.76, 83, 93,
    98, 237

Apostolic Constitutions   1.266;
    6.291; 12.106, 109, 111;
    13.192; 14.162, 280; 16.67,
    139

Ascension of Isaiah   17.180

Ascension of Moses   3.198, 319;
    15.167; 17.12, 14, 199

Baba Kamma   1.164

Books of Baruch   1.303; 2.182;
    3.318, 319; 5.197; 6.197;
    9.138; 12.183; 14.322;
    16.7, 8, 9, 10, 11, 174;
    17.5, 6, 14, 19, 46, 110, 187,
    188, 196, 198, 200

Book of Enoch   1.373, 374;
    2.182; 3.197, 290; 5.186,
    187; 6.122; 9.50; 13.111;
    14.51, 117, 239, 246, 322,
    325, 340; 15.80, 168, 183,
    196; 16.6, 7, 8, 9, 31, 158,
    167, 171, 174, 175; 17.5, 13,
    14, 15, 16, 19, 47, 48, 80, 81,
    113, 148, 187, 196, 198, 218,
    220, 231

Book of Esther   3.183

Book of James   14.18

Book of Jubilees   1.373; 2.22,
    182; 3.313; 16.7

Book of Judith   13.164

Book of the Secrets of Enoch
    6.153

Book of Wisdom   6.38; 9.50

Canons of Hippolytus   14.129

Catechetical Lectures, The
    14.280

Clementine Letters   14.130;
    15.38

Clementine Recognitions   5.76;
    14.10

Codex Corbeiensis   14.3, 9

Codex Fuldensis   11.173

Codex Toletanus   5.21

Commentaria in Epistolam B.
    Pauli ad Romanos   14.280

Concerning Anti-Christ **17**.25
Concerning illustrious Men **16**.41
Confessions, The **15**.6
Contra Celsum **1**.34, 289

De Amicitia **14**.279
De Oratione **14**.279
De Praescriptione **1**.267
Dialogue with Trypho **1**.24;
   6.25; **8**.41; **12**.76
Didache **1**.266, 282f; **4**.134;
   6.106; **7**.91f; **10**.147;
   11.189; **12**.65; **13**.53; **14**.315;
   15.90, 133f; **16**.12f, 42

Ecclesiastical History **1**.81; **5**.3,
   10, 17, 18; **12**.11; **14**.151,
   204; **15**.7, 38; **17**.79, 190
Ecclesiasticus **1**.54, 187, 234;
   2.154; **5**.29, 32f, 59, 150;
   6.178, 208; **8**.63; **9**.138,
   165; **13**.149; **14**.45, 46, 50,
   55, 63, 70, 75, 83, 85, 88,
   94, 110, 113, 119, 322;
   16.69, 141, 145; **17**.218
Epistle to Diognetus **14**.168, 308
Epistles of Seneca **1**.27
Esdras **1**.373; **2**.136, 162;
   3.313; **5**.29; **8**.80; **13**.19;
   14.82; **16**.169; **17**.13, 14, 15,
   113, 188, 198, 199
Ezra **1**.303; **3**.195, 196, 317,
   318, 319; **13**.145; **14**.57;
   16.6, 9; **17**.5, 196

Gospel, according to the Hebrews
   1.59; **2**.30, 215; **4**.228;
   7.96; **9**.144; **14**.11
Gospel of Nicodemus **6**.35

Gospel of Peter **6**.246; **15**.8;
   16.166

Histories of Herodotus **1**.25,
   365
Histories of Tacitus **1**.27

Koran, The **6**.31; **16**.156

Legatio Christianis **14**.280
Letter of Aristeas **1**.273;
   13.148; **17**.231
Letter of Barnabas **9**.15; **14**.137,
   301; **15**.38
Letters of Pliny **1**.378
Life of Adam and Eve **14**.50,
   53
Life of Joseph **15**.37
Life of Nero **1**.27

Maccabees **1**.387; **2**.28, 136,
   137, 239, 241; **3**.172, 210,
   266, 310; **5**.59; **6**.70; **9**.216;
   10.50; **12**.149, 150, 157;
   13.160, 168, 169, 170;
   14.246, 302; **17**.26, 79, 103,
   179, 216
Memorabilia **14**.304
Mishnah, The **1**.129, 303, 367;
   3.129, 164, 166, 195, 274,
   313, 349; **5**.121, 195, 202;
   6.2, 260; **9**.254
Monarchian Prefaces **5**.96
Muratorian Canon **5**.21; **12**.1,
   11; **13**.5; **14**.3, 152, 285;
   15.167; **16**.29

Nicomachean Ethics **14**.300

Odes of Solomon 13.180
On Prescription against Heretics
16.26

Paedagogus 14.280
Papyrus Oxyrhynchus 17.103
Peshitto, The 14.4, 152
Platonic Definitions 12.186;
    14.58
Protevangelium 13.18
Psalms of Solomon 1.304;
    3.197f, 265, 319; 6.54; 16.8,
    11; 17.177, 218

Sayings of the Fathers 12.67;
    14.55, 81, 91
Septuagint 1.93, 273; 2.68f;
    3.93; 8.198; 12.70; 13.19,
    114; 14.21; 15.183; 16.31, 70
Shepherd of Hermas 12.81;
    14.301
Sibylline Oracles 3.195f, 198,
    318, 319; 8.109; 14.40;
    16.7, 8, 10; 17.15, 90, 110,
    194, 199, 201, 218
Sirach 3.71, 129; 8.80, 99
Song of the Three Children
    16.182
Statutes of the Apostles 14.64
Stromateis 1.307; 14.277

Talmud, The 1.34, 268, 344,
    346, 268; 2.283; 3.37, 129,
    232, 274; 5.110, 121, 213;
    6.90, 226, 233; 9.136;
    17.155, 161

Babylonian 1.130; 5.121;
    14.37, 277
Jerusalem 1.130; 5.121
Targums 5.29f
    of Jerusalem 15.190
    of Jonathan 5.30
Teaching of the Twelve Apostles
    See Didache
Testament of Asher 3.320;
    17.218
Testament of Benjamin 5.187
Testament of Dan 3.296;
    12.62; 16.174; 17.175
Testament of Isaacher 3.296;
    8.161; 12.182f
Testament of Judah 1.234
Testament of Levi 17.175, 218
Testament of Naphtali 14.204;
    17.218
Testament of Reuben 1.233
Testament of Simeon 1.234;
    13.180
Testament of the Twelve Patriarchs
    3.296
Tobit 1.187, 273; 2.38f;3.129;
    12.76; 14.75, 119; 16.9, 31,
    174; 17.41, 175, 201, 217

Wars of the Jews 1.27; 2.38,
    307, 328; 4.258f; 6.104,
    233; 10.112; 14.37; 17.213
Wisdom 1.387; 5.33, 34; 6.38;
    8.41; 9.204; 11.117; 13.134;
    14.94, 117, 120, 322; 15.85,
    94, 189; 17.71, 148, 181